CW01261966

Wibb—A Flute for Life

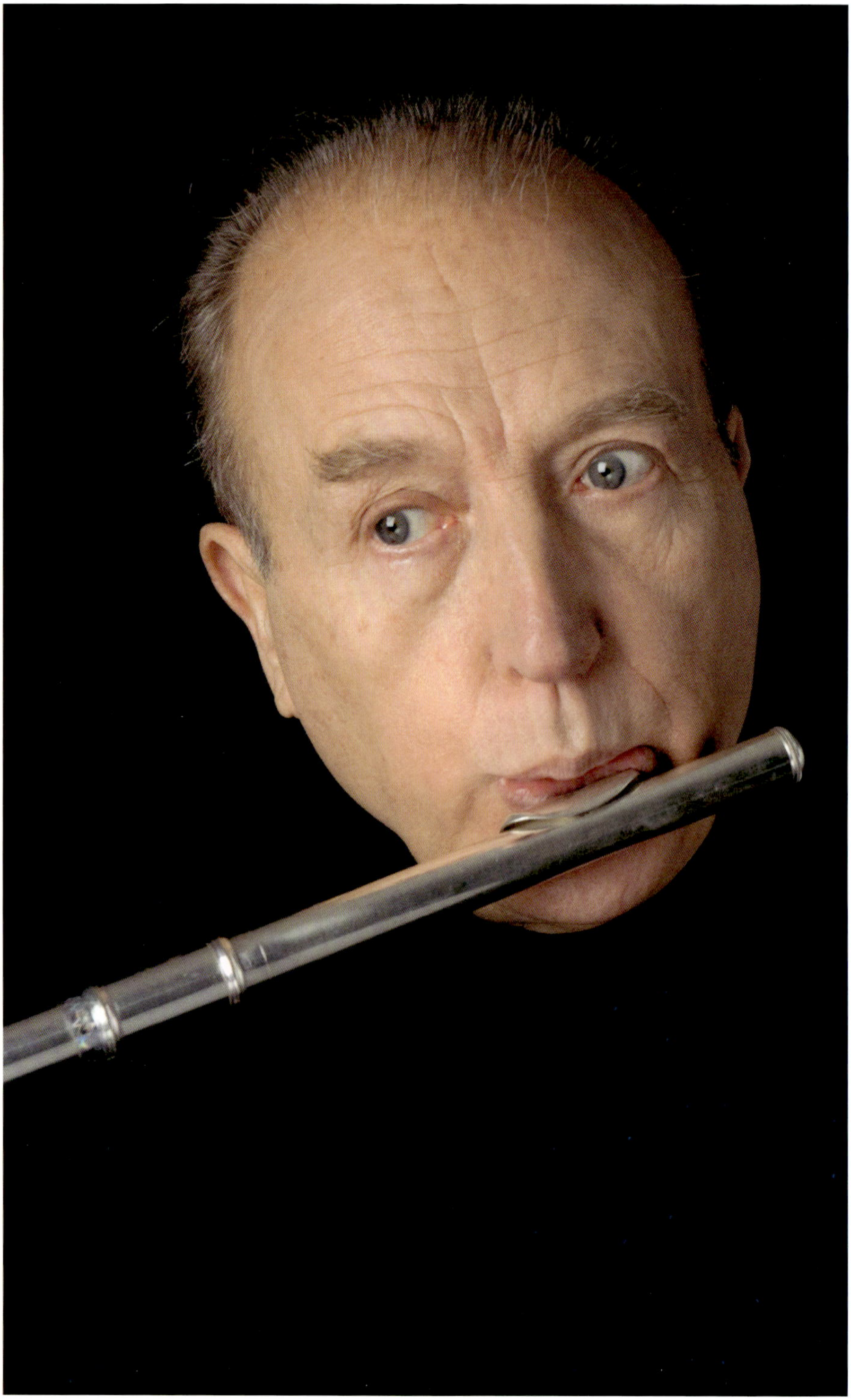

Wibb—A Flute for Life

Edward Blakeman

Tony Bingham
London

Copyright © Edward Blakeman 2016

All rights reserved. No part of this publication may be reproduced, stored in a retrieval system or transmitted in any form or by any means without the prior permission in writing of the publisher.

The author's moral rights have been asserted.

Designed and typeset by Robert Bigio
Set in Baskerville

Printed and bound in the United Kingdom by
W&G Baird Ltd, Antrim

ISBN 978-0-946113-10-1

British Library Cataloguing in Publication Data
A catalogue record for this book is available from the British Library

Published by
Tony Bingham
10 Willoughby Road
London NW3 1SA
England
Telephone +44 (0)20 7435 7578
www.oldmusicalinstruments.co.uk

Contents

Illustrations	8
Preface	13
Introduction	15
1—Beginnings	17
2—Teachers	35
3—Paris	51
4—Orchestras	67
5—Heroes	81
6—Flutes	95
7—Music	109
8—Recordings	121
9—Teaching	135
10—Playing	159
Conclusion	201

Illustrations

Front cover   Cartoons by Wibb
Back cover   Portrait of Wibb (Rena Pearl)
Frontispiece   Portrait of Wibb playing the flute (Rena Pearl)

Preface

12	Sketch of foliage by Wibb on tour in Brazil
14	Sketch of a cat by Wibb

Introduction

15	Self portrait by Wibb
16	Wibb on a penny-farthing bicycle

1—Beginnings

17	Sketch by Wibb, aged seven
18	Pastel by Wibb's father, Frank Bennett
19	Early pastel by Wibb
20	Wibb sketching with his mother
21	The Blitz in London, sketched by Frank Bennett
23	Caravan at Wibb's school
25	Wibb's letter home from school
29	Childhood sketch of a guitar by Wibb
31	Wibb with Jumble
32	Wibb's earliest sketch of a flute
33	Pastel of a boat by Wibb, 1951
34	Sketch of railway sidings, Bogotá, by Wibb

2—Teachers

35	Wibb with Geoffrey Gilbert
37	Geoffrey Gilbert
40	The wind players known as the 'Royal Family' in Sir Thomas Beecham's Royal Philharmonic Orchestra: Jack Brymer, clarinet; Terence MacDonagh, oboe; Dennis Brain, horn; Geoffrey Gilbert, flute; Gwydion Brooke, bassoon
42	Wibb with Marcel Moyse in Boswil

45	Marcel Moyse
47	Sketch of Marcel Moyse by Wibb
49	Marcel Moyse and Wibb

3—Paris

52	Wibb aged twenty-one
55	'Dear Old Buzzards' letter
57	'Drunken students' letter
58	'Rat on the stairs' letter
59	'Paris undertakers' letter
65	Wibb's award from the Geneva Competition of 1958
66	Watercolour of Paris rooftops by Wibb

4—Orchestras

68	Programme for the BBC Midday Promenade Concerts in Manchester in 1959
70	Handbill for a Mabillon Trio concert at Wigmore Hall in 1962
71	Handbill for a concert of French music at Wigmore Hall in 1965
72	Wibb at Dartington with three members of the Dartington Quartet in 1964
73	Early publicity photograph of Wibb
75	Publicity leaflet from the early 1960s
77	Handbill for one of many recitals with Clifford Benson
79	Publicity leaflet from the late 1960s
80	Sketch of Aix-en-Provence by Wibb

5—Heroes

82	Fernand Dufrène
83	Wibb with George Malcolm
84	Handbill for a concert with Wibb and George Malcolm at Wigmore Hall in 1964
85	Handbill for a concert with Wibb and George Malcolm at Queen Elizabeth Hall in 1977
86	Wibb with Yehudi Menuhin in the mid-1960s
88	Wibb with Yehudi Menuhin in the 1980s (Malcolm Crowthers)
91	Wibb with Clifford Benson
92	Wibb rehearsing with Clifford Benson
93	Wibb and Clifford Benson
94	Sketch of a Paris street scene by Wibb

6—Flutes

95	A corner of Wibb's workshop
96	Wibb playing a wooden flute
98	A publicity photograph from the 1970s
103	Wibb's No.1 flute with Louis Lot headjoint No.2828
107	Sketch of a baroque flute player by Wibb
108	Sketch of a Mediterranean harbour by Wibb

7—Music

110	One of a series of greetings card designs by Wibb
111	Christmas card by Wibb
112	Sketch for a card design by Wibb
113	Fingerprint sketch for a card design by Wibb
114	Fingerprint sketch for a card design by Wibb
116	Fingerprint sketch for a card design by Wibb
117	Fingerprint sketch for a card design by Wibb
118	Programme cover for Wibb's fiftieth birthday concert at Wigmore Hall in 1986
119	Programme of Wibb's fiftieth birthday concert
120	Sketch in Rio de Janeiro by Wibb

8—Recordings

124	CD cover designed by Wibb
125	CD cover designed by Wibb
127	Wibb in a recording session
128	Wibb with Trevor Wye
131	Letter from Geoffrey Gilbert
133	CD cover from 1992
134	Sketch from a holiday balcony by Wibb

9—Teaching

137	A young Wibb teaching
140	Wibb teaching
143	Wibb teaching
144	Brochure for the William Bennett International Flute Summer School in 2000
148	Wibb's notes on Note Bending
149	Wibb's notes on Essential Exercises

150	Wibb's Dohnanyi Type Exercises for the flute
151	Wibb's notes on the A-Z of What and How to Practice
153	Wibb teaching
154	Pages from Wibb's notes on getting back in shape after a holiday
155	Pages from Wibb's notes on getting back in shape after a holiday
156	Pages from Wibb's notes on getting back in shape after a holiday
157	Wibb's notes for a projected flute method
158	Sketch of a villa by Wibb on tour in 1975

10—Playing

161	First of a chronological sequence of twelve pictures of Wibb playing the flute
162	Wibb playing the flute
163	Wibb playing the flute
164	Wibb playing the flute
165	Wibb playing the flute
166	Wibb playing the flute
167	Wibb playing the flute (Photograph by Clive Barda/ArenaPAL)
168	Wibb playing the flute (Photograph by Clive Barda/ArenaPAL)
169	Wibb playing the flute
170	Wibb playing the flute
171	Wibb playing the flute
172	Wibb playing the flute
173	Wibb demonstrating a flute embouchure
174	Wibb at the piano
175	Wibb with a tenor ukulele
176	Wibb teaching
179	Wibb's notes on Sensitive Fingerings
187	Watercolour of sunlight on the sea in Ramsgate harbour by Wibb
190	Wibb's Octave Exercise
193	Handbill for Opera Flutastic! at St John's Smith Square in 1997
196	Wibb at the piano
200	Sketch of Copacabana Beach by Wibb

Conclusion

201	Sketch of his cats by Wibb
203	Wibb on tour in France
204	Wibb in relaxed mood
205	Sketches of Michie by Wibb

Sketch of foliage by Wibb on tour in Brazil

Preface

Imagine a cold, dark, wet, February evening in Central London. The Church of St Martin in the Fields, however, is all lit up and warm inside. The year is 2012 and I have struggled through the winter night to hear William Bennett and friends play a recital of baroque music.

Once again, in this soaring and resonant space, the music works its magic—and so does the playing, especially the playing. Such life in the sound! I find myself reflecting on the many years that I have admired and delighted in Wibb's unique artistry. There have been so many moments when something glorious in his playing has just made me break out in a broad smile. How many solo, chamber and orchestral concerts have I heard? And, of course, all those recordings... Some of them I was fortunate enough to produce at the BBC, and on an earlier one I played with Wibb and we talked about the French Flute School—a shared passion. That was back in 1985, half a lifetime ago. And here he is, in his mid-seventies, still playing wonderfully. What a shame, though, that he has written almost nothing about his life with the flute.

I congratulate him afterwards and hurry out into the cold, dark and wet again. There are many other things to preoccupy me... nevertheless a seed has been planted in my mind.

Almost a year to the day, I am back in St Martin in the Fields, this time to hear Wibb take part in a performance of Bach's *Art of Fugue*. The dual challenge and appeal of this music, to the head and the heart, is matched by playing of confidence, intelligence and restrained beauty. Time stands still. I know what has to be done.

A few weeks later, Wibb and I settle down to talk at his house in South London, the first of many extended and fascinating sessions. Over the next three years we explore his life and how it has been inextricably bound up with the flute. We listen to many recordings—from those that he made as a fifteen-year-old schoolboy, to the most recent one he is in the process of editing. We unearth recordings of other musicians who have been important to him. We pore over copies of flute music, much worn and rich with annotations and notes from lessons. Out come flutes, in various states of renovation and repair, for inspection and explanation. Out come portfolios of artwork, random jottings, photographs and concert programmes. Wibb talks, sings, plays. He demonstrates on the piano, harpsichord and guitar. Bit by bit we piece everything together.

The results of all this you are holding in your hand. This is the book born of that cold, dark, wet, February evening—a book of colour and laughter, I hope—the book that had to be written.

Edward Blakeman
April 2016

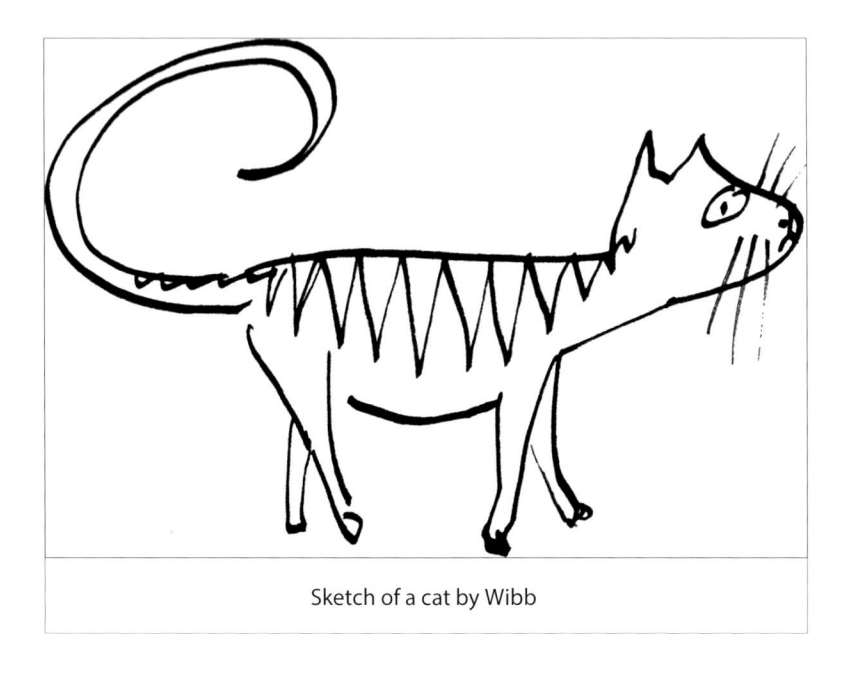

Sketch of a cat by Wibb

Introduction

William **I**ngham **B**rooke **B**ennett—Wibb—was born on 7 February 1936. In the *International Who's Who* he once listed his hobbies as *wine making and cockroach-baiting*. He has never kept a diary, but his opening gambit as we began to work on this book—and before I had even had time to turn on the recording machine—was:

All my life I've been dogged by good luck!

A characteristically forthright pronouncement. It made me keen to capture Wibb's own words in his own voice and communicate all that to you, the reader, as vividly as possible. This is not a traditional biography. Rather, it is an invitation to spend time with an extraordinary, mercurial personality. Wibb is larger than life and certainly not to be constrained easily between the covers of a book! But whatever this book is, you will be able for the first time to follow him in detail through his extraordinary life devoted to the flute. Wibb has played the flute, taught it, redesigned it, re-made it, and thought endlessly about it for many decades. It was fitting, therefore, that he was awarded the OBE by Her Majesty the Queen in 1995 for distinguished services to music.

There was a lot to talk about and I have sought to reproduce the immediacy and informality of our conversations as closely as possible. Wibb's words throughout are printed in italics, to distinguish them from my linking text and other quotations, and when you see an exclamation mark it nearly always means that he burst out laughing. We both laughed a lot! I have tried to minimise repetition, but sometimes the same or similar things came up in different contexts—and indeed could be illuminated in different lights—so please excuse what repetition remains.

WILLIAM BENNETT

Self-portrait by Wibb

I was greatly helped by Susan Campbell who transcribed many of the conversations—my thanks to her. Grateful thanks also to my wife Helen, whose unfailing support and encouragement are the reason the book ever got finished on time. The fact that there is a book at all is due to the skill of Robert Bigio who designed it, and the generosity of Tony Bingham who published it. My thanks to them both.

Finally, my thanks to Wibb himself. I discovered—as I knew I would—that time listening and talking to him is always time well spent and the whole project has been a rare joy. I am hugely grateful to him—and also to his wife Michie, who always knew where to find things, provided some important facts and dates, and kept us supplied with tea, chocolate, and the most wonderful dinners.

Enjoy!

1—Beginnings

It's unusual to be able to start anyone's story before they are born, but Wibb knows exactly how he got here.

I came into being because my Mum and Dad—Faith and Frank—were on a walk in Buckinghamshire and they passed Valley Cottage in Speen. It was May and they saw a cot with a baby inside it hanging from a tree, with the apple blossom everywhere in front of the cottage. And they thought: 'How romantic—let's have something like that...' and I was born on 7th February the following year.

Valley Cottage belonged to the composer Edmund Rubbra and later on the two Rubbra boys, Francis and Benedict, would play an important part in Wibb's young life. Meanwhile, 1936 was a turbulent year of social unrest, culminating in the Jarrow March—the miners' protest against unemployment and poverty—and the surprise abdication of the new King Edward VIII, giving up the throne for marriage to an American divorcee,

Sketch by Wibb, aged seven

Wallis Simpson. What, I wondered, were Wibb's earliest memories as a child in London.

> *Thornaugh Street, the flat where my parents lived, and a bedroom with a nasty picture in it. Nasty looking lady: Mona Lisa! I never quite liked it. I'm going back to when I was one-and-a-half, or two, or something... but I've got lots of memories about Thornaugh Street, especially about the gramophone that was there—the old, wind-up gramophone, which I broke so many records on! The gramophone was put away at the beginning of the war when we moved out to Buckinghamshire, and it came to light when we moved back to Hammersmith at the end of the war. I broke a lot of good records—there was a part of Beethoven's Fifth Symphony with a great big bite out of it and one record of Bach's Second Brandenburg, with Stokowski and the Philadelphia Orchestra. I liked that—a good military march!*

So, immediately we have art and music in the story. Not that there weren't some other things more associated with a little boy born in the 1930s.

> *I can remember the sandpit in Russell Square. I remember playing with my Dinky toys in it.*

But it's significant that Wibb's very first memory is of looking at a picture. Both his parents were artists, professional architects, so there were plenty of opportunities.

I picked up lots of pens and pencils and did this, that and the other. Some drawings have even survived. I always liked doing painting and drawing and, of course, my father was always drawing pictures and things.

Not surprisingly, Wibb's parents encouraged him to appreciate a great deal of art.

My parents had lots of friends who were painters and we used to visit art galleries, so I had quite a lot of the old visual stuff and I was quite good at painting and drawing things at school—with pleasure, with fun! I remember going and seeing exhibitions of Picasso, when I was ten or something, and it wasn't something strange to me.

Pastel by Wibb's father, Frank Bennett

Beginnings

Wibb was also encouraged to be creative is a very specific way by his art teacher at school.

> *We had a lovely art teacher, called Ron Morton, who taught us to break away from things. I remember doing a still life, and he said: 'Well, that looks rather good, but why not make the background more interesting? Why not a bit of purple or something?' In other words, change it, make the picture better. I was trying to represent what was there, but it might look better if you did something else! You're creating a picture, make the picture good—never mind what it looks like! A wonderful step forward.*

In fact, Wibb was surrounded by artists.

> *My godmother was another painter, Aletta Lewis, who did all sorts of things in Tahiti and Australia, and then there was Georgina York and Harry Valon, who were both painters, who lived on the other side of St. Peter's Square, and also had a caravan in Speen.*

Early pastel by Wibb

Speen was the neighbouring village to Loosely Row in Buckinghamshire (near High Wycombe) where Frank and Faith Bennett had a cottage and where Frank moved his family during the Second World War to keep them safe from the bombing in London.

> *I grew up in the War and was sort of shut away in this place in the country. Looking back I can see that I was making things all the time. I had a garden shed, lots of bits of wood and a saw. I'd make myself toys. I made a toy battle ship by getting a stout piece of wood and sawing a point on the front and sticking a lot of nails in it for handrails and somehow getting a funnel onto it. There was an awful lot of making things for myself because there wasn't anything else there. It didn't strike me at all unusual when I was at school, playing the recorder, but wanting a flute, to take a bicycle pump and bung some holes in it and see what came out! So I made my very first flute.*
>
> *Oh yes, and there was my statue! I made it at school with a piece of stone lying around the craft room. I got a saw and I turned it into a man's head. That's what bits of stone are for!*

You can just picture this little boy: open, enquiring, absorbing everything like a sponge, going off and making new things. You can't imagine Wibb being bored! It was an attitude to life inherited from his parents. In the

19

Wibb sketching with his mother

1930s, fathers were more likely to be distant with their sons, but Frank Bennett was an exception.

> *I thought he was terribly nice. Years later I went to an acupuncturist lady who kept on asking me: 'What about your father? What sort of relationship did you have with him?' And she was expecting me to say: 'Oh, he was terrifying', or something, and a lot of people obviously did have bad relations with their fathers, but I only have nice memories. Of course, I can remember occasionally he'd get angry with me—not very much—for something I'd done. I remember barging him in the bollocks and him coming up the stairs and clouting me, but that wasn't anything that would leave a great scar on me! No, he used to do lovely things: teach me how to make cement and things like that in the garden. Mixing cement was huge fun! I think I was very lucky.*

During most of War, apart from weekends, Wibb and his mother were alone in the cottage at Loosely Row while Frank Bennett stayed in London engaged in war work for the Ministry of Health. He wrote frequent letters back to them, illustrated with pen and ink sketches—one vividly shows the two of them looking from a great distance at the City of London on fire

The Blitz in London, sketched by Frank Bennett

from the bombing—and he was full of concern for how 'William' should be properly brought up, how he should be disciplined when necessary.

> *In one of those letters, he's talking to my mother about how they shouldn't both be angry with me at the same time. He was thinking about how I was the only child and it might be a bit too much to have the whole world turn against me.*

Frank Bennett was equally concerned to try to find children of Wibb's own age for him to play with, while at the same time providing an atmosphere in which Wibb could blossom through contact with adults.

> *He communicated all the time. He was very concerned about talking at mealtimes and having something pleasant running. He had been very depressed earlier in his life, and underwent a complete psychoanalysis. I think he sorted out a lot of problems at that time.*

Friends for Wibb, in particular those two sons of the composer Edmund Rubbra, were luckily not far away.

> The Rubbras were already known to my parents. We used to go over and see them from the cottage in Loosely Row, a couple of miles' walk over the hill which, for me, was a long, long walk aged three or four—it felt like an hour and a half or two hours to get there, though I suspect it wasn't as long as that really. I can remember doing it in winter with sheets of ice and slipping down the sloping hillside fields.
>
> The sons, Francis and Benedict, were the greatest friends in my life. The nearest things I've got to brothers. Ben is a painter—I have a painting of his out in the hallway. His mum was a violinist and her sister was a painter, so there was a lot of this sort of thing going on. Their next door neighbour was a painter too!

This easy mingling of art and music was taken for granted in the Rubbra household and Wibb continued to benefit from that as he grew older.

> We used to go to concerts and hear Edmund Rubbra playing in the Rubbra-Gruenberg-Pleeth Trio. He sometimes played through his symphonies at home, playing the piano and singing the melodies and we used to hear lots of music on the record player. He did record reviews and showed me a lot about music. He introduced me to Olga Coelho singing Brazilian folk music with the guitar. I was particularly intrigued with something called Il Caboclo *with lots of octaves and very fast—lovely. Then there was a wonderful slow tune. That record only got broken when I moved into this house and the cat jumped on the record player! It was at the Rubbra's house that I first heard a record of Jean-Pierre Rampal—an early long playing record of the Vivaldi Concertos and I remember being very intrigued with the quick double-tonguing.*

Near to the Bennetts in Loosely Row lived the Francis family. Hugh Francis, a doctor, was Wibb's godfather.

> He used to make his own cameras and he made his own gramophones—so that's part of this tradition of doing it yourself—and later, when I started playing the flute, he gave me all his cast-off 78 gramophone records. He was the world's greatest liar, so I never believed a word he said! So when he said: 'Oh this is a record of Marcel Moyse, the world's greatest flute player', of course I didn't believe him, but he nevertheless gave me the record of the Mozart Concerto. It wasn't the only thing. My godfather also gave me records of Egon Petri playing Brahms's Variations on Paganini... all sorts of things... Gieseking, playing Ravel's Undine *and* Scarbo—*marvellous!—and Segovia playing Bach and Sor.*

Even with friends relatively near, life for Faith Bennett during the War became increasingly lonely and frustrating, particularly when Wibb went off to school for the first time. Frank wrote sympathetically from London: 'You must have felt miserable in a way today. You've parted with him! Sent him out into the big wide world. He's going to be a man very soon now. He'll never be a baby any more! It is sad. I am rather miserable myself...' Wibb remembers his mother with equal affection.

> She was wonderful. Her father was the Reverend William Ingham Brooke. He was the son of the Archdeacon of Halifax, who was somebody quite important in those days. He liked horses and cattle and lost quite a lot of the family money on having a dairy herd. He would talk to himself about racehorses and apparently he was naughty and used to poke little holes in the window of the church in summer to get some ventilation. The Churchwarden used to find these little holes in the glass and mend them again. And he was told off for jumping over the gravestones in an un-Vicarly way!
>
> My mother's family did wild things. They all went off and lived in a caravan in the 1920s and then my grandmother was into Montessori teaching and was very interested in education and jobs for women. I think she was a suffragette, so she was an advanced thinker, interested in women breaking out, having jobs, professions. My mother became a photographer, went and studied drawing in Paris and then she became an architect. A sister, Barbara, became a dancer. She failed to get in the Folies Bergère because her tits were too big! Apparently that's not good if you're nude dancing—they flop around too much!

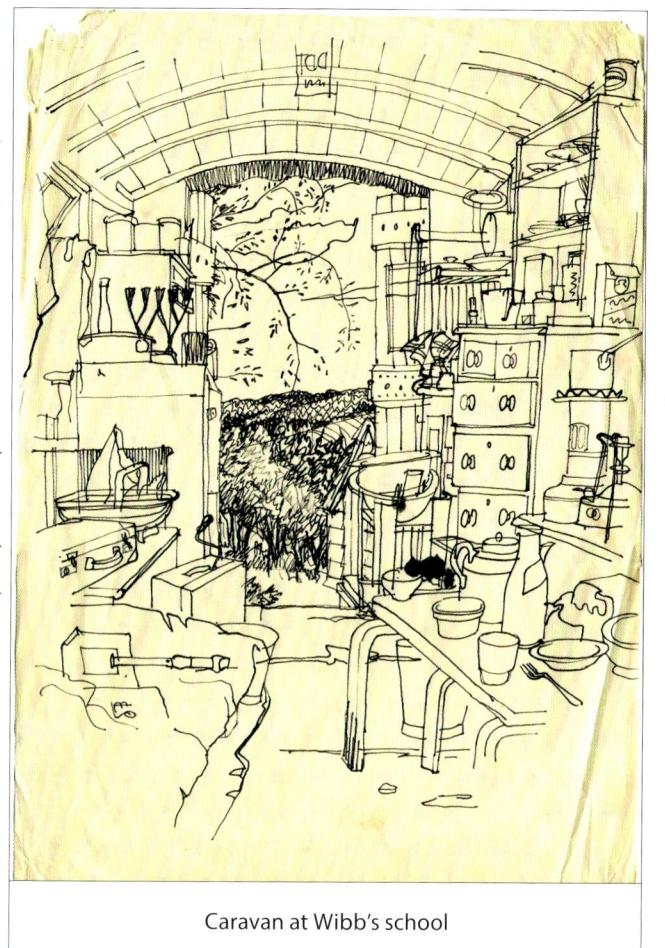

Caravan at Wibb's school

With a suffragette and the son of an eccentric archdeacon as grandparents, it's maybe not surprising that Wibb has always approached life with his own particular brand of originality. But did religion play any part in his childhood?

> *Little bits. I was baptised at some stage when I was about six and then I was sent to a Catholic school because the Rubbras went there and they were our friends. They thought it was a good place—they were Catholics. There was a shortage of anywhere to go, so I was bundled off to school with them for a while. It was in the place near High Wycombe where Eric Gill had lived—the printer, letterer and sculptor—and that was run on the lines of a medieval community. Then I went to Beltane School, in Wiltshire, when I was seven years old and I was full of all this stuff. I said something about God to one of the boys, and he said: 'Surely you don't believe in him do you? He died in about 1200!'*

Beltane School was a co-educational, private boarding school located in an old manor house at Melksham, near Bath. It was run on progressive lines—quite unusual for that period. The headmaster, Andrew Tomlinson, and his wife Joan were affectionately known as Tommy and Mrs Tommy.

> *It was a free school, but it wasn't without rules at all, they still controlled us a bit, but the interesting thing was that the pupils actually made half the things. They made the furniture. Before I was there, they arrived in Wiltshire, having decamped from London to avoid the bombs, and they sat down in the workshops and made steel chairs and welded them up. Tommy was always building things out of what was called 'Tommycrete', which was a sort of cement mixed with a lot of ashes left over from the boilers, and it was very frail, but it made breezeblocks and all sorts of buildings went up with these breezeblocks. I can remember the first place I stayed in at that school when I was seven was a converted stable—the cow stables, with gas lights—and in the first term, they were being modernised. Electric lights were being fitted, and a couple of the pupils in the middle school were doing all the electrical wiring!*
>
> *At the end of the War, Tommy acquired about fifty plywood pontoons which had been used in the Normandy Landings. They were a wonderful source of scarce building material and they had to be taken apart firstly by destructive small boys like me sawing away all the wooden struts on the inside!*

Wibb's letters home to his parent tell their own fascinating story and are characteristically quirky in style.

Dear Ma and Pa

I hope UR well. I.B BU? Thanks for the parcel that I got yesterday. It was most thrilling. We are down at Lavender Farm now, (where I was when I first came). We've got a much nicer matron. I.B. living in a caravan. No electric lights. We have to get into bed by torchlight. What a joke.

We went to the Quarry last week end, (about 2/3 of the middle school went). We've got some ghastly new people here. Because of the new people we aren't allowed to go to Melksham except on Thursday afternoons that was caused by some people queueing up for fish for about 2 hours and being late for supper. Could you send me my next month's pocket money its time. Four weeks

At that point the letter breaks off abruptly—was it ever finished, or did some of it get lost?

With Wibb away at school in term time, Faith Bennett was able to rejoin Frank in London. They moved to a new address and it provided Wibb with an unexpected diversion during the school holidays.

> They got a nice big studio flat just next to Chelsea football ground. I remember a sort of balcony where the hot water tank was and there was a shelf up there, which was my bedroom, and there was a window that overlooked the exit passage from the football ground. There was an apple tree in the front garden. I'd never been in the football ground but I used to drop apple cores on the crowds as they came out after the matches! I was about eight and well... that didn't last very long! Then we moved again into the St. Peter's Square house.

Wibb's letter home from school

After the War was over, Wibb stayed at Beltane School, which was later relocated to High Cannons, near Barnet, in outer London. By this time he was twelve.

> Again, we were roped into building things and altering the place, a lot of that. I went along before we moved and was helping knock things down and put them up again, to get the school to go to the new premises. I stayed there until I was sixteen.

I was a boarder all the way through those years. At first that was awful, being sent away from home. I think seven is a bit too young to be sent away. I can remember being very miserable, but then, maybe more so because I was an only child, much more dependent on my parents. But by the time I became eleven or twelve, I was more au fait with the whole business—and music was a sort of refuge in a way. When I got a recorder, I had my own thing to do and then I played the piano whenever there was a piano to be had. A little later, I started having piano lessons. Everybody played the piano a bit at school. We can't do without the piano!

Wibb's letters home continued through these years: spontaneous, ebullient, teeming with ideas, and questions.

The present situation for the Veggies, poor Fish can't stand eggs, and usually doesn't have any supper at all. Jack Norton is pestering me for my identity card, which I have already asked for once, I need my Debussy Preludes very urgently, 'cos I've got nuffink else werf pliyin', see? I would also like to know soon if this Norwegian chappie can come and stay for one or two weeks in the holidays...

Could you send me my paint brushes which I've left at home, I've been using the schools, which are frightful. My latest picture is one of Rudi digging his garden, in which Rudi's behind looks far more enormous than usual. Two of the sunflowers that I planted last term are sprouting out of the ground quite merrily, the largest is about six inches high.

How many times have you fallen into the river from the boat? How's Jumble? Have the new pram's holes been stuffed up yet? and millions of other such questions. I went into Bath with Christopher yesterday, and he bought some music for clarinet and piano by Gerald Finzi, I can play the piano for most of it. Lee Hunt got me some Grieg to play on the piano, it's awfully

Once again, at this point the letter breaks off abruptly and nothing more has survived.

Wibb's piano teacher at Beltane School was a Miss Fraser—*who was perfectly nice and good*—but more inspirational help was soon at hand for his emerging musical talent in the figure of a newly-arrived teacher at Beltane School called Rudolph Sabor.

Like many people in the school, Rudi was a Jewish émigré from Germany and both he and his wife were Germans. He was a very good teacher and later famed as a Wagner expert. He stayed until the school moved to High Cannons and then he was replaced by an Australian called James Bayley, who was super-imaginative and enormous fun and he opened our minds. Rudi was showing us classical music, introducing us to Brahms and music like that—and was absolutely wonderful—but James suddenly introduced us to Stravinsky and Milhaud and he could improvise and do Latin American rhythms on the piano. He got us all improvising—he brought it out in people. He encouraged everybody to go for it and improvise. That was pretty liberating! He and I could sit down and make music together, but maybe not too many of the others could do what I did. I never thought about that, but he sort of led us on... his antennae were out listening to what I was doing as well and he'd laugh at the right moments!

By then, Wibb was in his final couple of years at school and was already playing the flute seriously. His first instruments, however, had been a recorder and a plastic whistle.

I was eight or nine when a boy at school went to the nearby town and came back with a plastic whistle of some sort and I said: 'I want one of those!' I drew out my entire term's pocket money and jumped on a bike and went and bought mine. By that night I could play the song Clementine *with the aid of the fingering chart which came with it. Then a very little while after I graduated to a real recorder—plastic—and that was an awful lot better. I could steam around on that really rather fast!*

Then I got a record with a wind-up gramophone, Carl Dolmetsch playing Greensleeves, *which had fast variations, and I would play along with this record. But trying to play along with the record, I found I couldn't play one bit fast enough, so I slowed it down with the speed control lever, but then it was all in a different key! So I found out very quickly that you had to have it set in the middle. And I had all sorts of tricks: instead of double tonguing, I did something in my throat. I invented all sorts of techniques that were completely illegal, but I could sort of get through playing along with Carl Dolmetsch! A little later we bought a record of Robert Murchie playing the Rondo and Badinerie from the B Minor Suite and that was maybe my first flute record. I could very quickly play the Badinerie as fast as him, in some sort of way!*

So when did playing along to records on the recorder turn into a real awareness of the flute?

In my first school, I heard the flute on recordings or on the radio sometimes. It sounded so round and deep compared to this funny little whistley noise of the recorder! I liked that. Then I played in the Christmas holidays with a next door neighbour lady in London who played the flute—she was a tall lady called Julia who had a big, black, wooden Rudall Carte, and it sounded very nice and deep, a wonderful voice. A friend of mine and I both played recorders along with her—must have sounded frightful!—but we went round and did Christmas carols together. I thought: 'The flute is wonderful'. And then I heard it more on records and I just wanted one. So I made a thing out of a bicycle pump, and I can remember I painted all

> *sorts of patterns on the outside of it. It didn't sound like anything—I just drilled holes in it and just sort of found out what happened!*

The bicycle pump flute didn't really work at all, so Wibb persuaded his father that he needed something better to play on.

> *I went down the Charing Cross Road with my father and we bought a sort of six-key piccolo of some sort in a music shop. The six-key piccolo was awful and it probably didn't work and it was much too hard. Fingering on the recorder is nice and straightforward, but these keys went in reverse, there was something terribly difficult about it. I was always falling back on my cross fingerings for the recorder, and it was really most unsatisfactory. It stayed but I played the recorder most of the time.*

By this time, Wibb was also playing the guitar, an instrument he also loved—and still does.

> *I didn't really always think I was going to be a flute player. I mean, I just got interested in musical noises and then, suddenly, I got fascinated with the flute. I made myself a flute, a balalaika and a guitar and all that just because I was always making things. I got fascinated with the guitar too. I had a record that my godfather gave me, the Bach Gavotte being played by Segovia—a wonderful noise! The music master, Rudi, used to play the guitar a bit and I thought it was a marvellous instrument!*

Wibb's approach to 'always making things' was characteristically imaginative and resourceful.

> *I found some bits of wood and made myself what I thought was a balalaika. I didn't make a rounded shape—that was far too difficult woodwork for me—I made something with a triangular box on it and I stuck matchsticks on it for frets. I made a three or four string instrument, invented what the tuning was, and started making noises on it.*

Later on, while he was on holiday in Norway with a school friend, by chance he spotted a guitar fingerboard and tuning screws in a shop window.

> *I had enough pocket money to buy them and I came home and sat down to make a guitar. It took about two weeks. I started buying music before I'd finished the guitar and I had something by Frescobaldi and a Bach Gavotte. It took me about a week to start learning those. The guitar didn't last very long. I was still at school, and it was held together by a big wood screw where the neck joined on to the body and one day it folded in half. I had a moveable bridge on my guitar and it bent up. You put the tension on the string and the whole thing bent severely in the middle, and then the strings came up about a good half an inch more than they should have done above the frets. That in turn meant that the higher notes got terribly sharp, because of the stretching on the strings, so I moved the bridge down. Just pushed it. And so I learnt something about altering scales. Tuning a guitar is a very good way of developing your ear!*

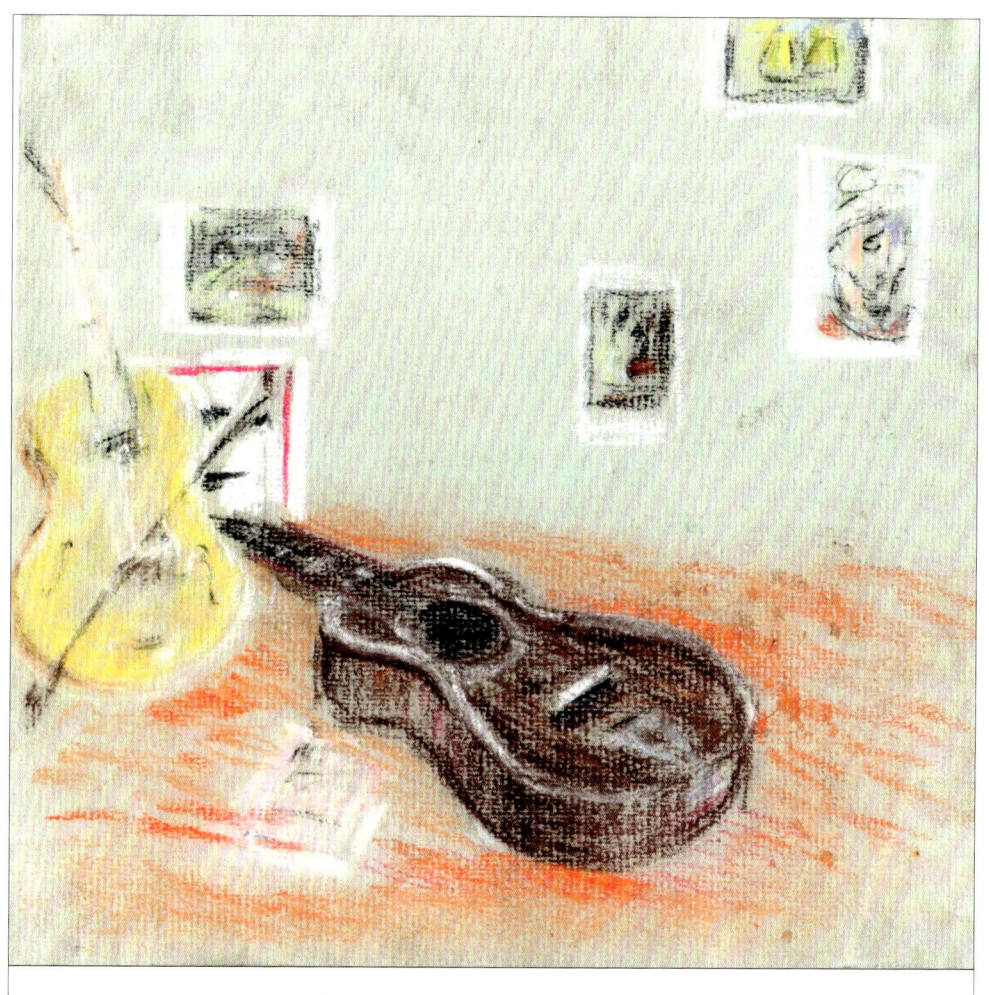

Childhood sketch of a guitar by Wibb

Always enquiring, Wibb was also picking up other information about tuning which was training his musical ear almost without him realising it.

> *I may have accidentally trained it, because people said things which interested me. Like about equal temperament. The harmonic series gives the true note and equal temperament is just a little bit off. If you play C below the bass clef on the piano, strongly and let it ring, you soon hear all the notes of the harmonic series singing out. You usually hear the fifth harmonic, which is middle E of the piano, more clearly than the others. I used to sit at the school piano playing bottom C, listen to the E and then play the actual middle E, which of course is terribly sharp. I used to play all the bottom notes, savouring the out-of-tuneness of the equal tempered piano.*

Meanwhile, Wibb was still persevering with both his piccolo and recorder, but he was quite clear what he really wanted and he kept pestering his parents.

> *I kept on saying: 'I want a proper flute'. I'd look at them in the local King's Street music store and there'd be these things with a few holes and a few bits of bent metal on them—six or eight key flutes—which were no good to anybody at all, but I couldn't possibly know that.*

Finally, as Wibb reached the age of twelve, his parents took some advice about flutes. More about that in a moment, but twelve was also the age that the famous Jumble (already mentioned in passing in a letter above) came into Wibb's life.

> *Somebody came round and knocked on the door with puppies for sale and I was entranced. I think my parents thought it was about time we had a dog and this wonderful dog came in, quite a young puppy still.*

There's a great photograph of Wibb and Jumble taken two years later, looking for all the world like Richmal Crompton's popular fictional character, William Brown, and his dog—who just happened to be called Jumble! Crompton had begun writing her *Just William* books about a mischievous schoolboy and his gang called the Outlaws back in the 1920s and the year that Wibb was photographed with his Jumble the latest book appeared, with the title *William the Bold*. That said it all!

> *The photographer said to my Mum: 'The dog's perfect, the boy won't keep still!'*

Well… Jumble wasn't quite perfect.

> *He was the randiest dog in London!*

He was particularly enamoured of a pedigree cocker spaniel bitch and fathered at least three lots of puppies by her, despite her owner, the local tobacconist, trying to keep her locked up.

'I reckon he comes down the chimney', he said. 'A regular Houdini he is!'

But back to the flute…

> *My parents found out that Edmund Rubbra knew this chap called Joseph Slater and he said he was selling a flute because he was going to go away. So my mother capitulated, I think to my father's horror, and spent £50 on a flute. And I can remember going and getting this flute, which was a flute in only two pieces—head and body—and showing it to everybody at school in front of Rudi. All my other colleagues in the music gang at school were slightly older than me—they were vastly superior. 'Oh, how are you getting on?' one of them said. So I played low C. I could actually get the bottom note out of it and that was enough of a demonstration!*

Not surprisingly, having waited so long for a flute, Wibb didn't need to be encouraged to keep practising.

> *No, it was only: 'Stop!' I remember there was a school song, written by the French master called Tom, and one of the verses was: 'From up in the attic*

Wibb with Jumble

there comes a faint toot / Oh it's Wibb with his flute!' And it ended with: 'Re-giblet my Wiblet for me!'

Wibb was lucky: it was no ordinary flute. Made in 1919, it had been chosen by the celebrated flute player, Albert Fransella, for his pupil Joseph Slater. Fransella had gone to the Rudall Carte factory and selected the best wooden tube he could find. The keywork was Boehm system, with open G Sharp, which was Boehm's original design and which Wibb has played ever since. It served Wibb well for some years.

Geoffrey Gilbert said it was an unusually good flute for a wooden Rudall Carte. I went to Geoffrey for lessons when I was not quite sixteen and I was carrying on, doing frightfully well, getting steamed up with all my scales and studies and things. Then one day I came in to a lesson and said: 'I think I need a new flute', and Geoffrey said: 'Oh, really? Why?' He never pushed anything, being most incredibly ethical. I said: 'It doesn't make the right sound in the high notes'. I was convinced that my nasty sound in the high notes was due to the wooden flute! Geoffrey said: 'What is the right sound then?' And I said I'd got a record with the Paris Conservatoire Orchestra playing En Bateau by Debussy, and he was very pleased. He said: 'Oh, that's

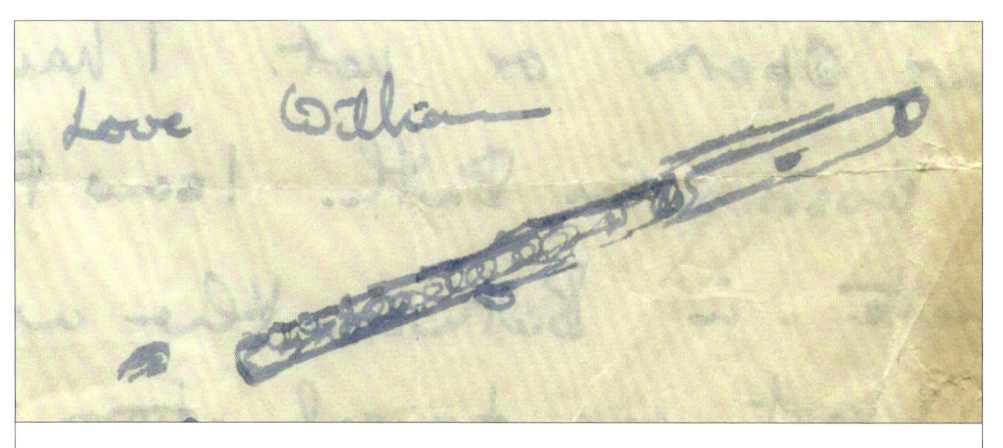

Wibb's earliest sketch of a flute

Lucien Lavaillotte and he plays on a Louis Lot, and so do I, and that's the sort of flute you ought to have.'

Soon after, Wibb and his parents saw an advert for a silver Louis Lot flute that had been rebuilt by Charles Morley, the eminent flute maker and repairer. They bought it—the first of many Louis Lots that would pass through Wibb's hands over the years.

Incidentally, it was Charles Morley who had first told Wibb about Geoffrey Gilbert.

I went to see Mr Morley first because some accident had happened with my wooden flute at school—I think one of the corks had come off a tail, and I thought the thing needed bending, and I bent it, and of course the tail of the key broke! While I was there, he said: 'Look at this'—he had a metal flute foot joint—'This is platinum! I'm making this for Geoffrey Gilbert, England's greatest technician on the flute.' He called him a technician! Anyway, he told me it was twice as heavy as silver and twice as expensive as gold.

Shortly after that, Geoffrey Gilbert played the Mozart D Major Concerto in a radio broadcast. Wibb was at school and Rudi Sabor switched on the Third Programme for his music appreciation class.

I heard this most amazing sound coming out of the flute. It was wow! I realised: 'This man is phenomenal'.

A defining moment. Wibb was fifteen and he immediately resolved to have flute lessons with Geoffrey Gilbert. But first he had to persuade his parents.

There were several flute players who played quite regularly on the radio and I remember my father trying to be sensible: 'Well, who are the leading flute players in the country?' And I said: 'Geoffrey Gilbert, Gareth Morris and John Francis... but I think Geoffrey Gilbert's the best'. Without knowing it, I was relating it to records I already had of Marcel Moyse and others. My parents happened to know the Principal of the Guildhall

Pastel of a boat by Wibb, 1951

> School of Music, and they spoke to him and he said: 'Yes, I think Geoffrey
> Gilbert is the right person'.

For Wibb, it was a moment that focussed not only his vocation as a musician—at the age of eleven he had been thinking he might become a cartoonist—but specifically his vocation as a flute player. Wibb's parents, however, although they were both artists, were not at all sure about such a choice of career. They shared a widespread mistrust of music as a serious profession.

> If I'd wanted to be a poet or something like that, they wouldn't have
> flinched, but a musician? Dirty people in dark suits! It wasn't a side of
> life they'd ever thought about very much. The fact that they knew Edmund
> Rubbra... they didn't connect. They thought it meant that I would end up
> in the Lyons Corner House!

In other words, playing background music in a restaurant orchestra—albeit a smart restaurant.

> *They thought that was what musicians did. At first they were supportive of me wanting to study, but when I said I wanted to do this for a living, they went and had a private meeting with Geoffrey Gilbert and asked: 'You know, is this alright?' Apparently Geoffrey said: 'Yes, it is. Quite often it isn't a very good idea, but in his case it's alright'. From then on I got absolute full support.*

And with that support guaranteed, Wibb's mind was made up: nothing else was going to divert him, or hold him back—not even the prestigious National Youth Orchestra. He had established a pattern for life of resolutely pursuing his own path.

> *I left the National Youth Orchestra after one course because I decided I didn't want to wait to go up the ladder in their hierarchy and I thought that since Ruth Railton considered I never washed my fingernails properly, I wasn't going to succeed! I could feel that I wasn't the sort of smart, young gentry she would have fancied—there wasn't any future for me in that particular regime. So, I decided: 'No, I'm going to get on. I'm going to go to the Guildhall now'. So I joined the Guildhall when I was sixteen.*

Sketch of railway sidings, Bogotá, by Wibb

2—Teachers

In any conversation with Wibb, two names come up time and time again, like complementary talismans of the flute: Geoffrey Gilbert and Marcel Moyse. As already noted, Geoffrey Gilbert was Wibb's teacher from the age of fifteen, at first privately and then at the Guildhall School of Music and Drama. Marcel Moyse didn't arrive on the scene in person until Wibb was almost thirty, but the influence of his playing on recordings pre-dates even Wibb's first encounter with Geoffrey Gilbert—an encounter that might not have led to flute lessons.

> We went to his house—very nice—I played and he said: 'Excuse me a minute', and went out of the room. We only learnt many years later what had happened. He apparently left the room to say to his wife Marjorie: 'Come to the sitting room, you've got to hear this'. The situation was that he had been having some health problems, I think it was angina, and he'd decided to cut back on his teaching. Being thoroughly ethical—he was concerned with ethics to a fault—he said: 'What shall I do? Well, I'll get rid of the best ones; they can cope best without me'. So he kept all the bad ones—he was that much of an idealist—and he had decided not to have any more pupils. But on this particular occasion he said: 'Come and listen to this. I've got to have him'. So I was accepted.

Wibb with Geoffrey Gilbert

Lessons began a week later.

> *He made me play all the major and minor scales straightway in the first week and to come with the Moyse Daily Exercises. I asked him: 'How fast should I play?' and he said: 'As fast as possible'. Then he proceeded to show me in the lesson that as fast as possible was terribly slow! It wasn't just a question of the notes, it was to get complete control, absolutely even in time, with equality of sound, and so a lot of slow practice was necessary. The standard of accuracy that he was demanding was extremely demanding! He had to slow me down so I could control everything perfectly. But he was always very nice and never put you down for anything at all. He was utterly kind.*

Wibb had had a couple of lessons previously from a saxophone player in Bath who, among other things, had talked to him about vibrato. He'd been impressed on hearing the Concertgebouw Orchestra that the flute and oboe actually matched their vibrato speeds. Vibrato on the flute was an entirely new concept for Wibb.

> *I questioned Geoffrey about it: 'Do you do anything about vibrato?' and he said: 'Oh yes, you've got a very fast one—we must learn to control it'. I had no idea that I had a vibrato! And sure enough, within a very little while, maybe four or five weeks, we were practising little vibrato exercises and learning to control it at all the different speeds. That went along with work on the tongue, which I'm now more and more grateful for. He taught me, tongue out, loosely, withdraw the tongue—and without him saying so, that involved putting the jaw forward—so you can do a softer attack by doing that movement slowly, and finishing the notes by continuing to blow afterwards. Now, he'd learnt that, probably from René Le Roy, as part of the French style.*

This technique was to become a mainstay of Wibb's playing and eventually his own teaching, as we will see later.

> *I'm finding all over the world that people don't have this basic technique. Practically everywhere I go, people are ruined because they can only make one sort of beginning to the note. But the tongue can work in all sorts of different places. Geoffrey said that when it goes very fast, it just moves a little bit at the top of the mouth, but if you're a bit slower, you may move the tongue a bit further backwards and forwards. So, I don't think it was an idea of a fixed place. He was trying to get that French 'ah', but I think I'd already caught the old 't' from maybe the saxophone player or somewhere, I don't know. Now I'm constantly saying: 'Why do you tongue? It's not necessary—it's a vowel', but people haven't really learnt that the flute is a voice, and not all words begin with a consonant. But I'm just constantly grateful to Geoffrey—gosh, wasn't I lucky!—he got rid of this habit more or less before I was sixteen.*

Not surprisingly, although lessons were meant to last an hour, they always overran. The study plan was logical—as was everything Geoffrey did—with a secure technical grounding.

> *We did sonority, scales, studies, and then later, a piece or two. Geoffrey didn't demonstrate very much. You had to learn his quite dry, logical language. 'If you do such and such, then...' and so forth. He didn't swamp you with words—he was quite a genius I think.*

Geoffrey's father had been an oboist and his mother a schoolteacher. From his mother he had inherited a concern for good use of English and clear expression and he was very meticulous in how he used words.

> *I can remember saying: 'You said something', and he said: 'Oh no, what I said was this' and he corrected my reportage. He was right.*

Geoffrey Gilbert

Geoffrey had also inherited a very English way of playing the flute, rather tense and rigid in style, concerned almost exclusively with technical brilliance. A breakthrough for him had come when he listened to Marcel Moyse recording the Brandenburg Concertos in London in 1935, realising that there was another, wholly different approach to flute playing that placed a premium on suppleness, expression and colour. He took lessons from another French player, René Le Roy, and rebuilt his own playing from the basics. It was an extraordinarily visionary and brave move from someone who was already an established professional player.

> *Sometimes Geoffrey said to me: 'You don't know what an advantage you've had over me, because you have all the benefit of my experience learning the flute the hard way, and I've sorted out the problems before I told you about them'. He said his teacher, Joseph Lingard, when somebody was playing, would say: 'Stop, hold it!' and if they were playing a high G, they'd have to hold it as long as possible, until they burst or something! Control! Tremendous focus on control, but in holding it you became hard and rigid, and Geoffrey found out that there were other ways of doing things.*

> *I think his big shock come when he studied with René Le Roy. Everything was different. He said that the War had helped him tremendously because he'd had this total new, vast dumping of other ideas and he was suddenly removed from being in the profession, so he had time to implement all this new knowledge. Then, when he could practise, he could just concentrate on the new way of looking at the instrument. He was trying to relax things and do it in a different way, and he said: 'You're very lucky, you haven't grown up like I and some of the other players did'. But he was sorting things out in a really super-intelligent way.*

Fundamental to that sorting out was rethinking the flute embouchure: what to do with the lips to ensure the required suppleness.

> *Geoffrey talked about relaxing the lips and turning the corners down rather than pulling up. In fact, as a student, I learnt a lot from rubbing shoulders with Jimmy Galway, who arrived on the scene—he was sixteen and I was nineteen. He could play the flute blowing over the end and I couldn't get a note out of it that way. I wasn't going to have him able to do something that I couldn't. So, the next day, I practised that sort of blowing for about eight hours until I could do it—and I could.*

The results for Wibb were astonishing.

> *I found the most colossal sound coming out of the flute. You take the head joint off and just blow over the top. And I found out much more about turning the corners down, because it would only work that way, and I use that to this day for stopping somebody pulling up the old 'British smile'. The sardonic smile of the wooden flute players comes from pulling like hell to try and get some brilliance out of a very dull flute. That was the big issue: the English had the tight, sardonic smile, and the French had, what was called 'loose lip', the upside down embouchure. But when we met other players like Rampal, they never thought about it, they just had flexibility, naturally.*

While Geoffrey was rigorous and exhaustive in his advice for solving the technical issues of his students, he usually took a step back when it came to artistic matters.

> *He had a principle, which he stated at our first meeting in 1951: 'I don't teach music, I teach the flute. I try and sort the technique, remove the obstacles and let the player's innate, natural musical sense guide them to make music'. So he didn't actually say very much about musical things. He was talking about logic, strong and weak beats—which I give my pupils hell with!—and that sort of thing, but he thought that his job was only to give his pupils the ability to express themselves. That's what I noticed was so fantastic when I went to Moyse: all those that had studied with Geoffrey Gilbert had much more ability to do what Moyse was telling them. So Geoffrey was right!*

With hindsight, Wibb can see how the process of his musical education was proceeding along two parallel paths.

I was picking up what to listen for in recordings and concerts, and Geoffrey was showing me the mechanics of getting everything in a well-ordered frame of things and getting the technique right.

I'm constantly remembering what he said, the basic things: the tongue and the jaw movements, the actual mechanics of blowing the instrument and overcoming its problems of going sharp and flat. What a brilliant man he was. How economical he was with his words and with the clarity of his ideas. I can remember particularly wishing I could do that as well as he did. He'd learnt it from René Le Roy.

Wibb can also see how comprehensive and yet specific to each student was Geoffrey's approach.

I'm constantly amazed with what Geoffrey did and didn't tell me. He didn't tell me a lot of things, but maybe he perceived that I already had my own inkling and I just needed training. I think he had the good taste to know. He knew when not to put the pressure on about creating something, he referred to people's innate natural musicianship. He would do the guiding and what you had to do was to get the technical problems ironed out.

Musically speaking, Wibb's first lesson with Geoffrey actually dated from that Proms performance on the radio of the Mozart D major Concerto.

I wanted to know what to do with the shaping and the phrases. I had my pen with me and marked the crescendos and diminuendos that I observed Geoffrey doing (I've still got that part at home) and that's very much what you need to do. So that was a lesson for me: he did this and it sounded right. And I said: 'I'll put those marks in, what I observed him doing'. But that wasn't him telling me to do anything, and I didn't tell him when I played that piece to him—I covered his marks!

There were, however, definite moments of musical illumination coming directly from Geoffrey which have stayed with Wibb ever since.

I do remember playing the Trio Sonata from The Musical Offering *to Geoffrey once, the Second Movement, and he said something about the upbeat: that it can sometimes be long, meaning that there's something leading through. It's an indeterminate length, and that might apply to all sorts of other music.*

I was doing something like that with a pupil the other day in the Schubert Arpeggione *Sonata (which really must have been written for the flute!). 'You've got to make those upbeats longer, and you've got to slide...' and I thought: 'Oh yes, that's one of those upbeats that Geoffrey was talking about in the Bach'. You couldn't possible play Hungarian-style in the Bach, but there's an element of it there, sometimes in an upbeat.*

The wind players known as the 'Royal Family' in Sir Thomas Beecham's Royal Philharmonic Orchestra: Jack Brymer, clarinet; Terence MacDonagh, oboe; Dennis Brain, horn; Geoffrey Gilbert, flute; Gwydion Brooke, bassoon.

Behind Geoffrey's apparent reticence to talk much of musical matters, lay a world of experience and insight that could take Wibb and his fellow students completely by surprise.

> *Geoffrey knew much more than he taught. He'd suddenly play the piano, for example. He wouldn't actually say what he did, but in one class he played the piano part in the* Carmen Fantasy, *without the music. He just knew all the harmonies—fantastic ear. He wouldn't tell anybody what to do with the vibrato, but he did it!*

Geoffrey did, however, have a guiding principle to inform any musical decision.

> *He would often say: 'If you do something, you must consider why, because if you do such and such, it means such and such'. He was trying to impose a certain logic on the whole thing.*

That logic came into its own in building an absolutely secure technique.

> *When I went to Geoffrey I was doing the Boehm Opus 26 Studies and I think he thought that was a little bit more advanced than I should have been doing, but he didn't want to discourage me, so he let me go on. But I had to do trill studies, making sure all the trills were the same. That was*

> *frightfully boring—all trills at the same speed—and I could trill very fast on most notes! Of course, we got onto the Marcel Moyse Sonority Book and some of his other books. Then sometimes Geoffrey got a thing about fingers and said: 'Now we're going to do Lorenzo Studies', which was boring! But that's what he'd learnt in Manchester, that's what they were concerned about—even fingers—that was the English school. He wasn't totally throwing out everything he'd learnt.*

Geoffrey was very unusual, however, in introducing Moyse studies at that time in England.

> *Oh yes... and he told me afterwards that some of the players in London laughed when they heard Moyse's playing. They couldn't take it seriously. (And I know lots of admirers of Moyse who laugh when they hear the English style!) But it's difficult to go a different way, isn't it? Geoffrey Gilbert said that when he started playing French style with vibrato, a lot of the conductors used to consider it effeminate. Henry Wood, the conductor of the Proms, didn't like it. But it's funny, isn't it? They said that, but then Albert Fransella quite frequently appeared at the Proms. So they did like the French style...*

With that style went a rich repertoire of contemporary French music that Geoffrey championed.

> *His group, the Wigmore Ensemble, played an awful lot of French music and modern works—he was very Francophile. He liked the Ibert Concerto, works by Roussel, and things like that.*

Wibb counted himself fortunate to continue learning from Geoffrey even after he had left Guildhall, been to Paris, won a prize at Geneva and embarked on a busy playing career.

> *I went on having lessons. I'd be going and asking questions about what to do in such and such a circumstance. If I was going for an audition, for instance, and I would have to answer questions about orchestral playing: 'What do I need to know?' And he said: 'Watch the music and the beat, and don't turn round and look behind you when somebody else is playing a solo'. (Obviously, he'd been clouted by somebody!) And he said: 'Play quietly enough'. (In other words, don't play too bloody loud!) 'Play quietly, play in time and in tune, and watch the beat. If you have a few bars rest, memorise what's coming up and then watch the conductor more when you're playing'. Practical things.*

Very practical advice for a young professional—and it wasn't the last lesson.

> *He went off to Florida in 1969 and, of course, I went on knowing him and visiting him. In fact, I even had a lesson in Florida, so the last lesson was later than I thought. Then Trevor Wye had started the summer schools and Geoffrey came to Ramsgate and I remember playing the Ibert Concerto to*

Wibb with Marcel Moyse in Boswil

him (which I was performing somewhere) and he gave me bits of advice. It wasn't really an official lesson, but it was still a useful experience. It turned into a lifetime's connection: he was a father figure.

But not the only one.

Moyse was the biggest father figure of all!

Long before Wibb met Marcel Moyse for the first time, at a masterclass in Switzerland, he had got to know his playing intimately. From childhood he had spent hours listening and carefully analysing his recordings—and sometimes just enjoying them.

I used to put Moyse on when I was feeling despondent—it used to put the smile back inside!

It was all part of getting to know the French approach to playing the flute, which Wibb had always felt instinctively drawn to.

One day in Boswil, Moyse asked: 'What is French style?' Nobody said anything for a long while. Eventually I was very brave and put up my hand—you had to be brave to say anything in front of Moyse, he could take it the wrong way! I said: 'In England, it's a flute player who uses vibrato!', and he said, raising his leg: 'Oh, no, never!' and he roared with laughter.

He said that the French school started when great players like Taffanel began listening to the other instruments and finding out they inflect or articulate like this, or do that, and they imitated the violin, the voice, the trombone, the triangle. He said the French School is being able to play the notes like the other instruments—and I was already quite into that. In fact, by the time I went to Moyse, I was into listening to Janet Baker and many other singers. In fact, I'd done a lot of work with them.

For Wibb, that first summer at Moyse's masterclasses in Boswil was the great illumination of his musical life. So how did it come about?

I went to hear my friend Jimmy Galway play at Wigmore Hall with Michel Debost—it must have been in 1964. Afterwards, Michel said to me: 'Oh, you'd be interested. I've just been on a course with Marcel Moyse!'. 'Is he still alive?!' 'Yes'. Immediately I got in touch with Trevor Wye and we decided to go, of course.

They arrived in the summer of 1965—it was Moyse's second year of masterclasses—and stayed for a month. The village of Boswil had an Artists' Association connected to a decommissioned church and that was where the masterclasses took place. The organisation was totally informal: you paid a fee and then waited your turn.

Somebody would get up and play without there being any preference. You had to think: 'Looks like everybody has had a go, so I'll get up next'. You made sure you played when you felt it was time. We started watching how often various people had played and if you really were bursting and you saw a chance, you'd take it!

Wibb duly waited (though not for long) then seized the moment and got up to play Philippe Gaubert's *Nocturne et Allegro scherzando*.

It turned out that that was the piece Moyse had played for his passing out parade at the Conservatoire. He got awfully enthused when I played. The thing I remember about it, we were working at a certain section and he said: 'Here, no vibrato!' So I used less—and that passed—and we went on to the next point. Then the next day Trevor got up to play his piece, and suddenly Moyse said: 'No, vibrato'. Trevor, being confrontational, suddenly started playing that straight English noise: 'Do you mean like this?' And Moyse said: 'Oh, no, never! He not do that yesterday when I asked no vibrato!' Trevor got a very clear answer, but we spent a long time beginning to understand that whenever Moyse said 'no vibrato' (he pronounced it 'vybrato') he didn't actually mean vibrato. When somebody went 'wow... wow... wow... wow...' and you heard lumps in the sound, he called that 'vybrato' and he said: 'Living tone, but not vybrato'. They were separate things for him—he didn't call it vibrato to have a normal sort of sound.

Eventually Wibb made a connection back to his earlier training.

Geoffrey used to say: 'I'm not going to tell you how many wobbles to put on a note any more, I'm going to say merely, more expressive, or less expressive.

> *You must use your judgement. If I can count your vibrato, it's probably wrong!' And Moyse would say 'expressive tone', or something.*

Moyse's reactions could still be hard to predict, however, and it took some time for Wibb to fathom him.

> *We found out that he had curious ideas about what was good in terms of tone. One day a Swiss bloke was playing and it was pretty poor, and Moyse suddenly said: 'Very good. He has nice life in the tone!' and I never found out what it was that he liked! But he talked about life in the tone, and he didn't mind which sort of life it was—it wasn't 'it has to be this way'. That, of course, is encouraging, because it's not fixed. Fernand Caratgé had tended to say: 'This is the sound of the flute'. Moyse hadn't any fixed idea. If it was good, if it was alive, it was nice.*

Moyse could famously be very critical of some of the players who came to the Boswil masterclasses. Did Wibb emerge completely unscathed?

> *I was very blessed! He was very pro me, yes. Maybe because I could play 'elephants' well! 'Catch an elephant, catch an elephant!' he was always singing.*

Where Geoffrey's approach had been fundamentally technical and his musical sympathies had extended to the modern age, Moyse was the great Romantic of the flute. He was a child of five when Debussy composed his *L'Après-midi d'un faune* and he had grown up in the musical world of Gounod, Massenet and Saint-Saëns.

> *Elegance was something he was after. I remember going to Saint-Amour, Moyse's home town, after the course, and I had a lesson with him. He said at the end: 'You do not need to come to me any more; you have found elegance'. I was terribly sad, I thought he was giving me the boot—you won't need to come any more. I didn't feel that was right at all! I went on coming, so it was alright, but I had this awful feeling: 'Oh, no, nothing more for you', but it wasn't true and it didn't happen like that.*

So Wibb's learning relationship with Moyse continued, just as it did with Geoffrey. Moyse's teaching was unfailingly inspiring but, as Wibb found, it was not always easy to know exactly what he meant. What about 'elegance', for example?

> *I don't know, except that he had it! Elegance was something he was after and that was the thing that was so wonderful about those French flute pieces: they had elegance. I had a lesson from him in Boswil on the Godard Suite. I'd had a copy before and tried it, and I wrote on the cover: 'Suite by Benjy Goddard, ha ha ha!' I thought it was absolute rubbish, but then I found I rather liked it and I thought: 'Hey this is Moyse's kind of stuff' and I played it for him.*

That was when Wibb began to extend his knowledge of the repertoire that had grown up around the playing of Paul Taffanel and Philippe Gaubert, in response to the new flexibility and expressivity of French flute playing.

Teachers

Marcel Moyse

> *It really made me interested in playing French music properly. Moyse just showed me all sorts of things. One day, for instance, he said: 'Oh you should look at Reynaldo Hahn... good piece'. It was the* Variations on a Theme of Mozart *and I went straight down to Zurich and bought a copy and it became one of my pieces. I think he just got a feeling I would be able to play it, make it work. It was one of the pieces that people weren't playing and suddenly he had this wonderful memory of it.*

As for knowing exactly what Moyse meant, Wibb's copies of the flute music he took with him to Boswill are peppered with Moyse's observations, aphorisms and advice—some clear, some cryptic. Here are a few of them, collected by Wibb over the years from various classes.

> *I practised a long time Andante to observe everything...*
> *I rush a little, but a little bit by pleasure...*
> *When Mozart say something three times, the third time he smile...*
> *Fauré look in distance, far away... yellow fingers, cigarette holder, chain smoker...*
> *When we do something the teacher tell us, we must practise every day for a long time until we understand and we feel inside...*
> *Oui, oui, je t'aime!... [I love you]*
> *Monet, Cézanne, Van Gogh, always try and get the light—we must always try do same thing with flute...*
> *Make me afraid...*
> *This is only expressive by the sound you make...*
> *Natural tone in the middle—not like frog...*
> *Richer, not by strength, but with love...*
> *Sometimes conductors make wit, when others make crescendo...*
> *En fermant les yeux je rêve [closing my eyes, I dream]. That's how you get the top note in the Schubert Variations. And we will be happy...*
> *I never practise something without trying to evoke something...*

That last affirmation struck a particular chord and has become fundamental to Wibb's own philosophy of playing and teaching. The flute is a character in the music. It's like going on stage, isn't it?

> *Oh yes, he's talking about how you deliver it to the audience. 'Develop'—or as he said it, 'deevelop'. That was a word he used all the time: 'Deevelop!'*
>
> *It opened up things vastly for me. I felt he was expressing in a more direct, tangible way things that I had sort of half known, half dreamed of. He made them strong in me and made it possible to use them. I was so delighted: it was confirmation of the truth and it made me own all these things for myself. I remember thinking: 'Well, I suspected that... thank you... I always felt something like that... yes, that's it!' It was a revelation the whole time.*

Sketch of Marcel Moyse by Wibb

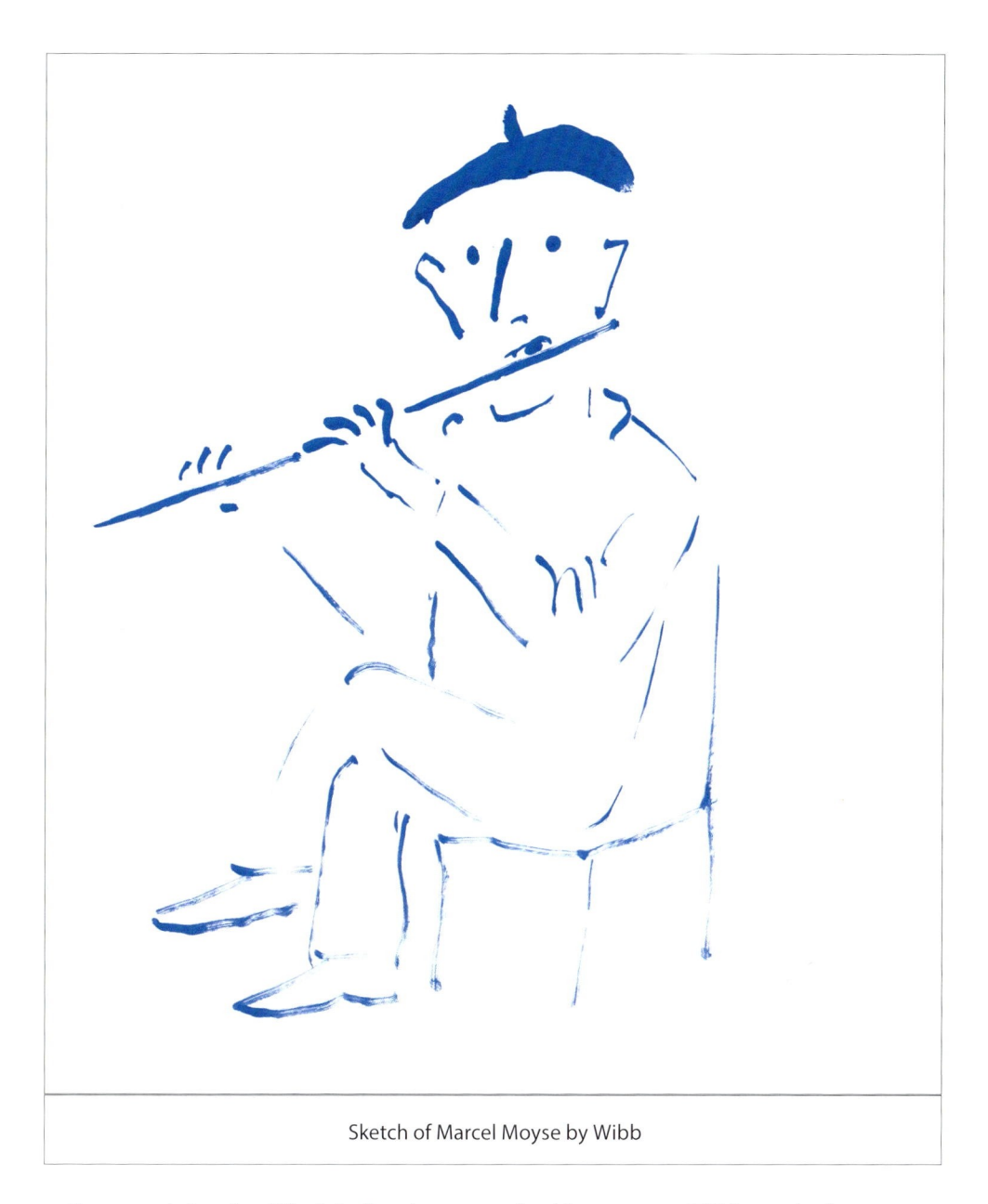

It was advice for life. Maybe the most significant note Wibb made from these masterclasses was jotted down in his much used, now crumbling copy of Moyse's *Etudes et Exercices Techniques*. 'Try to be what you play—like actor!—take the atmosphere with whole body'.

Moyse himself—ever the actor—obviously noticed the effect he was having on Wibb, because Wibb and Trevor always tried to get the best seats at the front of the class.

> *We realised that was definitely the best place to be. And one evening at drinks after the class, Moyse said: 'You notice I always talk to you?' I hadn't really noticed, but he said: 'I talk to you because I see you understand'. Obviously it was registering on my face and he was appreciating the recognition of what he said, so he spoke to me.*

With so much to take in, Wibb found that he also learned a lot from what others at Boswil were observing of Moyse's approach—the American flutist, Eleanor Lawrence, for example.

> *Ellie said: 'You notice he has a strong principle? "Melodic versus rhythmic". It's either rhythmic or melodic'. I use it now all the time, but I actually learnt it from Ellie, not from Moyse himself. When you have an articulation, for instance, is it smooth and lyrical or more staccato and incisive? Moyse also used to say: 'Not more forte, but more généreuse [generous or full-bodied].' Forte meant tight for him—a rhythmic, very concentrated sound.*

Observing how others were playing and responding to Moyse's teaching was also inspirational.

> *Once you heard something that sounded good, you could go away and practise what was beautiful and try to emulate that, and practise what Moyse had suggested, instead of frantically cobbling together a mountain of notes for your next appearance. What we learned was practice from observation and enthusiasm—love.*

What was it like then, to sit in the class at Boswil, watching Moyse for many hours each day? What did he look like, how did he act?

> *He had deep set, sunken eyes and an intensity in the eyes, which was quite fantastic. Always something going on. He used to tell stories. You couldn't always immediately get the connection, but lots of good stories were thrown in.*

Here is one of the most vivid of those stories, as remembered by Wibb, in Moyse's characteristic Franglais—a curious blend of French and English!

> *'I dream I die, and I go to Purgatoire [Purgatory]. They take me down and many terrible things happening. They take me through many places. Finally they bring me to a big lac [lake]. In this place I see many heads in the water and the lac is full of shit! I look and I see all these heads, I see my friend Schneider. I say: 'Hello Schneider. How long you got?' Schneider say: 'Two hundred years!' Me, I rejoice—myself, I only got one hundred years for my crimes against music. I take my clothes off and prepare to jump in! He say: 'Moyse, Moyse, take care. Don't make wave! 'Lac full of shit... don't make wave!'*

And the musical interpretation of the story?

> *That's about vibrato—or 'vybrato'. 'Don't make wave! Don't drown us!' Vybrato was obvious waves—like a bad baritone!*

Marcel Moyse and Wibb

All of this intensely colourful approach to flute playing, of course, needs to be viewed in the context of Moyse's many books of studies—in his own way he was just as concerned about technique as was Geoffrey Gilbert. But the rare moments of specific technical advice in the masterclasses were always driven by the music.

> *He said to me one day: 'You should take C sharp'—that's the upper C sharp—'with these fingers'. It's like high D, with an extra two fingers of the right hand. I didn't like that fingering then. I'm telling people all the time to use it now, but at that time I wanted the pure, open C sharp and I could play the right pitch. He said: 'It is more sensitive if you take it this way'. He used sensitive fingerings quite frequently—playing C like F without the thumb; or B flat like E flat without the left hand middle finger.*
>
> *My big success with Moyse, the first year we went there, after I played the* Nocturne et Allegro scherzando, *was with the tune from Weber's* Oberon, *for soprano and horn. Moyse kept on playing it and I happened to have learnt it with Caratgé. I didn't think much of it as a piece, but one day I thought I'd chance my arm and see what Moyse had to say about it. He went over the moon! I was his golden boy after that! And when he*

demonstrated it, he used the sensitive fingerings for B flat, C, and D flat. He would play 'sensitively', but he didn't spend a lot of time telling people they had to do this. He would only suggest it to a very advanced player, I think. But we noticed him doing it. We were watching his fingers no end!

It's significant that Moyse was working at that time on a new book of musical studies, *Tone Development Through Interpretation*. At one memorable lesson he also produced a copy of his *24 Petites Etudes Mélodiques* which had been published back in 1932.

We had a Saturday morning when Trevor went through the whole book with Moyse. That's when I got to know them. Moyse was referring to them all the time and I became very fascinated. I practised those 24 Studies like mad, because they have the real basics in them: like how do you make repeated notes... how do you finish a note... how do you start a note….? Moyse was one of the few French players who could do a soft attack. Most of them are stuck with a clear beginning because they can't avoid tonguing, but I've got Moyse's recording of the L'Arlésienne *Minuet and he can do a soft attack alright. Marvellous! That's how it has to be.*

Wibb has lived with the 24 Studies as a mainstay of his playing and teaching ever since.

Yes definitely... but Trevor doing the whole book in one session... I can't get through the book as quickly as that. When I've tried to have a class on the 24 Studies, it's taken me three hours to get through the first six. I had a class in the States with Clifford Benson in attendance to play the piano accompaniments (as yet unwritten!) and it took two days to do the 24 Studies. I've also done that on a masterclass at Wildacres in the States. I insisted: 'We are going to do the 24 Studies—get the basics'. And it's still my intention to do it with the Royal Academy students. They keep on saying: 'But I'm playing in a competition next week...' and so they miss out on it. Instead of doing the real work, they learn half a million more notes!

And in case anyone is in any doubt, Wibb has inscribed the title page of his own copy of the 24 Studies with the word *BIBLE* in capital letters!

Wibb continued to go to Boswil for masterclasses for five or six years. Afterwards he often followed Moyse to Saint-Amour in the Jura mountains and remained in regular contact with him for the rest of Moyse's life. I well remember visiting Saint-Amour with Wibb to meet Moyse in the early 1980s. He was very old by then and in ill health, but his passion for the flute was undiminished. Wibb and I talked to him about his memories of Taffanel and I shall never forget what he said: 'His playing was like the rising of the sun: it did not astonish you, it transfigured you, as the sun gently but powerfully brings light everywhere. There were so many colours in his sound... I learned to sing from Taffanel.'

Wibb, of course, learned exactly the same thing from Moyse.

3—Paris

After completing his studies at the Guildhall School of Music and Drama and three years of military service in the Scots Guards, Wibb was free to gain experience of French flute playing at first hand. French Government scholarships were available for short-term study of three months and Geoffrey Gilbert encouraged him to apply.

> *He was saying: 'You need to go for a period to get the finishing touch in Paris'. He was definitely for it. He thought that was a splendid thing that everybody ought to do and it was my natural inclination, because I was already a complete fan of Fernand Dufrène as well as Marcel Moyse.*

Geoffrey Gilbert thought Moyse had 'the most wonderful clear sound' and he was also an admirer of Dufrène and of René Le Roy.

> *He had a great respect for Le Roy as a very intelligent man who did things the right way, but he said he didn't play in tune. He didn't control things like Geoffrey would have liked them to have been done. He threw a lot of stuff out of the window. But Geoffrey could nevertheless hear through that that there was something very good.*

Neither Le Roy nor Moyse were available to give lessons in Paris at that point, and Dufrène didn't take pupils, so a different teacher had to found.

> *I knew this player called Albert Honey, who was with the BBC Revue Orchestra. He was a pupil of Fernand Caratgé and was always singing his praises. Albert made a wonderful sound and so he persuaded me I needed to go to Caratgé—who was the one everyone went to in Paris in those days anyway. Caratgé wasn't at the Conservatoire, but he seemed to be the favoured one. Geoffrey wasn't against that at all. So I applied for 'leçons particulières'—private lessons—with Caratgé and I got my three months—that's all I had—plus an extra three or four weeks my Dad paid for.*

Those crucial months, beginning in January 1958, are documented in the detailed and hugely entertaining letters Wibb wrote home to his parents. Luckily they kept them safely. Their letters back to Wibb haven't survived, but what we do have paints a vivid picture of an eager young flute player at liberty in the City of Light.

Wibb aged twenty-one

Wibb's letters must have greatly amused the postman. He addresses one, on 2 February 1958, to
> Mr and Mrs Fitzjumble-Bennett R.I.B.A etc

and on the reverse announces
> N.B. I have passed the first month's probation, and this address is now permanent.

The back of the envelope is also decorated with a sketch of a sleeping cat and a further message.
> How's Thornton managing in my room with all that Gramophone and so forth strewn all over the place? And that ferocious puss? How's that peace loving dog?

The envelope of a later letter is addressed to
> Mr and Mrs Frank E Jumble (R.I.B.D.) (Royal Institute of British Dustbinlids)

and embellished on the reverse with a sketch of a skull's head smoking a pipe!

Wibb's new address was the Hotel Stella in the rue Monsieur le Prince (still there) in the heart of the student quarter, close to the famous boulevard Saint Michel, the River Seine and Notre Dame. It was a lucky find.

Dear Ma and Pa. I hope you are all alive still. I spent one night in that hotel I booked, and then Philip Jones helped me to find another in which I am staying for at least a month. The first room I had was about 4 feet square, and very smelly—the one I am in now is enormous, with 3 tables, 2 settees, 2 wardrobes, and everything else—(water [sometimes], and a radiator). This is cheaper than the first room, and I am also allowed to practice in it until 10-00 at night. A woman moved out of the next door room on Saturday, and gave me a large methylated spirit stove, upon which I am now brewing some soup that the previous inhabitant of this room left in a cupboard. Whoever it was appears to have lived on soup, tea, Nescafé, Alcohol, and Veganin pills. There are about a dozen glasses, some plates, a cup, a small quantity of cutlery, some tea and sugar, eleven empty Nescafé tins, three of which have Veganin tablets inside. Also there are the remains of a crystal set (partially devoured). Practically all the restaurants in this street are Chinese...

Daily life in Paris was meticulously and amusingly documented.

Lavatory paper in the hotel is usually newspaper, if not, it is glazed paper from coloured picture magazines. The Newspaper is usually 'The Observer', and from this I learnt yesterday that the Oxford team were likely to win the Boat Race, because their coach had been giving them an utterly new and far more complete method of training, which included; football (for the legs); fencing (for the arms); running (for getting out of breath); Marbles (for concentration of mind over matter); and Ballet (to make them unappreciative of mediocre music, such as they might hear from massed portable radio sets on either sides of the river). Perhaps if I peruse enough lavatory paper I shall discover the result.

Today at lunch we had a very good piece of meat, without any fat or gristle, served (as usual) 'bien saignant', extremely rare. Now somehow an elderly English couple (tourists) had got into the restaurant, and sat quite near to where I was. This is what I heard:

'Oh Archie, this meat's absolutely raw'

'What do you expect me to do? Cook it?'

—silence—

A little while later a woman came around clearing away salt and mustard pots. The Englishwoman pointed to what, by French standards, was an extremely well cooked, if not overdone, piece of meat, and said (in English): 'Ere, could we 'ave this cooked a bit?' This was answered by a loud guffaw (in French) and the equivalent of 'it aint me wot cooks it', which the Frenchwoman found very amusing, and she pushed her way through the crowd of chairs and coats and bodies, spilling salt and bits of bread everywhere she was laughing so much.

There were evidently few problems about settling in and feeling at home.

The next letter is headed

> TELEGRAMS ETC. WIBBFROG!
>
> *I played in an orchestra in the American House of the Cité Universitaire last night—they are rehearsing for a concert on Friday, for which I have only to play the piccolo in one piece. I get paid about 600fr for each of the rehearsals, and 1000fr for the concert. The conductor is enormous, American & useless.*
>
> *As far as the bureau is concerned;—you can empty all of it except the bottom drawer (at the side), which is full of such precious things as the closed g sharp keys for the Haynes and Selmer. Could you put all the little bits of silver tube and wire rod etc that are in the corner of the Gas Meter, in this drawer please.*
>
> *As far as the kitchen cupboard is concerned:—you can empty everything in it into a box, but make sure my special flute tools and fine screwdrivers don't get mixed up with Pa's 'garden' tools!*
>
> *Could you send:—*
>
> *1. Assimil book (French without toil) which is Red, and on top of the chest of drawers.*
>
> *2. ½ lb of Tea (Strong, as in workmans cafe) (This is impossibly expensive here, and I already appear to have eaten a large quantity of my money)*
>
> *3. A pot of honey (large) (for similar reasons)*
>
> *I went to the flea market on Sunday—(even these are taxed over here),— and found some Moyse records—about which I am highly pleased. I have met a Chinese painter called Sing, who plays the flute vertically. He inhabits the American House, and most important, owns a gramophone.*
>
> *P.S. I have just received the Powell measurements, Thank You*

Time was short and not to be wasted.

> *I am doing a lot of practice to make up for the time I spent in bed doing nothing... Mr Lefèvre, (who is the Mr Morley of France), is doing my Louis Lot up, and said it should be ready by the end of the month...*
>
> *I have not yet received any parcel with Alarm Clock, Jacket, Assimil Book etc—the Alarm Clock is needed seriously as it is sometimes necessary to get up before 10.30, which is when I am now in the habit of waking. Could you get me some music from <u>Augener's</u> of Gt Marlborough St?—a Trio by John Addison for flute, Oboe, and Piano, which I need for a concert here?*

Wibb's parents duly obliged and were sent in return the first progress report on Wibb's flute lessons with Fernand Caratgé.

> *My flute was overhauled by Lefevre at a cost of 12,000frs, and works no better than before, if anything, rather worse. (This is somewhat annoying).*
>
> *I heard Caratgé playing the other night, and was rather disgusted,*

so now I can't believe anything he tells me about tone production—at lessons he sometimes tells me that I am playing flat, and picks up his flute to show me what pitch he thinks the note should be played at, but when I heard him at this concert, he was sharp most of the time. If I decide I can afford it, I shall try and take some lessons from Dufrène (of the Radio Orchestra) who is the best flautist I have heard here. Caratgé makes a noise like a pillow, and wants me to do the same, and also insists that Moyse's tone is not what a flute should sound like. Go to the French institute on the 23rd February, where he is giving a recital, and see what you think.

'Dear Old Buzzards' letter

I'm afraid that there 'aint much more to tell you, except that I have invested some valuable lolly in a box of watercolours, and also that Philip Jones, an oboist, and myself, had to walk out of a rehearsal of the 'Orchestre Nationale de la Cité Université', because everybody else was playing so out of tune that we couldn't stand it any longer!

The next letter addresses Wibb's parents affectionately as

Dear old Buzzards

with a sketch of two actual buzzards sitting on the branch of a tree smoking cigarettes!

I hope you are still well and alive in spite of I.T.V's Third Programme, strikes at Beecham's Pill factory, and Jumble's smoker's cough!

History doesn't relate what poor Jumble thought of this slur on his character! But on to more serious, musical matters.

I am having a flute specially made for me by Lefèvre (the foreman of Marigaux's flute factory). It will be an exact copy of Caratgé's Powell, and will have all the luxury extra keys such as the low B natural, and a special vented D key. The fact that Lefèvre is making it privately in his spare time cuts out any purchase tax, and also there will be no maker's name on it, which disposes of customs difficulties. Lefèvre is the man who made Gilbert's Louis Lot, and has the reputation of being the best craftsman in France, so I should get a better flute than a factory built Marigaux or Modern Louis Lot of which Lefèvre only makes the head joint. My flute has to be in Maillechort (a special alloy developed for musical instruments) and not silver because Lefèvre has not the necessary licence for silver, but I don't think that that matters a hoot, because Moyse played a flute of Maillechort, and, also some of the best Louis Lots I have come across have been made of ditto.

This will cost me 65,000fr with case (£50 if I can get it changed at tourist rate in England), and I hope to have a flute with the sound of a Louis Lot and the scale of a Powell by the beginning of May...

I have just been filled with cheap champagne at the expense of the American house of the Cité Universitaire, after a concert there, in which I played the solo in Bach's 5th Brandenburg (everyone seemed pleased, and even I wasn't too distressed, after having finally influenced the leader to make the orchestra tune to the same pitch as the piano!).

I had an enormous stroke of luck just before the concert,—I arrived at the dressing room quite early, and the janitor of the house saw me playing the flute, and told me that he had an instrument like mine, but shorter; that someone had left behind, and would I like it,—so now I own another piccolo—all metal, closed G sharp, in excellent condition,—and I only gave the chap 1,000frs tip, with which he was delighted. (This may save me a lot of money!)

Also today I met 'the Bootlace' (Rainer Schuelein), who is in Paris on his way back from Rome, (where he has been having lessons from an Italian called Gazzelloni). Rainer is bringing back my Haynes, and will leave it with Gilbert; perhaps you can ring up Gilbert and arrange what to do with it—ask £110, and try not to let it go for less than £100, (but I must get <u>at least</u> £80 to pay you back what you lent me).

Rainer has improved most tremendously with his 4 lessons in Italy, and, (I am very glad to say) seems to have the same opinions of Caratgé as myself. (It is very relieving to find someone else who thinks the same way as I do!). He has managed to acquire a solid gold Haynes headjoint from Gazzelloni without having yet paid for it! Also I lent him £5 on condition that he manages to get the money back to me by the beginning of May. So if you hear of anyone coming over, give Rainer a ring.

The next letter picks up on Wibb's parents' enthusiasm on hearing a concert given by Richard Adeney and their interest in Wibb's mention of Gazzelloni. Wibb himself, however, had other plans in mind.

> I'm glad to hear that you liked Richard Adeney—because he makes what I consider to be 'the right sort of noise'—also he plays in tune and doesn't indulge in anything vulgar. As I may have told you before, the best flautist (according to me) is Dufrène of the National Orchestra, who is also highly musical, (doesn't use too much vibrato, as all the other Frenchmen do) and has the most super tone I've ever heard. I asked him for some lessons after a concert the other night, but unfortunately he doesn't teach at all, (probably much too busy). So I will have to make do with Caratgé only, for the moment. This isn't so bad since I seem to be learning a lot from him even if he is a lousy performer! One of my main objections is that he plays much sharper than is necessary in England, and when he discovers that he is playing sharper than me, he insists that I am playing flat. In my last lesson I got fed up with this and donged my trusty tuning fork to prove that he was utterly up the pole (or, in other words, <u>sharp</u>!).

> What's all this nonsense about me going to Gazzelloni and staying with the Tommy's and so forth? You realise that I am going to be broke when I have paid for my flute etc? If I have any money left I shall want to use it for one of the International festivals at Geneva or Zurich or some such place. (Perhaps you could acquire some information for me on this subject?) I would also like to be able to have my home made flute repadded over here, but I'm not sure if I can afford it...

'Drunken students' letter

'Rat on the stairs' letter

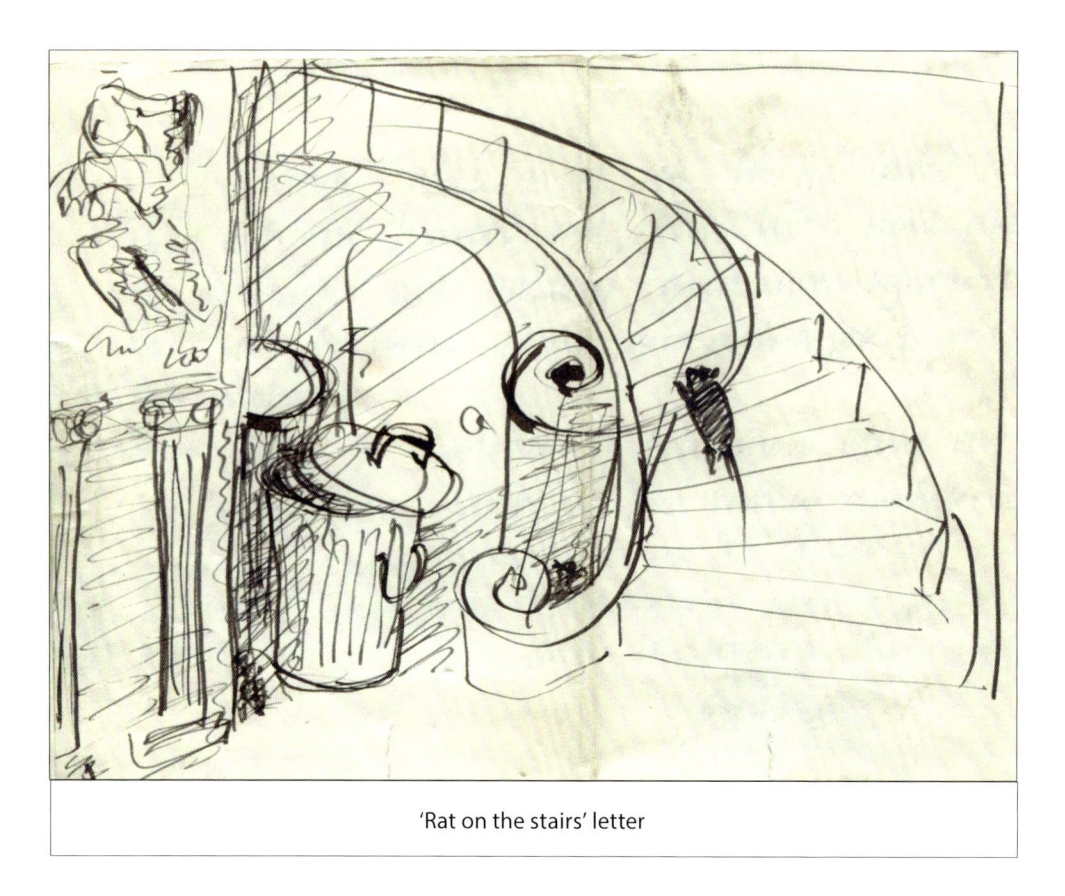

Meanwhile, daily life in Paris continues to be a source of keen fascination—and artistic inspiration. Wibb copiously illustrates a letter with sketches of a rat, policemen, drunks, and himself playing the flute to a cat!

> *I have met a large and very athletic French rat, who lives next door to a posh art gallery, and goes upstairs two at a time. (Quite good going for a rat.)...*
>
> *I saw a carload of policemen jump out of their car, stick up two rather drunken students, and search them for concealed weapons. This was probably an excuse for getting out of the car to stretch their legs.*
>
> *My inventiveness for making up true stories has dried up, so I will tell you a true story...*

The style and transport for French funerals—*in small taxis (very fast)*—supposedly with a coffin strapped to the roof, is eagerly reported on, with a sketch of a fleeing cat and a Frenchman looking on, holding an enormous baguette.

> *But I doubt if funerals are one of your main interests!*

Wibb then moves on to the real point of the letter, which is to request more music to be sent to Paris and to speculate about his future.

> *Lan 5391*
>
> *Wednesday*
>
> *Dear Ma and Pa*
>
> *WANTED. (also!) Bathing Costume, (which is in one of my frog feet), and Bach (J.S., not C.P.E.) Triosonatas. (in Triosonata folder in Kodak box).*
>
> *French funerals are done in small taxis, (very fast),*
>
> *(This one smells of garlic).*
>
> *but I doubt if funerals are one of your main interests!.*

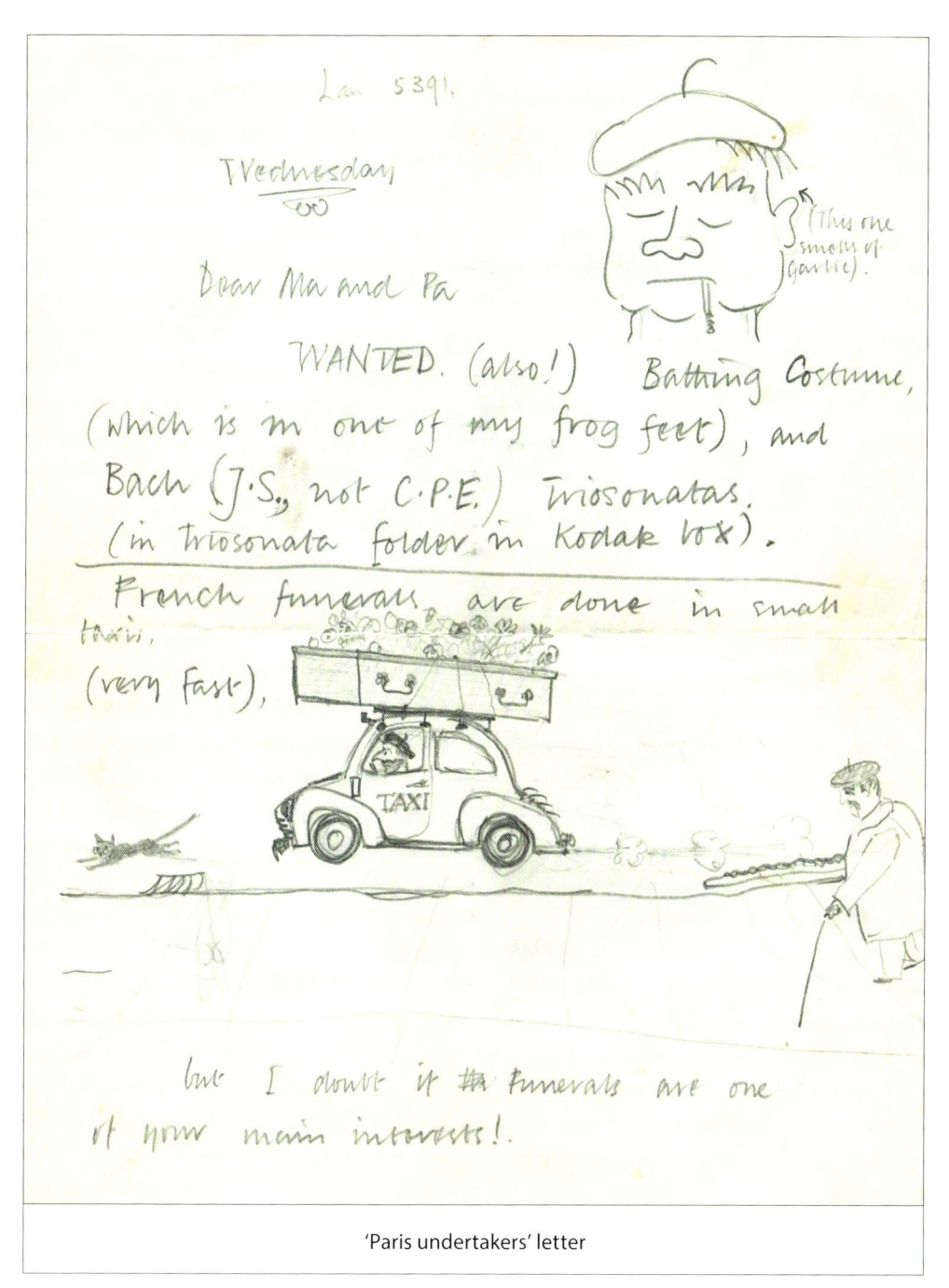

'Paris undertakers' letter

I have decided that, if possible, I would like to stay on here until the end of June (the scholarship expires at the end of May, so that it would be a fair guess to say that I am asking for some money! Is this likely to be possible?). I am already making rigid economies, but money doesn't seem to weigh so much

> as in London. (The cheapest seats in most concerts are 300fr and one that I went to the other night cost 600fr,—and I don't consider it wise not to go to concerts, as there is a lot to be learnt from these French players even if I don't like <u>everything</u> they do). I heard Caratgé again during the week, playing in the Orchestra of the Opéra Comique, and much to my relief he sounded quite OK there (not, however, as marvellous as Dufrène!).
>
> Please fill in the following as regards the condition of the following (Mark with an X)...

And the letter concludes with a grid of family members and six categories to choose from.

> *Dead. Drunk. Groaning. Chasing Cats. Almost Alive. In Prison!*

There's also a glimpse of what the French student Wibb must have looked like.

> *Since the first time I went to the barbers after I was here 3 weeks, I decided that haircuts were too expensive; however I will probably get one in England one day.*

That letter is signed with a sketch of a wild-haired flute player

> *Otherwise known as StruwelWibb!*

In the next, written on Easter Monday in April 1958, with Wibb's time in Paris fast ticking away, his preoccupations are shirts and yoghurt—and of course the flute.

> *I got the parcel with all the shirts in it. I now have so many shirts, that I can save on laundry bills by not having any more washed at all. (It should be possible to last out!)*
>
> *Otherwise there is no news. Practice takes up too much time, and it's still impossible to get enough done every week. Apart from that, I am consuming a lot of yaouhrt [sic] which is available in lots of different flavours. (Lemon Yaouhrt is colossal!)... Down with the Revolution.*

With the funds for an extension of time generously donated by his parents, Wibb stays in Paris through May and early June and is able to explore its musical world in more depth.

> *I really am most grateful for all your help, without which I would already have to be back in London—which would be a terrible pity since there is still such a tremendous amount for me to learn here. Although I seem to get a lot out of every lesson and I hear so many good things in concerts I can't seem to get hold of enough of these things quickly enough!*
>
> *Last Saturday I persuaded someone to take me along to listen to the flute class at the Conservatoire, which was extremely interesting and instructive—so much so that I wish Rainer Schuelein and Albert Honey had not said that the Conservatoire class was not worth bothering about. Crunelle, who is the teacher there, is quite an old man well past his prime, but still an excellent flautist—I have heard some of his records, which sound as good as Moyse himself (which is miles better than Caratgé!)*

> *I have decided to take a few lessons from Rampal, (the celebrated virtuoso who does practically all the solo work and recordings over here), to see what he says about everything, and particularly tongueing, which is at present my weakest point, and is Rampal's strongest.*
>
> *Geoffrey Gilbert is in Paris at the moment with the Glyndebourne Opera, and came to see me on Thursday—I very cunningly arranged that he should come and listen to my flute lesson yesterday. Having two teachers at a lesson must be a very rare luxury! but very instructive, as I got Gilbert's opinions and differences about everything afterwards.*
>
> *The Glyndebourne Opera is feeble after seeing (and hearing) the French National Opera. However the one consolation was that the Royal Philharmonic plays much better in tune than any of the French orchestras.*
>
> *I have been to some most colossal concerts recently. One with Pierre Monteux conducting was by far the best concert I have been to here (or been to hear). Monteux just plants his feet firmly on the rostrum and conducts with the minimum of movement (which got terrific results). Whereas Stokowski who I heard three days later outflashes even 'Flash Harry'. (Caratgé calls him 'Polichinelle', who is the hero in French Punch and Judy shows.)*

But this was also the time of the 'May 1958 Crisis' in Paris. Provoked by an attempted political coup during the Algerian War of Independence, it spelt the end of the Fourth Republic and swept Charles de Gaulle back into the political arena and to an eventual return to power on 1 June.

> *People who have read the English papers say there is a revolution, or civil war, or something. It's true that there are lots of policemen hanging around, but this isn't unusual. The Metro and buses are somewhat erratic, and there is a shortage of sugar and salad oil. As yet no Guillotines or old ladies dropping stitches in their knitting.*
>
> *I am going to have a lesson from Rampal this evening. (It should be interesting).*
>
> *Apart from the Piano, Gramophone, and Jumble, I find the prospect of coming back to London rather dismal. I shall be back somewhere between 12th-20th of June (groan!).*

Wibb was busy plotting his next move. Among other things, he was keen to compete in the Geneva Flute Competition. But money, the lack of it, was the challenge.

> *There are more muddy money matters to ask about:*
>
> *1. I have told James Mosley that I will go on holiday with him to the Tommy's place in Italy. Can you lend me money for this?*
>
> *2. <u>Geneva</u>—I will have to try to arrange payment through the Swiss Embassy in £. Also I have to to send 20frs (Suisse) as an inscription tax with my entrance form. (I don't know how much this is, and I certainly*

> doubt if I can afford it here!). Could you enquire about this possibly?
>
> 3. Are there any possibilities for continuing my studies here next year? I would like to know about this before I come back, as if there are, I will be able to arrange lodgings (with practice rooms) in the American House of the Cité Universitaire. (This is much cheaper than a hôtel, and has many other advantages, but it is impossible to inscribe for less than 3 months).

Business done, the subject of Wibb's letters soon switched again to music.

> I went to hear the Philadelphia Orchestra conducted by Eugene Ormandy on Monday, and walked out halfway through in disgust. It was terribly unmusical after hearing the French National Orch every week, (concerts will be unbearable in London!). Apparently the Philadelphia got very good write ups in London—shame! It was also just as out of tune as any French orchestra, and the flute, oboe, and clarinet were appalling. (The illegibility is caused by trying to write in the Metro!)
>
> There is no news other than that my new flute is nearly ready—it is at the platers—and should be ready by the end of next week. I have three concerts to play next week, and in the third I am playing the Prokofiev Sonata which is frantically difficult.
>
> Damn the Metro!

Wibb's plans are still up in the air in the final letter, but he has received some significant encouragement and advice from Jean-Pierre Rampal.

> I had a lesson from Rampal on Wednesday. Very interesting—he showed me lots of useful things. At the end of the lesson he asked if I was going to Geneva, and said it would be a good idea if I did. This makes it <u>imperative</u> that I go, because he (Rampal) is one of the judges! He is going to coach me in some of the pieces next lesson!
>
> Can you consider leaving some Swiss francs in Geneva for me to use in September—Also can you find out quickly about the payment of the inscription tax for the Concours?
>
> This is idiotic. (Always talking business). Also this pen has got indigestion.

So how does Wibb feel now about this period looking back almost sixty years? Did he ever keep in touch with Caratgé?

> I went to visit him once afterwards, but I just wasn't an admirer of what he did. He was quite nice, but I had this notebook: on the left-hand page—'Caratgé says this'—on the right hand page—'Whereas Geoffrey Gilbert says this'. I was pitting them against each other in my notes. Which is the right one? And I was listening to Fernand Dufrène and discovering that some of the things that Dufrène did related to what Caratgé said, but they had to be done by Dufrène to prove it. He was my hero of the extant Frenchmen. I asked him for lessons. He declined. He said: 'I don't teach. I'm just a humble orchestra player'.

And that visit to the flute class at the Paris Conservatoire was never repeated.

I wasn't interested to go again.

Crunelle's recordings may have interested Wibb while he was in Paris, but of course it was the playing of Moyse that really captivated him. Moyse by then had left France for Argentina, so how did his fellow French flute players remember him?

If I mentioned Moyse in Paris, they weren't enthused in the same way, but I always had my enthusiasm, and I was buying his records all the time in the flea markets.

I met Caratgé myself, years later in the early 1980s, and it was obvious that he had nursed a grudge against Moyse all his life. For whatever reason, although Caratgé had studied with Moyse, he appeared not to have been in his inner circle as a young player—and that meant that he wasn't likely to get the good playing jobs in Paris. Not surprising, therefore, that when Wibb mentioned Moyse to Caratgé in 1958, he also got a cool reception.

At my first lesson, Caratgé said to me: 'Play Syrinx'. At the end he said: 'That's not the sound of the flute!' And I said: 'Well, I've always tried to make the sound I've heard Marcel Moyse making on records. And he said something very disparaging: 'Ah, Moyse, not a very good flûtiste...' Well, that didn't help my relationship with Caratgé. Moyse was my hero! When Geoffrey came to Paris, after the lesson he said: 'Oh, you make a much better sound than Caratgé does!'.

As for Dufrène, Wibb's other hero,

He didn't like Moyse—didn't like him as a person. The word he used was 'méchant', making trouble. I never saw that side of him... just occasionally.

Fortunately the reaction from Jean-Pierre Rampal was quite different.

I went to my first lesson with Rampal and thought: 'Well, it didn't go down very well, me talking about Moyse at the Caratgé lesson, but I'm going to do the same thing!' I told Rampal that I most of all admired Moyse, but he was perfectly generous about it: 'Oh yes! I always used to go and hear him. Moyse dans la Belle Epoque—c'était merveilleux. I was always in the front row, if I could be there'. And I thought: 'I can accept this man now'. It helped. So I immediately could take much more of what Rampal had to say. I must have felt that anti-Moyse thing from Caratgé quite strongly. Poor old Caratgé!

Wibb's relatively brief encounter with Rampal in 1958 has stayed vividly with him and obviously at the time it had a crucial influence on him. Once again, it was thanks to Geoffrey Gilbert.

Here's the rest of that story, which I didn't tell my parents. Geoffrey came and heard my lesson, and he heard Caratgé tonguing—'t, t, t'—a lot of effort going into his playing and right after the lesson, he said: 'You might learn a lot if you went and had lessons with somebody else like Rampal'.

> *And I had this friend, Dorothy White, who studied the flute with Rampal, and the harp with Lily Laskine—she had the best of both worlds—and she had kept on: 'Why don't you have some lessons with Rampal?' So when Geoffrey said that, I got straight in touch with Dorothy and said: 'Can you fix me a lesson?' and I went straight there!*

But what was it that worried Wibb about his tonguing?

> *Well it was difficult to get the clear beginning on the note. I was trying to get a clean attack and I certainly knew that Rampal had a very good attack. I didn't approve of his sound, to tell you the truth. I thought it was a bit wishy-washy, and you can understand that if I was a Moyse-ist!*
>
> *My friend Philip Jones, the oboist, was always on about how you must get a clean beginning, because that was the essence of French playing. His was over-pronounced, in fact, but that was his little obsession, a clean beginning.*

Rampal's reaction was encouraging.

> *He was utterly nice, and said: 'Oh you already have a good understanding of the French style. What do you want to get from me?' and I said: 'I was hoping to find something about wonderful tonguing like you in the low register'. He laughed—I think everybody said that to him—and then he proceeded to show me how to use Taffanel and Gaubert exercises and to practise 'da' and 'ga', not 'ta' and 'ka', to get the tone to be like a bell and with a little vibrato. And not pressing too much, he didn't like me over-focusing, which of course as an imitator of Moyse I was prone to doing... still am! He wanted his easier way, but he was aware that the harmonics had to be in tune in the tone, just as a matter of course.*
>
> *He showed me how to make the note a long bell tone—'doinnggg'—quite relaxed and then again, to overlap before you actually died to nothing, to reiterate it. That would seem to be the basis of it. Then to make the 'ga' sound exactly the same as the 'da' sound, so you didn't have 't', 'k', different sorts of sounds. He said you should be able to use either form of attack anywhere and that he sometimes did slow double-tonguing—a lot of people reserve double-tonguing for only the quick things. As a result of that, I often pronounce 'da, ga, da, ga'. When I was teaching in Germany, to try and soften the Germanic language attack, I got some of them to do 'na'. That was my invention, but that's slowing the attack down, slowing the release down. That had quite a good effect on at least one of the pupils. But I use 'la', 'ga', 'da', very occasionally 'na'.*

Along with technical help, there was also musical insight from Rampal.

> *A lot! I'm constantly talking about two things that I learnt. Something about encouraging you to really develop the phrase to the top. Finding the top of every phrase and doing it the easy way, and with tremendous carefreeness about it. Somehow a very cheerful attitude to making the music flow. When you hear the good Rampal records you can hear how*

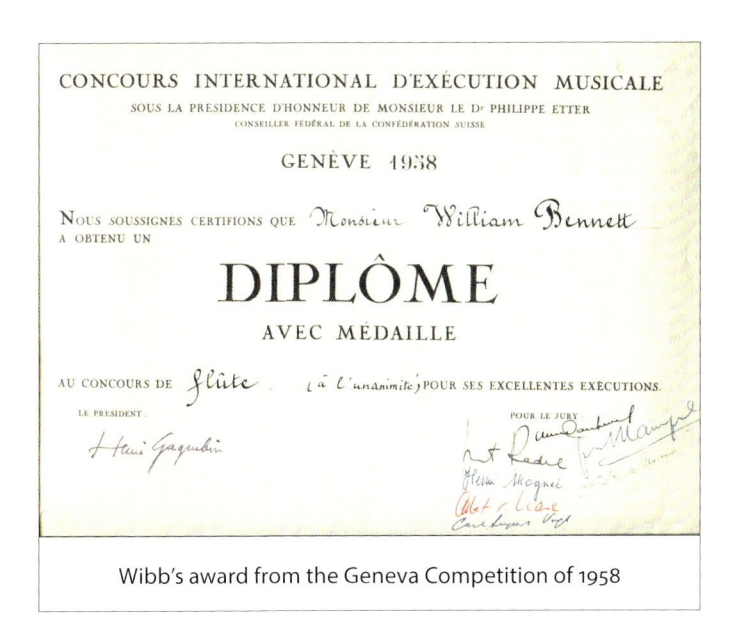

Wibb's award from the Geneva Competition of 1958

> *phrases build nicely. He had one bit in the Prokofiev where he wanted the phrase to go up to the top and he couldn't stop using his body to show this, just like Moyse, and I'm trying to get students to do just that. The audience think it's just lovely, they understand it. Pulling a phrase to the top, instead of doing bugger all with it! That's where Rampal taught me a lot—getting me to feel everything. Looking for the top. By contrast, if it goes the other way you should find it out, by contrast it's easy!*

Later, their relationship would mature from the relative formality of teacher and pupil to a shared respect and admiration as flute playing colleagues. The genial Rampal, hailing from the sun-drenched South of France, was just the sort of personality to appeal to Wibb.

> *He was always nice and friendly. I even once went as a jury member for the passing out parade of his Conservatoire class. He gave me a ride to the airport afterwards and somebody did something mad on the motorway and he said: 'Oh, he won't last long, will he?' and laughed. Lovely attitude! He wasn't angry or anything.*

So Wibb's Paris interlude was over. Geoffrey Gilbert had urged him to go there for 'the finishing touch', but in a way it would never be over. 'Paris is eternal', as someone once wrote. The French influence would remain and intensify in Wibb's playing in the years to come. For now, however, returning to London, the next steps in his career were beckoning.

> *I came back and did the Geneva Competition, got in the finals, and then I started working. Well, I mean, I'd already been working a bit playing in television shows and things. I continued to work more and more after that. And that was it!*

Watercolour of Paris rooftops by Wibb

4—Orchestras

The musical world that Wibb returned to in London after Paris and Geneva, in the Autumn of 1958, was one full of opportunity for someone with his eagerness and ambition.

I said to Geoffrey Gilbert: 'I feel as if I can do anything now'. I came back full of the joys of life, kicked my heels, and then the Royal Philharmonic rang up and said: 'We need a fourth flute, get down to the Festival Hall, rehearsals have started. Creep in quietly'. And there was Sir Thomas Beecham conducting, and it was Strauss's Heldenleben. I sneaked in and did my bits as best I could. Sir Thomas was stopping occasionally and telling inaudible stories and the people at the front would all be laughing and everybody behind was talking! There was one bit that was very difficult. He did a gesture and three of us flutes had to come in pianissimo. I said to the second flute, Gerry Markham: 'Where the hell do we play?' He said: 'Don't come in first, old chap!' That was the most frightening thing... but the concert at the Festival Hall was perfect!

That was the only time I played for Beecham, but there was a tremendous atmosphere backstage, just before the concert. You could feel it. It had to be good and you could sense some special aura about the whole proceedings, which was part of Beecham's magic, getting everybody wound up the right way—like God being present. Fun, definitely. You know how they were in the RPO, they couldn't stand anybody who wasn't Beecham in the end. It was all a bit extreme.

Geoffrey Gilbert was the first flute in the RPO and no doubt responsible for giving Wibb this first break. Another followed soon after.

That Autumn suddenly there was a need for somebody to play first flute in the BBC Northern Orchestra and I was sent up by Geoffrey: 'Go and play an audition'. I was the only one there! You know, they were just testing me. Geoffrey had said: 'This is the person for you'. So I went and played to them and they said: 'Can you start next Monday?' and I did!

An orchestral position in Manchester, however, didn't stop Wibb from pursuing many other playing possibilities.

When I wasn't in Manchester, I was back in London for my weekends and catching up with my chamber music and various little groups. I was doing

TOWN HALL. MANCHESTER
By courtesy of the Manchester Corporation

THE BBC PRESENTS

MIDDAY PROMENADE CONCERTS

BROADCAST IN THE BBC HOME SERVICE

FRIDAYS 9 JANUARY TO 20 MARCH 1959

1.10 TO 2.0 P.M.

THE BBC NORTHERN ORCHESTRA
(LEADER, REGINALD STEAD)

CONDUCTORS
GEORGE HURST
STANFORD ROBINSON
GORDON THORNE

COMPLETE PROGRAMMES PRICE SIXPENCE

BBC NORTHERN ORCHESTRA

1st Violin
Reginald Stead (*Leader*)
Ben Horsfall
Harry Thorniley
James Davis
Lawrence Daley
Margaret Ward
Sadie Hardy
Ethel Richmond
Hugh Bradley
Edward Batten

2nd Violin
Don Hyden
Herbert Smith
George Roche
Harold Hilton
Phyllis Russell
Jeffrey Booth
Kenneth Willmott
Helen Silverman
Frank Horner
Philip Hecht

Viola
Paul Cropper
Thomas Mather
Norman Cunliffe
Norman Mansell
Ronald Gould
Jean Soni

Cello
Leonard Baker
Alan Morton
Robert Haworth
Alexander Young
Albert Dyson

Double Bass
Wilfred Collinge
John Norris
Robert Barratt

Flute
William Bennett
John Snowdon
Cecil Cox

Oboe
Alfred Livesley
Bernard O'Keefe

Clarinet
Norman McDonald
William Mainey

Bassoon
Arthur Thornton
Albert Entwistle

Horn
Sydney Coulston
Robert Aspden
Frank Taylor
Peter Rider

Trumpet
Cecil Kidd
Harold Hall

Trombone
Clifford Crossley
Michael Payne
George Cottam

Tuba
Thomas Atkinson

Tympani
David Greenwood

Percussion
Harry Massey
Michael Blakey

Harp
Wendy L'Evesque

Librarian
Frank Lee

---

music club concerts and things—all sorts. There was a lot of freelance stuff going, which was very healthy, and I started being invited to play with the freelance crowd. The ECO was beginning and I played the first time for them in Manchester within two weeks of starting in the BBC Northern Orchestra.

The job in Manchester began to bring Wibb to the notice of a whole range of visiting conductors.

> Colin Davis came to conduct the BBC Northern and he was marvellous! He kept the Orchestra guessing about certain things. He'd rehearse the first half of the first movement of the 'Jupiter' Symphony and we'd get to the double bar, having made lots of things happen, and then he'd say: 'Alright, let's go on to the next movement'. He left a lot of it unread for the show and this got us sort of electrified, a little bit like Beecham. You thought: 'Hey, we haven't rehearsed this bit', so everybody switched on and became more alive than they were normally. It was a marvellous week or two. We

> *did Fauré's* Dolly Suite, *which he did just superbly. I can remember the surge to the bottom of the phrase and his great Colin Davis gesture. I had a marvellous time playing with him—it was always exciting, all the time.*

That wasn't an opinion shared by everyone: Colin Davis had a reputation as a firebrand as a young man and orchestras didn't always like him.

> *But they don't always like people who have a real spark, do they? There was a culture: the conductor was the 'other side'. George Hurst, the conductor of the BBC Northern used to come down to London at the weekends and he often gave me a ride in his Bristol sports car—which was nice, saved me a bit of train fare—but the people in the orchestra used to say: 'Eeh, you're a bit pally with the conductor. You must remember that they're the other side, it's them and us, you know'. But I'd been to a progressive school where you called teachers by their first names, so that wasn't something that was natural for me. The conductor was a person like everybody else—and George was lovely!*

Wibb stayed in the BBC Northern for about twenty months and then it was decided that there should be a proper audition for his position, to make it official.

> *Of course, I was petrified of that audition and I was terribly nervous, but I got the job.*

Almost immediately, however, another, more attractive opportunity back in London presented itself. Once again, there was no formal audition.

> *I had a couple of very great friends in the Sadler's Wells Orchestra, Philip Jones, the oboist, and Tom Kelly, the clarinettist. They wanted me to apply for Sadler's Wells and I was offered it and didn't stay in the BBC Northern. And I said to the Leader of Sadler's Wells: 'Why didn't you give me an audition?' He replied: 'Oh, we gave you an audition, we just switched the radio on occasionally!'*

The benefits of playing in a BBC radio orchestra had paid off! The year Wibb spent playing in the Sadler's Wells Orchestra was full of a new repertoire for him of opera and ballet scores. It was very stimulating, but he had also been getting into the contemporary music scene in London.

> *I was going to play the Boulez Sonatina for a BBC Invitation Concert, but Sadler's Wells wouldn't give me time off. I had a discussion with them—Edward Renton and Colin Davis. It was the first night of* La Traviata, *which had been done a million times, anybody who'd done it before could come in and do it, but they wouldn't let me off. So I had to leave Sadler's Wells—I wasn't going to turn down a chance like the BBC concert—and they had quite a good person down the line who took over. That was Jimmy Galway! But I remember walking out of Sadler's Wells wondering if I was ever going to play the flute anywhere again.*

The pianist for the Boulez broadcast was Susan Bradshaw whom Wibb had got to know in Paris. Susan had also been there on a French Government scholarship—actually studying with Pierre Boulez—and together with Wibb and the oboist Philip Jones they had formed the Mabillon Trio, named after their favourite Paris restaurant where they could eat cheaply and well! Another student friend in Paris had been the composer Richard Rodney Bennett (no relation to Wibb) also studying with Boulez. Richard and Susan formed a piano duo partnership and he also composed a three-movement work, *Winter Music*, for Wibb and Susan and dedicated it to them.

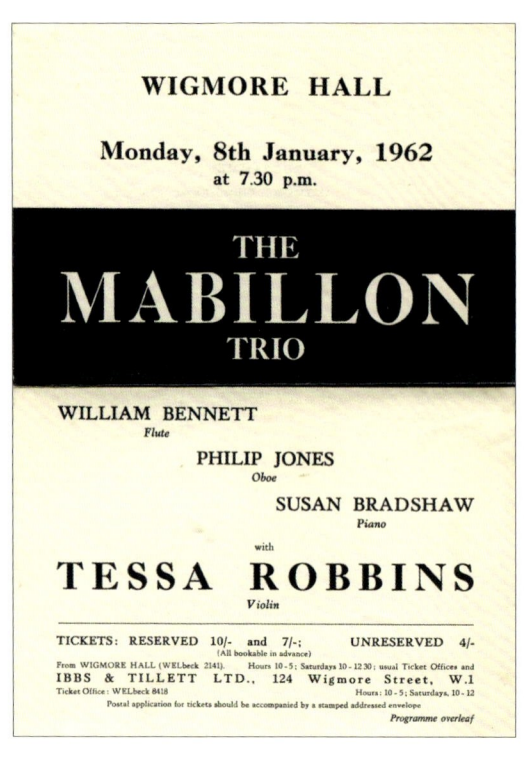

I was doing a lot of stuff with the pianist Susan Bradshaw then. We had started playing concerts in Paris—a whole range of repertoire, everything that we could get our hands on—and after Sadler's Wells I got heavily into being involved in contemporary music. We had another ensemble going and Susan Bradshaw said: 'We can go to Dartington, there's a workshop group to play modern pieces'. So suddenly there was a need to find a name for the new ensemble. I said: 'Contemporary music... lots of explosions and things... eruptions... what about Vesuvius?' That became the name of the ensemble!

The original core members of the Vesuvius Ensemble, with Wibb and Susan Bradshaw, were the violinist Kenneth Sillito and clarinettist Thea King. Later they were joined by the cellist Charles Tunnell, and the violinist John Tunnell replaced Ken Sillito.

It led me into all sorts of occasions playing contemporary music for the SPNM [Society for the Promotion of New Music]. There was also William Glock, Controller of Music at the BBC, pushing new stuff and I was rather good at it. I became a quasi expert in contemporary music. I could do the frenetic screeches and gentle cooings of the dove that flutes were meant to do. I could do extreme dynamics and I had another feature: I could actually keep it in tune most of the time!

After a while, however, Wibb knew that his musical heart lay elsewhere, not primarily with contemporary music.

I didn't really like it that much, although previously I had been very taken with being in the avant grade and doing something shocking! But I didn't

> *want to be one of those people who only plays contemporary music. I was offered a chance early on to be in the London Sinfonietta, but it was just after I started studying with Moyse and I wanted to do classical music. The idea of doing more Schoenberg—more silly noises—didn't appeal. I declined and Sebastian Bell was the next on the list and made a very good career of it. He became one of my really great friends—he was intelligent and fun.*

Having given up Sadler's Wells, for a while Wibb wasn't regularly in an orchestra.

> *But then I started getting invited: Northern Sinfonia, occasionally the Bristol Sinfonia, the Pro Arte Orchestra, the Academy of St Martin in the Fields, and the English Chamber Orchestra—I was getting used quite a lot by them.*

The ECO's principal flute was Richard Adeney, then in his forties and well established on the London scene. Richard was also principal of the London Philharmonic Orchestra and the Melos Ensemble—juggling a busy diary—and Wibb was able to benefit from that.

> *Richard helped me tremendously. He gave me an awful lot of work when he wasn't doing the ECO and I also quite often deputised for him in the Melos Ensemble. I played the Debussy Trio and the* Prélude, Marine et Chansons *by Ropartz. It was fantastic to play with Cecil Aronowitz, Manny Hurwitz and all the rest. I did a lot with them, even some recordings. One of the first things I did after I left Sadler's Wells was a whole month playing in the LPO for Richard, for the Festival Ballet. It was nice—filled the pocket! There was a lot of freelance stuff happening. Sidney Sax was one of the big time light music fixers—he was a violinist who was a great fan of Heifetz—and I was getting enough work to keep me going.*

In March 1961 Wibb married his first wife, Rhuna Martin, a cellist whom he had met in the Sadler's Wells Orchestra. Rhuna was also a pianist and she taught in the Junior Department of the Royal College of Music. Among her students were the cellist Julian Lloyd Webber and the pianist Clifford Benson, who would eventually become Wibb's longstanding duo partner. Wibb and Rhuna were together for nineteen years and had two daughters, Vanora and Sophie.

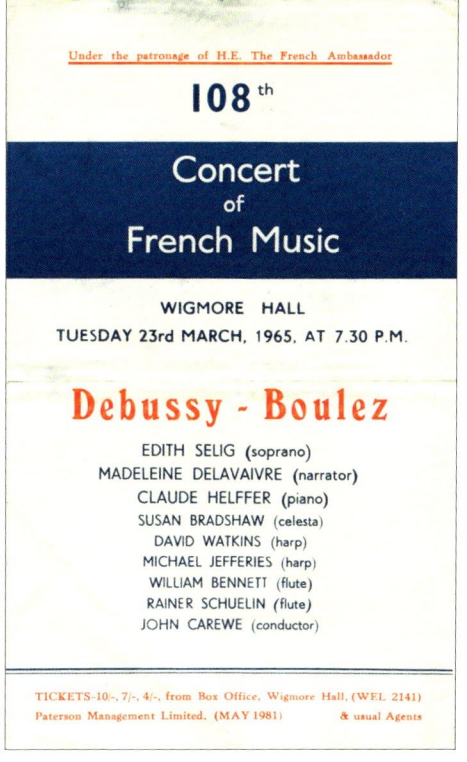

Wibb at Dartington with three members of the Dartington Quartet in 1964

Meanwhile there were other new musical partnerships developing for Wibb.

> *The fire was burning very quickly, very strongly. George Malcolm fixed up for me to play a concert with him and Yehudi Menuhin at Westminster Abbey. Then I was playing in the Menuhin Orchestra, with the oboist Michael Dobson who was one of my great supporters. We played a lot of chamber music together and we had a group called the English Baroque Ensemble. Michael also put on concerts at the Queen Elizabeth Hall with the Thames Chamber Orchestra and that was a fantastic amount of activity for me. Things were happening all the time.*

Another big orchestral job, however, was just around the corner. The 1960s ushered in a golden period for the London Symphony Orchestra, with a succession of high profile principal conductors—Pierre Monteux, István Kertész, André Previn—world tours, television appearances and frequent recordings. The LSO quickly came to be widely regarded as the leading orchestra in the UK. When Alexander Murray, the principal flute, left to move to America there was a tempting vacancy—or actually, two vacancies.

> *I was busy freelancing in 1965, the year I went to Moyse for the first time, and about the Christmas of the same year, suddenly Jimmy Galway burst into the LSO. He got there about a month before I did! We shared it. We were co-principals. The LSO was working so hard that they needed two players and I had been doing stuff with the LSO before. I was quite often*

there recording and I would play down the line, piccolo and third flute and everything—and sometimes on first. So, they knew me. Anyway, when Jimmy was appointed, very soon I was appointed too, without any formal audition.

So how did it work out, with two strong and very different personalities sharing the role of principal flute?

Well, we managed. We balanced it sort of, more or less...

After a year or so, however, James Galway was approached by the Royal Philharmonic Orchestra with (in his own words) 'an offer I could not refuse' and he moved on to a new principal flute position. Christopher Taylor took over from Jimmy for an LSO tour to Florida, but he was suddenly taken ill after rehearsing his half of the concert in the morning.

Early publicity photograph of Wibb

So I had to sight read his half of the programme in the concert. But having been in the Scots Guards and transposed ninety percent of the parts, and in the BBC Northern Orchestra which sight read everything, sight reading was just fun! I had great fun sight reading a Rachmaninov Symphony with the public there! That's how I was—I enjoyed living on the edge.

The players of the LSO, as a self-governing orchestra, now had to decide what to do about the co-principal flute vacancy.

They asked me whom I would like to share it with, and I said: 'Peter Lloyd', whom I knew and respected very much. That was a very happy collaboration because he was so nice and it went on for another four or five years.

All was indeed well for a while, but then James Galway left the RPO for the Berlin Philharmonic and his successor, Laurie Kennedy (one of Wibb's former students), was tragically killed in a car crash. So the RPO was once again looking for a principal flute.

I thought: 'Time for a move, take a risk' and I did a deal. I said: 'Give me two solo dates a year', but I didn't get them until after I'd left, a year-and-a-half later. What a rotten deal! They kicked me out because I was

> *doing a world tour with the ECO. I hadn't had my solo dates and I said: 'The ECO is offering me dates playing the Mozart Concerto in Bangkok and things like that'. So I went off to do them and while I was away they said: 'Don't come back!' I told my colleagues in the ECO about that, and they said: 'Oh good! We'll have a party to celebrate!'*

By this time in the early 1970s Wibb had succeeded Richard Adeney as principal flute of the ECO. He was also principal of the Academy of St Martin in the Fields, so his diary was pretty full, but he did also go back to the LSO for another brief period, once again sharing the principal position with Peter Lloyd. In the end, however, there were just too many claims on his time.

> *I still had quite a good relationship with the LSO, but it fizzled out because I was doing too many other things. Peter got rather fed up, because I was having most of the fun doing the outside solo dates. Freelance was bubbling. The ECO and Academy of St. Martin's were the mainstay, and work for the fixer Sid Sax. There was a wealth of stuff happening: Denham Film Studios and all over the place, a lot of session work, driving everywhere to different studios. I got to know London frightfully well!*

There was a moment some years later when Wibb was sounded out for an orchestral job in America. Bernard Goldberg was retiring from the Pittsburgh Symphony Orchestra and the management invited Wibb to spend a week with them. The principal conductor at that point was Lorin Maazel.

> *I thought: 'Why not? I'll go and do a week there' and it turned out I wasn't playing for Lorin Maazel, I was playing for Charles Dutoit, who was lovely. So, I went and did my week there and just before I went, the manager rang me up and said: 'Could you do another week?' Without looking at my diary, I said: 'No, I'm not free!'*
>
> *I knew that my life was here in Britain—quite simple. To go for a week and see what it was like in an American orchestra, that was interesting, it was different, but it wasn't as good as the ECO, or the other orchestras here. Pittsburgh had some good players, but it wasn't the super-playing that you got in the Academy of St. Martin's and the ECO. I remember we did Mozart Symphony 35 in Pittsburgh and it was very primitive compared to the ECO.*

Wibb continued to play in the Academy of St Martin in the Fields until the 1990s and in the ECO for many years beyond that, into his mid-seventies, appearing regularly in London and touring all over the world with them.

> *I thought: 'This is where all my friends are', and it seemed to be... I don't know... just my place.*

That's a telling comment from someone for whom orchestral playing and the shared experience of music making have always been paramount, however important solo playing has also been for him.

I love playing in orchestras. I can tell you what it feels like. I can remember going into the National Youth Orchestra for the first time somewhere in Scotland and hearing this wonderful surge of sound—Dvorak's Eighth Symphony—and I'd never had the thrill of being in the middle of it before.

I can remember also getting the same thrill a few years later when I was late one morning with my dog—Jumble was lodging with me in Manchester. We had some trouble getting on the bus and I was delayed. I got to Milton Hall a bit late and they were doing Scheherazade. *I dropped the dog in the band room and rushed in and sat on my chair and it had started, but the sound of this piece—it was so thrilling to be there! All these colours going on. Like when you go in a church and all those stained glass colours are everywhere. When there's a thrilling sound the whole place is incandescent.*

For Wibb, the thrill of orchestral playing is also about the actual repertoire and the inspiration from the players around him.

William Bennett . flute

William Bennett began playing the flute at the age of twelve and, four years later, went to the Guildhall School of Music as a pupil of Geoffrey Gilbert. In 1957 he won a French Government Scholarship to Paris where he studied with Fernand Caratgé and Jean-Pierre Rampal. In 1958 he obtained the Première Médaille at the Geneva International Competition, and then took the position of principal flautist with the BBC Northen Orchestra, where he stayed for nearly two years, commuting regularly with London in order to fulfil his chamber music engagements. He then became principal flute at Sadler's Wells and has now left in order to devote more time to solo and ensemble playing

Publicity leaflet from the early 1960s

You play more substantial music than if you're playing solo flute pieces—most of the time. It's very fascinating to play in a good orchestra. In the LSO when I was there, Gervase de Peyer was the clarinet, and later it was Jack Brymer. Roger Lord was sitting next to me on oboe and Roger Birnstingl on bassoon. Pretty marvellous!

One major challenge remains, however, even in the greatest orchestra, and it has always haunted Wibb.

In any orchestra, you have problems with tuning, and that's part of my thing, trying to make the flute in tune. I was fascinated by my hero, Fernand Dufrène, because he always sounded in tune in his ghastly, out-of-tune orchestra. I never worked out how he did it. He just sounded right all the time. Like Oliver Bannister in the Hallé, all the time. That's part of our problem, to get the flute to sound tolerably in tune. Somebody once asked Dufrène: 'What do you do about tuning?' Apparently Dufrène said: 'Oh, you know, in our orchestra we try and play in tune, but not too much —it's boring!' But he always sounded right. He wasn't going to have a sort of 'intonation-freak' life. I'm afraid I've got to intonation-freak level!

And there are practical, survival skills to be acquired in an orchestra that audiences—and even conductors—don't really know about.

Common sense about what you do in certain moments, like playing Beethoven's Seventh Symphony with 'Mickey Mouse' at the front conducting in circles! I said to Roger Lord: 'How the hell do we play with this stirring going on at the front?' Couldn't tell what the tempo was or anything. He said: 'For heaven's sake, don't watch the conductor. Listen to the violas'. They're in the middle of the orchestra, they've got the pulse. He knew, in whatever passage, where to direct your attention to get the sound to come out right.

When not to watch the conductor was of paramount importance to Roger! In this passage you listen to the violas, but in another passage you might play with the basses. Roger said: 'The LSO became a great orchestra when we had a lot of recording sessions, that was our main meat, and we had conductors with whom you couldn't tell where the beat was at all, but we had to make good records, so we all had to listen to each other and find out where everything was. You couldn't rely on the stick. We had to work out for ourselves where to play'.

So does Wibb miss playing in an orchestra?

Yes—I miss being in the swim of the sound and the pieces themselves, but you can get frightfully upset with the conductor doing a piece you like completely wrongly. I think that's why conductors are disliked so frequently. You have your favourite pieces and most of the time you do what you believe, but the conductor doesn't always see it the same way as you do and there are moments when you've got to do things which you believe are totally wrong. If the conductor asks you to play pianissimo when you think it's fortissimo, you've got to do it, but that doesn't happen very often.

I remember Jeanne Baxtresser with the New York Philharmonic saying she was very upset having to play Brahms Four—I think it was Rostropovich conducting—with no vibrato in the flute solo. She did it, because she was told to, but it sounded frightful and she was so ashamed of herself. But what a thing to be told!

Orchestras

Greater London Council

PURCELL ROOM

Director: George Mann OBE

William Bennett & Clifford Benson

Romantic Music for the flute and pianoforte

Thursday 17th February 1977 at 7-30pm

Tickets priced £1.50, £1.20, 80p, available from the Royal Festival Hall Box Office SE1, telephone 01-928 3191, and usual agents, from 17th January. Please enclose a stamped addressed envelope and remittance with postal applications.

One of many recitals with Clifford Benson

For Wibb, the basic challenge and fascination is always there: how to make music, really make music, whatever you are playing.

> *You've got a row of dots in front of you that you've got to transfer into notes. Sometimes you just do them as abstract notes and get the pitch right and the rhythm right, and that's it. I remember being in a choral concert in the Royal Albert Hall, the choir going full belt behind you, and you could hardly hear what you're doing. 'Am I playing the right notes?' and suddenly you realise: 'Gosh! Roger Lord made a nice phrase out of that!' I could tell that it was completely pointless making a phrase at all with all that racket going on, but he'd found a phrase in the notes and that was an inspiration to keep my soul on that path. To try to make a phrase as often as possible…*

From time to time throughout his career, Wibb has directed orchestras from the flute for concerts and recordings of concertos, but unlike so many other instrumentalists he has rarely been tempted to put down his flute altogether and take up the baton. He did, however, have some conducting lessons as a student at the Guildhall.

> *They were very interesting. Aylmer Buesst was the professor. The first thing I did—I think it was the* Magic Flute *overture—I had to learn to breathe in order to give a beat, which was most useful instruction. You don't just lift your arms and push them down, which is what I did. He told me that I had to breathe in time, and take the breath in the time that I was going to put the down beat down, and it made all the difference. That's been invaluable advice to me, leading chamber music. When you're playing chamber music, you've got to show a new tempo somewhere and I'm using that information ever since then.*

So far, so good, but then as a young player he was suddenly put on the spot.

> *One day I went along to play in the Ben Uri Orchestra at St John's Wood Synagogue and the conductor Jimmy Verity wasn't there, so they asked me to get up in front of the orchestra and conduct. Ghastly experience! You do something with your hands, make a gesture, and the note doesn't come out—a sort of strangled noise comes out some time afterwards! It's not like playing an instrument when you blow and a note comes. It was quite terrifying and I thought: 'I don't like this!' I didn't attempt it anymore. Well… I have conducted once since. At King's Place there was a Royal Academy concert a few years ago, with the best of the Academy flute players. They asked me to direct it and conduct it, but my God it was difficult and I thought: 'I don't want to conduct!'*

Directing from the flute, however, has been more satisfying—and indeed can have real compensations.

> *When you've got a sensitive orchestra like the ECO, it's often better without a conductor, because they're switched on to finding some other way of getting together and there are usually lots of ways. It was like playing with Clifford*

> REPERTOIRE INCLUDES:
>
> *Concertos*
>
> with strings only:
> ARNOLD, HAYDN, JOLIVET, HONEGGER, KENNAN, FOOTE, GRIFFES
>
> with strings and continuo:
> J. S. BACH, C. P. E. BACH, DITTERSDORF, QUANTZ, PERGOLESI, STAMITZ, TELEMANN, VIVALDI
>
> with orchestra:
> J. S. BACH, CIMAROSA, MOZART, ARRIEU, HUE, IBERT, CHAMINADE, GODARD, NIELSEN, REINECKE, WIDOR
>
> *solo flute*
> | | |
> |---|---|
> | J. S. BACH | Sonata in A minor |
> | C. P. E. BACH | Sonata in A minor |
> | DOHNANYI | Passacaglia op. 48 no. 2 |
> | DEBUSSY | Syrinx |
> | HONEGGER | Danse de la Chèvre |
> | BONNEAU | Caprice en Forme de Valse |
> | IBERT | Pièce |
> | BLAVET | Grave and Rondeau |
> | TELEMANN | Fantasias |
>
> *solo flute—modern*
> | | |
> |---|---|
> | W. ALWYN | Divertimento |
> | R. R. BENNETT | Sonatina |
> | BERIO | Sequenza |
> | HAUBENSTOCK-RAMATI | Mobile for flute and tape-recorder |
> | LUTYENS | Variations |
> | MICHAEL ROSE | Pan Plays |
> | RICHARD ORTON | Eloquy |
> | VANRAJ BHATIA | Flute Music |
> | HINDEMITH | Eight Pieces |
>
> *with keyboard*
> Sonatas, Sonatines, Suites and other pieces by:
> ARNOLD, ARRIEU, J. S. BACH, C. P. E. BACH, BEETHOVEN, R. R. BENNETT, BERKELEY, BOULEZ, BRUNNER, CLEMENTI, COUPERIN, DOPPLER, DUTILLEUX, GAUBERT, GODARD, HINDEMITH, HOTTETERRE, LECLAIR, DAVID LORD, MARCELLO, FRANK MARTIN, MARTINU, NICHOLAS MAW, MILHAUD, PROKOFIEV, QUANTZ, REINECKE, ROUSSEL, SCHUBERT, SCHUMANN, TELEMANN, etc.
>
> # William Bennett
>
> WILLIAM BENNETT first studied with Geoffrey Gilbert, then went to Paris with a French Government Scholarship and studied with Rampal and Caratgé. He won the 'Première Medaille' at the Geneva International Competition, and later studied with Marcel Moyse. He was awarded the first place in the 'Prix de Marcel Moyse' in 1965.
>
> He has been principal flute with various orchestras, including the BBC Northern Orchestra, Sadlers Wells Opera, and now with the London Symphony Orchestra. He has appeared as soloist with the London Symphony Orchestra, the Royal Philharmonic Orchestra and the English Chamber Orchestra, and plays with many chamber orchestras and ensembles. He is Professor of Flute at the Guildhall School of Music.
>
> WILLIAM BENNETT can offer a wide variety of recital programmes with both harpsichord and piano, his partners including George Malcolm, Harold Lester, Clifford Benson, Susan Bradshaw and Alex Kelly.
>
> Management:
> BASIL DOUGLAS LTD
> 8 St. George's Terrace, N.W.1. (01-722 7142)

Publicity leaflet from the late 1960s

Benson on the piano—he didn't actually have to see you to know when you were going to play—and that's an extra sense. I've found a few other people who'd got that too.

A final word on touring—a huge part of Wibb's career. Whether with orchestras, or on his own, Wibb can always be seen with his trademark bag of flutes. Really it's a portable workshop, full of all sorts of useful things, as he found once on tour in Mexico with the ECO when he and several friends decided to go exploring.

We had two days free and we hired a car and went off to see pyramids and things. We were driving along a road and it was foggy and suddenly we found ourselves in a herd of wild horses—most peculiar thing—and we hit one of them and it dented the whole front of the car and damaged the radiator. It was pierced and the water was coming out. And I managed to repair the radiator with plasticine which I had in my flute bag! But then we had to take the damaged car back to Mexico City and explain—and they didn't quite believe it...

Wibb also always has materials at hand for sketching and painting on tour. Much of his free time has been spent observing and recording new sights from around the world. Some of these pictures are included in this book and there are many more. Whether consciously or unconsciously, visual and aural sensations have always run parallel, and sometimes intersected, in Wibb's imagination. More about this in the chapter on Playing, but for now it's worth noting how enthused he is by the visual world and how natural it is for him to be an artist as well as a musician.

I'm drawing all the time, really. Pictures just happen!

Sketch of Aix-en-Provence by Wibb

5—Heroes

Alongside Wibb's flute playing gods—Geoffrey Gilbert, Marcel Moyse and Fernand Dufrène—there are a number of significant musical heroes, mainly not flute players, who have helped shape his outlook and imagination. Other flute players, however, have also played a part.

Plenty! Joseph Mariano in America. Then I had a record of the Boston Symphony Orchestra with Georges Laurent, a Taffanel pupil, which is absolutely wonderful. I was very fond of Oliver Bannister, who is sort of French School despite playing a wooden flute. There's André Pépin, one of Moyse's pupils—wonderfully singing sound. There are a whole lot of recordings with Stravinsky and the Stuttgart Chamber Orchestra, with Pépin playing the flute, which are just fabulous! He played on one of those Couesnon flutes, shorter than Louis Lot flutes, and so did Aurèle Nicolet when he first started. Even Gaston Crunelle I've got quite a lot of time for. I've got some records of his, which I've enjoyed...

The list goes on. Wibb has always been open to recognise elements in many other flute players from which he can learn—and not only players in the Western tradition.

I can remember in Paris, as a student, I bought a record of a Jewish chap playing an Arab flute, a nai. He was called Hillel. His wife, Aviva, had an Israeli nightclub where she played the drums and he played the nai and they sang together and danced. This record was an absolute inspiration of what might be done on the flute with its range of expression and changeability, colour and attack and everything.

Hillel was blowing the nai out of the side of his mouth and he could do incredible things with it. He goes from this sometimes completely straight, primitive sound and then the vibrato creeps in like a very slow wave coming over a calm sea, and then it becomes excited, and hysterical when necessary. He has a great number of different attacks and you hear him playing a passionate note at a special pitch, which isn't quite the right note, but you know that it's on purpose—it has a musical effect. I met Hillel in Israel sometime after I'd studied with Moyse and he was quite well established. I was very excited to meet him, he could make the nai really sound like a voice. That's what the flute is in its elemental colour.

Actual voices have been crucial to Wibb's understanding and vision of the flute—and not just the voices of classical music. *I was very fascinated by Josh White, the American blues and ballad singer, when I was at school. Whenever I heard Josh White on the radio I was always glued to it and I was fascinated by his pitch. He would sing something in a major key and then there would be odd notes that had a special pitch which was just slightly off where you would expect it—off equal temperament, I mean.*

He had the jazz thing, with a major third which is flatter. Not just a properly pitched major third, which is flatter than the equal temperament, but one that's a little flatter than that.

Fernand Dufrène

And then there's a sharp fourth, which is sharper than an F Sharp in C Major, which is leading to a G—it's really quite a flat G pushing up. Josh used these quite often, but he wasn't just singing them, he would also get them by bending the note on the guitar, stretching the string sideways. He had an exact pitch and I noticed several jazz players had special expressive notes. Hillel had the same fifth—or sharp fourth—I think it's a flat fifth rather than a sharp fourth.

I've been bending notes for ever! Even before I had proper flute lessons, I was trying to do jazz things, smears and things by using my lips because I wanted to.

As we have already noted, before Wibb had proper flute lessons he was also fascinated by the guitar—and has remained so.

Wibb with George Malcolm

I wanted a guitar because I had records of Segovia. My godfather gave me records—the Bach Gavotte and a piece by Fernando Sor—and that was something marvellous, those deep sounds. I just loved the guitar. Then somebody told me about Julian Bream, so I went to hear him and that was the big enchantment—all those colours! On the guitar, if you pluck near the bridge, it makes a hard 'dig, dig, dig' sort of noise, and if you pluck in the middle it goes 'phum, phum, phum' and you've got all the colours in between. Julian was doing marvellous things all the time—changing the colours, the inflection. I thought Julian Bream had better taste than Segovia. I loved Segovia, but when I heard Julian Bream I thought: 'Even better'. By then I was already a flute player, but all I wanted to do was play like Julian Bream. I could still afford to do that!

Listening to Julian Bream soon led Wibb on to another musical hero.

It led me to George Malcolm. I went to hear Julian's concert, and there was this chap playing the harpsichord. Seemed to be doing all the same things as Julian was doing.

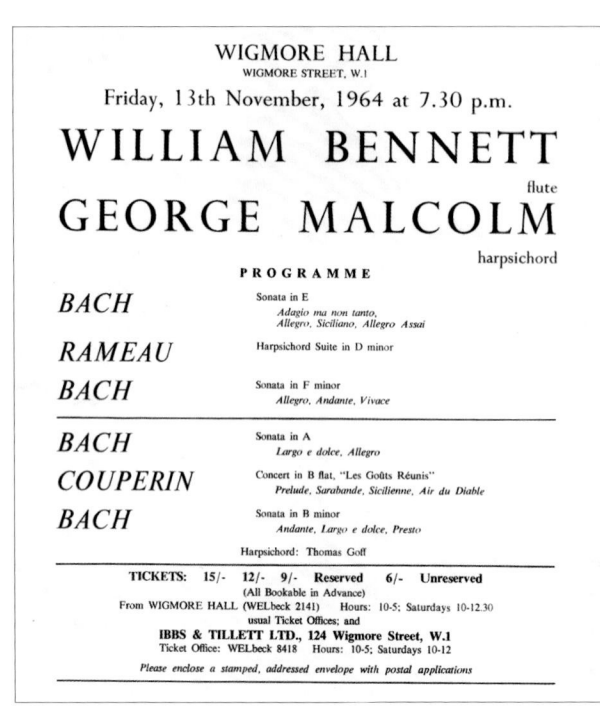

> So how was George Malcolm achieving that same range of colours and inflections on the harpsichord?
>
> *He was using the pedals and making crescendos and things—very anti the baroque crowd! He would do a little crescendo by putting one of the pedals sensitively down slowly, making the phrase go up and down, and using the frowned upon 16-foot stop, played an octave too high, which gave a lovely singing sound. He often used the combination of 16-foot and 4-foot. The 8-foot was the standard stop, but just the 16 and the 4, without the 8 in the middle, made a wonderful sound. Of course, it was a Thomas Goff harpsichord, which again wasn't authentic. Didn't half sound good! In fact, my first Handel recording, with Harry Lester, was on the 'Goffsichord' as we called it, with a roaring bass! I loved that instrument—George made it sound like a magic instrument, not just skeletons on a tin roof!*

George Malcolm would soon introduce Wibb to another hero, Yehudi Menuhin, but Wibb's ears were already tuned to what a flute player could learn from violinists.

> *In those early days, my friends with whom I played chamber music were always saying: 'Oh listen to Busch and Kreisler!' which I still do. Geoffrey Gilbert talked a lot about what you did with the bow on the violin, so maybe listening to other instruments—other musical entities, as it were—had also been inspired by that. I'd certainly got into listening to the violin in a different way.*

Adolf Busch and Fritz Kreisler became particular favourites and Wibb remembers spending many hours during his military service in the Scots Guards polishing his boots to their recordings!

> *I was fascinated by Kreisler, he had a different sort of way of beginning and ending notes than the others. I was trying to puzzle out what he did in the way he shaped the notes to make that different attack. Kreisler would sometimes make the notes very detached, sometimes join them together without articulating, in a very different way, and he had so*

many different ways of tying things together and sliding between notes. It just sounded so good. The Beethoven Concerto recording was marvellous—tremendously dignified, and alive and smiling. When you hear Kreisler double-stopping, it's not like one violin playing a double-stop, you hear two wonderful violinists playing together and it's somehow better than anybody else.

Adolf Busch was more... well I don't know which I liked better. I think I was initially more of an Adolf Busch fan. He was very classical and when he played short notes they were very short. But he could also play very romantically and do the proper connecting between the notes, which is a wonderful thing you can do on the violin. It's very hard to get a portamento on the flute, because you can't actually slide—not too often anyway!

Back to George Malcolm, and Wibb was quick to take advantage of an opportunity that soon presented itself.

I went along to play the Haubenstock-Ramati Mobile *for solo flute at a BBC Invitation Concert (and I think a Trio by Hugh Wood for flute, viola and piano) and George Malcolm was playing a Bach Suite in the same concert. There was an opportunity to turn the pages for him and afterwards I said to George: 'Is there any chance that I could ever play with you? There's nothing I'd like to do more'. George immediately fixed up for me to come and play with him at Tom Goff's house and that was how it started. A little while later, George arranged for me to play a concert with him and Yehudi Menuhin at Westminster Abbey and soon after I was playing in the Menuhin Orchestra.*

Menuhin had already made a series of Bach recordings with his Bath Festival Orchestra in the early 1960s, including the Brandenburg Concertos, Orchestral Suites and *The Musical Offering*. Those were with the American flutist, Elaine Shaffer, a friend of his and of his pianist sister, Hepzibah. Impressed with Wibb's playing, Menuhin invited him and George Malcolm to tour the Bach Triple Concerto (for flute, violin and harpsichord) with him in Germany and then take it into the recording studio in June 1965.

Wibb with Yehudi Menuhin in the mid-1960s

> *Yehudi was terribly amenable, he wasn't like a god you couldn't talk to. He would welcome ideas from me, even though I was only quite young. It was early in my musical life. I was trying to do my best and do the Caratgé live staccato (it was before I met Moyse). We were both experimenting—I'd never played the Concerto before and it was a new piece for him as well. That's why I was able in rehearsals to say: 'Do you think it does this or that?' It was equal, it wasn't him saying: 'You must do this'. But I remember that wonderful attack of his in the First Movement and the shape of the line—and he made that orchestra play like devils! It was so right and I've never heard anybody else play it as well as that. It was a centipede with a pair of balls between each set of legs! I was very lucky to be included on that recording.*

Menuhin did, however, have a reputation for being a somewhat uneven player, something that Wibb experienced at first hand—and took inspiration from.

> *Once he played a Mozart Concerto and made a complete cock-up of the First Movement. He often used to get very nervous about some challenge to do with the bowing and it was a total embarrassment—a real Menuhin scrambled*

> egg job! But then he went into the slow movement and all the problems fell away. Anyone else would have been praying for a hole to open up in the ground and to disappear into the flames, but we were all transported completely. I've always thought: 'If something goes wrong, I want to do it like that: recover and make the next thing so beautiful, like Menuhin did'.

It wasn't only Menuhin's playing that appealed to Wibb.

> I even liked his conducting! He wasn't very good at it, but somehow he could convey something which surpassed his sometime awkward gestures. He used to get shape into things and I couldn't understand it. Adrian Boult had the same ability: somehow he conveyed the architecture of a Brahms Symphony better than other people could. With Menuhin, I could sense the magic going on and sometimes it was so stunningly good.

Observing closely that Menuhin magic, Wibb was keen to ask him exactly how he achieved certain effects, particularly the smoothness and continuity of line across the registers.

> 'How do you make those shifts, when you change position?' I wanted to penetrate what he did that had that wonderful feeling about it. He said: 'You know, the curious thing about the violin? Sometimes I can't do that sort of thing if I've had too much for supper!' The amount of food in the gut affected his ability to do a good legato. I can relate to that on the flute! And breathing was part of the sound for Yehudi. I had recordings of him playing unaccompanied Bach that were absolutely marvellous. I can't play it like that...

As Wibb said, his recording of the Bach Triple Concerto was before he met Moyse—although only a few weeks before, on 30 June 1965 at Abbey Road Studios. He had, however, already instinctively picked up the French Flute School's preoccupation with the flute as a vocal instrument and therefore the inspiration to be gained from studying singers closely. It would be a soprano, April Cantelo, who would unknowingly give Wibb a moment of great revelation about his playing one evening in a concert, when his keen ears and concentration were searching for some ideal of sound and expression (more about that in the chapter on Playing) and he has always admired a variety of other singers.

> I like the soprano, Sumi Jo—wonderful, great phrasing and tremendous fun with it. I remember being fascinated by the countertenor Alfred Deller—he was always exciting to hear! I'm a great fan of his. It was wonderful the way he used his voice, and when he did dotted notes, he had a sort of jazz lilt.

Eilidh McNab was another soprano Wibb worked with early in his career in the 1960s. He particularly remembers her approach to Ravel's exotic song cycle, *Chansons madécasses*.

> I did Scottish tours with the Lyric Trio and got to know Eilidh McNab quite well. She had passion and drive—what I thought was real

Wibb with Yehudi Menuhin in the 1980s

> *understanding—and a fantastic intensity of expression, which wasn't commonplace amongst singers. She was something! And whenever I heard the* Chansons madécasses *done by anyone else they were floppy and useless. She showed me a few vocal exercises, vocalises, which I've incorporated into my practice and give to others. That was about the same time as I was with Moyse and I was consciously trying to apply getting the sound into my body, then rolling it out in front.*

Interestingly, the *Chansons madécasses* are more often sung by a mezzo-soprano than a soprano and it's a mezzo among all the singers who has had the most profound influence on Wibb: Janet Baker. Only a couple of years older than Wibb, she was a young singer just beginning to make her name when he returned from Paris in the Autumn of 1958.

> *One of the first things I played in was Gluck's* Orfeo, *at Morley College, conducted by Anthony Lewis, Principal of the Royal Academy of Music. Janet Baker was singing Orpheus, but she wasn't doing all the performances. I told my parents: 'You've got to come and hear it, there's this wonderful singer'. So they came along to the show, but it was the understudy that day and I was so upset—I was her greatest fan. Janet was bloody marvellous, straight away when I first heard her!*

So what was it that Wibb was hearing in Janet Baker's voice and music making that so impressed him?

> *Well, there was a good sense of melody and I was always enraptured by Janet's solid, well-produced sound and the way she phrased. It just sounded one hundred percent right the whole time. She had more conviction in her voice than anybody else I'd heard. I used to listen and ask myself: 'What sort of vibrato does she have?' and things like that. Not that I could actually get it, but every time I heard her I thought: 'That's it!'*

And there was something about colour—a word and a concept that is central to Wibb's own artistry.

> *The colours in her voice were changing all the time. I remember doing a session with the Melos Ensemble with two flutes in Conway Hall. Janet was placed right behind me and we were doing a lot of French music and we had a very fine recording engineer. I always used to think that when he was in charge of a session you got a marvellous quality of sound. But I can remember hearing Janet behind me, with these wonderful changes of colour and subtle things, and then going to hear the playbacks in some other room in the back of the hall. Only about half of what she did got onto the recording. It was quite interesting to notice how much got lost, but the people doing the recording couldn't possibly know. I'm making an unfair comparison now—they heard a very good recording going on—but I was there, I was in the hall.*

That glorious recording was made by Decca in 1966, with music by Chausson, Delage and Ravel—including the *Chansons madécasses*—and Wibb playing second flute to Richard Adeney. He was also deputising a lot for Adeney at that time, including in Benjamin Britten's English Opera Group, where he worked again with Janet Baker in *The Rape of Lucretia* and began to get to know her better. On one occasion he met her by chance on a train travelling down to Wales and had a chance to compare notes about flute playing and singing (see the chapter on Playing for more about this). Then Wibb was invited to record Gustav Holst's Fugal Concerto with the ECO. That gave him an opportunity to experiment with what he had observed and absorbed from Janet Baker.

> *I did the recording with the oboist Peter Graeme and Imogen Holst conducting. She was wonderful. We did the first movement and at the end of the first take the producer said: 'That's a bit slow don't you think?' Imogen looked up and said: 'Absolutely no, that's the perfect tempo!' and she was dead right. She had a really good sense of rhythm and she wasn't going to take any nonsense from anybody bossing her around. You can hear the record and you can tell it's the right speed.*
>
> *It's in the slow movement of that piece that I was thinking: 'How can I make the flute sound like Janet Baker', because that was one of my ambitions. 'I want that sound'. There was a melody that would have been good*

> *had Janet been doing it and I was trying to make that creamy, mezzo-soprano sound. That's what I wanted the flute to do.*

It's worth noting that Joachim Quantz, in his great treatise *On Playing the Flute* (1752) also likens the ideal flute sound more to that of the contralto than the soprano voice. There is something here about richness and nobility of sound which has always struck a sympathetic chord with Wibb.

Meanwhile, the 1960s also saw the beginning of the longest lasting and maybe most significant of Wibb's musical partnerships. The pianist Clifford Benson was ten years Wibb's junior but he was destined to become just as significant a hero and influence as many of his elders. Wibb's wife, Rhuna, was responsible for bringing the two of them together when Clifford was only fourteen.

> *Rhuna said: 'You must play with my brilliant pupil' and that was Clifford Benson. She had taught him marvellously and he came to the house and we played the Bach E Flat Sonata. He seemed alright—good, quick witted—and it sort of grew from there, but I didn't really appreciate quite how good he was straight away.*

Clifford then encountered problems with his playing when he moved on from Rhuna to join the senior Royal College of Music as an undergraduate student.

> *He got transferred to the wrong teacher at the College and we wanted some help for him. Then George Malcolm heard him and his remark was: 'Oh it sounded like a football match!' So it ended up with Clifford having a few lessons with George Malcolm on piano. That was very instructive, George helped him very much, neatened up his playing no end and gave him some very technical advice. Then Clifford ended up with Cyril Smith as his teacher, which was alright.*

Since his Paris years, Wibb's main pianist had been Susan Bradshaw, but now he began increasingly to work with Clifford.

> *Bit by bit I found out that Clifford had dimensions that Susan didn't have, although she was fantastic. He picked everything up incredibly quickly and already he'd been writing his own music forever, so he was madly fertile in his mind. He just knew everything about music. I can't tell you a precise moment when it clicked with Clifford—I think I just went on learning more and more, because he was better and better and better than I thought before.*

When Trevor Wye organised his first masterclass course for Moyse at Ramsgate, Clifford was invited to be the pianist.

> *There he was, lapping up all the information from Moyse.*

Moyse was happy and Wibb and Clifford were now seriously embarked on a musical journey and partnership that would last until Clifford's tragic death at the age of sixty in 2007.

> *Clifford had a very good touch, he could make the piano sing and be sensitive. He capitalised on all that. He was learning a lot of the music*

along with me and we developed it together. Later I found, looking back: 'Clifford showed me how to do that', but only through playing it. Things like the Reinecke Concerto, nobody ever taught me that except by playing it with Clifford. Later on I would hear it with someone else and think: 'It doesn't go like that—I've heard God play that piece!' Clifford would play something in a way that was much more musical than anyone else and I would just accept it. I wasn't consciously picking up ideas, but I realise that he was pointing the way very often.

When Geoffrey Gilbert first heard Clifford, he was knocked over. He said: 'I haven't heard piano playing like that since Cortot. He had that ability to make it sing.' Geoffrey had already lent me a record of Cortot playing Chopin studies, as guidance, and Geoffrey was a pianist himself.

Wibb with Clifford Benson

Wibb particularly admired Clifford's ability to get right to the heart of a piece and really make it work.

He put musical life in without my telling him how I wanted things to go. Occasionally we would discuss something, but very seldom did I have to ask Clifford about anything and I found that if I did have to discuss something and Clifford said: 'No', I completely accepted it. It was always right! You can't argue with a Scorpio, it doesn't work! We didn't often discuss fine points or anything. He would sometimes say: 'Oh, can you do something here...', but most of the time it was both of us leading each other, I think.

So often pianists in a duo are judged and valued for how well they support the soloist. For Wibb, Clifford didn't stop there.

It was more than supporting, it was actually creating, because he would do something with a phrase and you'd just feel you had to follow it. Like in the RPO, they used to say: 'It's very nice when we have Alan Civil coming to play the horn with us. Everybody plays better'. They listen to Alan and hear how he does the phrase and everybody sounds better if Alan is in the orchestra. I think that's what happened with Clifford: as soon as anyone heard something going on in the piano part that was really convincing, they knew, like me: 'That's how it goes'.

I used to think that Clifford was absolutely psychic. I'd often hear it in masterclasses. Somebody would be fumbling away, and getting a bit out, and without Clifford having to watch anything he was totally aware of where they were wrong. And if they were having difficulty with the breathing, he used to be part of their breathing—he was very aware of breathing—and that helped me enormously to cope with all my inadequacies!

Wibb rehearsing with Clifford Benson

And off the concert platform?

Oh yes, we had a lot of fun! A lot of swimming and drinking and all that!

Even onstage, and particularly during masterclasses, there was a playful quality to Clifford that delighted Wibb.

He was fascinated with words and doggerel. In masterclasses he'd be doing nothing for a quite a while, when I was working on some point of flute playing, and at the end he would come up with another limerick.

Clifford's limericks were almost invariably rude—and unprintable! Here's one of the only ones that wasn't.

> A flutist whose playing bewitches,
> Had the audience one evening in stitches.
> When he asked why it was,
> They replied: 'It's because
> Of the way your moustache always twitches!'

> *That's pure Benson and he came up with lots of them, taking the silly words that I used—'taxis' and 'elephants'. We were both into finding words to scan with the music, to make it say the right thing and show where the comma was, etcetera. That was all part of getting the musical stresses into the words. We both enjoyed it very much and he was brilliant at it.*

I have my own memories of this unique partnership, particularly through a series of recordings I produced at the BBC in the 1990s. After Clifford died, Wibb and I put together a CD of some of them on Wibb's Beep Records label (BP 38)—works by Hahn, Schubert, Franck and Prokofiev. In the sleeve notes I wrote:

> Time and time again, the way that Wibb and Clifford set a mood, turn a phrase, and ride the wave of a great musical climax, illuminates the music in a truly marvellous way. I only wish you could also hear the gaps between the tracks, particularly the laughter! Even though the sessions were hard work, and the music demanded to be taken seriously, the whole experience was also such fun—there was so much joy in the music making.

What more telling tribute could there be then, from Wibb to Clifford, than his response to my asking how Clifford's death had affected him?

> *I haven't recovered from it yet. With other pianists I think I'm always asking for things I remember hearing Clifford do...*

Sketch of a Paris street scene by Wibb

6—Flutes

For some flute players, the close relationship they build up with a particular instrument is fundamental to their playing. Wibb has never limited himself to one, or even a few flutes, although he does have favourites. He is famous for the huge number he has—and they are everywhere. All around his house you will find flutes and bits of flutes, in and out of cases, and each with a particular story attached. Flutes on their way in, and flutes on their way out! Open the door of his workshop and there are even more, in various states of repair, or disrepair. As we have seen, Wibb's first flute was made of wood, his second of silver. Already as a young player he was searching for an ideal of sound.

> *There was a big divide in England between the French and the English styles, associated with metal and wooden flutes. I wasn't aware of it. If there were flutes I was interested in—and I gradually found that out without realising why—they were mostly the French ones or the French style. But I wasn't into analysing why at that stage. It was an emotional reaction to it.*

A corner of Wibb's workshop

Wibb playing a wooden flute

Could he identify this emotional reaction?
> *When I was fifteen or sixteen... I would hear some flute sound and: 'Wow!' It was a wonderful sound and then you got different versions of this wonderful sound and that's really still how it is. You get these big differences of ways that people play. Some of them are very convincing and beautiful and some of them just sound like a little computer. And that's not necessarily fixed and associated with only being one style.*

But it is about the quest for a certain colour, or range of colours.
> *I wanted to do all the things that other people could do with their flutes. I wanted to have that sound. Like a painter, you want to be able to buy such and such a tincture or colour.*

And for Wibb there is potentially something even more, latent in the flute. You hear him bringing it out time and time again in his playing—something visceral.
> *Yes, that animal thing... there is a vitality there and it's wonderful. In the instrument there is a basic vitality, which you pick up on when it comes out.*

So how have the actual instruments he has played helped Wibb in this search for sound and colour and vitality? How important has it been to him what materials the flutes have been made of?

I played a wooden flute to start with and then Geoffrey Gilbert pointed me at a Louis Lot. He didn't say anything about whether it should be plated metal or silver. He at that time had a platinum flute, but he locked it in the safe because it didn't sound right for him. He played it for about a year and then gave up on it and went back to playing on his ordinary Louis Lot. But he wanted to be known as the man with the platinum flute.

Then after Wibb had been in Paris and had his few lessons with Rampal, back in London Albert Cooper offered to make him a gold flute.

He built me a silver flute first and then he said: 'Oh, I'll make you a gold flute if you like'. I thought: 'Oh yes, I'd like that, that might help me', because I was impressed with Rampal and his gold Louis Lot (that was before he got a Haynes). So I gave Mr Cooper a set of key work (I'd got an old wooden Louis Lot, and we used that for the key work) and he sold me the tube.

Rampal himself came to London soon after and Wibb arranged an evening of chamber music.

Jimmy Galway and Rampal came round and we had homemade wine and played trios with three gold flutes. It sounded terrible! Rampal had just discovered the fingering for high F Sharp—above the Boulez top note—and he would spit it out and try and get an F Sharp. Terrible noise! But we had great fun making terrible noises!

Wibb carried on playing his gold flute for a while, but it wasn't a success.

It sounded bloody awful! But I have to say that it was only nine carat gold. Rampal's Louis Lot was eighteen carat—a very lovely sounding instrument. Anyway, I wasn't getting the sound I wanted—which was the Dufrène sound—and I very quickly abandoned the gold flute. It just sounded thin in the top register. I couldn't bear it and I found that I had a voice when I was playing my rebuilt, silver Louis Lot. It had nearer to what I was hoping for.

I've always wanted to have a singing ability. I've always wanted to have that width of sound that the few really great players have in the top register. I like Louis Lot flutes because the good ones have some space in the sound—openness of voice in the third octave—and it can be the hardest thing to get right. I know that that's my concern when I'm trying a flute. Can I get a fairly good low two octaves and something in the third octave that matches in with the second? Many flutes simply contract, and there's nothing I can do about it.

Louis Lot and various other French makers in the late-19th Century used not only silver, but also *maillechort*, usually referred to as nickel silver because of its silver colour, but actually a mixture of nickel, copper and zinc.

Moyse played a nickel flute, a Couesnon. I didn't like the Couesnon flutes when I first tried them when I was in Paris. I didn't bite. Then when we met Moyse, Trevor Wye had a Lebret metal flute, which he'd retuned. One night a whole lot of us were trying flutes, and Moyse came in: 'Oh, what is this?' And I said: 'We're trying flutes and there's a flute here by Lebret'. Moyse said he used to play a Lebret before he moved on to a Couesnon and it seems that his first recording of Carnaval de Venise *was done on his Lebret in 1927. I've got quite a few of those cronky old French flutes. I've got three Lebrets, in maillechort, and a couple by Rive, because I love that metal. Nowadays, I play half the time on one of my Louis Lots in maillechort—I find it has more zing in it than silver.*

A publicity photograph from the 1970s

A lot of this is of course personal taste, but Wibb does feel that the actual metal influences the playing.

Very definitely the metal influences it. To me, gold is a very hard metal, particularly nine carat gold, and it induces a thinness in the high register, which, as I said, I couldn't overcome. I actually had Cooper take the tube off my gold flute and rebuild it with a silver tube. However, it sounded exactly the same on the silver tube so I abandoned it altogether—so it may not have been that at all! But gold wasn't my favourite stuff at all. There are plenty of gold flutes which sound pretty good up the top, but I haven't been lucky with the ones I've had.

Nevertheless, later on Wibb tried once again.

Cooper sold me another gold tube and I had a complete set of mechanism put on by Altus. I've got one recording somewhere of me playing on that. It's alright. It sounds quite pleasant, but there aren't any changes of colour in it. It's the same colour throughout. It just didn't do what I wanted it to do. So I sold that and Michel Debost bought it for one of his pupils and they were very happy. He said: 'Why are you selling this lovely gold flute?' He sold me his Louis Lot, so he was happy with his bargain, and I was terribly happy with the other one, which is now my wife Michie's flute. It's

> a superb Louis Lot, one of the really great ones that vibrates. It has that quality: it vibrates in the hand and there's a wonderful resonance in it.

There is a sense, of course, in which every flute is really two separate instruments: the body and the head. Over the years Wibb has combined many different flute headjoints and bodies and for him the choice of headjoint makes or breaks any flute.

> It's supremely important. The old French players used to have a personal headjoint. Taffanel is supposed to have carried his in his jacket pocket and if he wanted to demonstrate on someone else's flute, he put his headjoint on it. Each one has a different dimension somewhere on the mouth hole and that will affect how it works. You've got to learn to play your own particular headjoint. I play several, but they're very much within a small range of proportions.

Along the way, Wibb has had some intriguing experiments with headjoints.

> I once tried a Gazzelloni-style large embouchure. When Rainer Schuelein came back from Italy with a Gazzelloni headjoint, Geoffrey Gilbert said: 'Oh, the mouth hole is bigger than a lavatory seat!' Rainer had an alto flute made with this mouth hole on it and when I did my first alto flute job I hired it and had to learn to play this enormous mouth hole. It was quite cumbersome. I have been able to play it a little bit, but Rainer persevered and played it always.

So what are the important factors in designing and making a good headjoint?

> The exact diameter at the centre of the mouth hole is of very much concern to a flute maker and somehow some headjoints suit certain bodies and some don't. I can't venture explanations for that, but if you've got a good headjoint, you hang on to it for life—even if you hang on to half a dozen or so, which I've done.

Which makes it sound as though there is an inescapable element of chance.

> Yes! Even if they're made on a machine there are differences in every headjoint. A tiny micro cut in a different place completely changes the resistance on it.

Is that the same then for the body of the flute?

> It's much less sensitive on the body. Up here, the blow hole is where the sound originates. That's where the division of the air is—'le biseau' as Caratgé called it. That edge, or wedge, is the place where the sound is formed, coupled to the actual dimensions of the hole, and then how much you cover it. If you take a drinking straw and you blow through it, you get a very fine jet of air coming out. You can blow quite gently and a coolish jet comes out the other end, but if you take a larger tube, like a drainpipe, all your air comes out at once and it doesn't come out cold, it will come out warm as it leaves your lips. That means that the actual width of the

> mouth hole and the length of the mouth hole affect it very much—and then the dimensions of the diagonals too.
>
> You might have a mouth hole which is completely round. That can happen on some Indian flutes. There's also the old English oval shape, which is often seen on piccolos. Then there's the rounded off square, which the French ones have. Some flutes have even had an actual square mouth hole. All that affects how the air travels through that first little bit. The angles of undercut, particularly at the front edge, also affect the sound colossally. There are so many minute things that can affect it. It's the most sensitive bit of the whole flute. None of us know very much about it. It's just: 'This one works, that one doesn't!'

Trying to find out why a headjoint works or not, however, has been a major preoccupation for Wibb over the years.

> For instance, if the front wall's slightly curved: with my Haynes that I bought, I thought: 'It shouldn't be curved like that, I'll straighten it out!' I was fed up with the flute by then anyway, so I filed it flat. All the resistance went out of the top register because the air was getting in too easily. The air passes through it more quickly, but it needs to stay. The air has got to work on something in that tiny hole actually to create the note.

And the way the note is created sets up the basic resonance for the whole instrument.

> Yes, it's initiating the vibrations. Now, on a headjoint, it's been found that if there's a sharp edge at the bottom of the hole, it creates a whistly sound—which we associated with Cooper's headjoints. They were too clinically made, with sharp angles. We believed that they needed rounding off at the bottom. Quite a lot of people also believe that the tone holes have to be rounded off at the bottom. I believe that too.

Johan Brögger, the Danish maker who worked with Brannen, developed a special, mathematical curvature gauge.

> The Brögger cut on the keys was supposed to open up the sound and quite a lot of people have had a specifically Brögger cut. I believe that does affect it, but not anything like so markedly as it does for the headjoint. If you've got very sharp edges at the tone hole, it may affect the sound. Quite often I have rounded off the tone holes at the bottom of the flute in order to see if it would make the sound any more round, avoiding the thin noise that I don't like. The trouble is, you do that and you can't really tell if it's different, but you can't go back to how it was before—you can't try it again! It's all subjective in your memory.

What about the mixing of metals in the headjoint, using gold for the lip plate, and more significantly for the riser, even if the tube is silver?

> Well, a lot of the people believe very strongly in that. I've got two Rainer Lafin lip plates, and he talked me into having gold risers. I can't see that

> *that tiny length of gold makes much difference at all, but a whole lot of people have a little bit of gold or platinum inlaid. They tell people it makes the thing speak better. I don't subscribe to that idea, but I don't know how you can prove anything...*

What you certainly can prove, however, is that Boehm flutes, although based on scientific measurements, are fundamentally out of tune—or at least they were until Wibb and some other colleagues came along.

Wibb had been working on his first Louis Lot flute (serial number 4780) when it was lost on the London Underground on New Year's Eve, just before he was due to join the Band of the Scots Guards for his military service.

> *Catastrophe! Then Geoffrey Gilbert found me a sharp pitch Louis Lot, which I had rebuilt, again by Mr Morley. That took too many months and I was struggling along with my old Rudall Carte flute, but I was so staunchly a silver flute man (or metal flute man) by then. I didn't want to play wooden flutes—I thought they had a horrible sound, which of course was a big mistake because they don't! But I was eighteen, you see... I was delighted because I had the sound of a silver flute. I thought the high register was going to sound better at once, but of course I soon found it sounded just as bad on the silver flute as it did on the wooden one! That's one of my preoccupations: trying to get a decent sound in the high register.*

There were also other problems with this rebuilt Louis Lot which no amount of practice could put right.

> *I started playing, but very soon after I thought: 'But it's out of tune—my C is terribly flat'. Then I discovered F Sharp was horribly sharp. It was all over the place. But C was the most distressing note. By this time I was turning nineteen, and was going to America in the Army, and I was always pitching the C up madly on my rebuilt Louis Lot. It was agony.*

Drastic measures were called for and Wibb knew what he had to do.

> *Somebody had showed me a flute where Mr Morley had moved the E hole and filled the little gap with a large wodge of solder, so I knew something was possible. I'd already bought a cheap Selmer flute, and I'd tried altering one of the notes, which was particular obnoxious, by scraping a bit out of the hole. It was a cheap flute, it didn't matter!*

Wibb's Louis Lot was anything but a cheap flute, but somehow he had to get that C sharper.

> *So I carved it out. I got a file and a knife and I cut as much metal as I could out of it. It got a bit better. Finally I put something in the F Sharp hole to try and make it lower.*

The visit to America in 1955 with the Band of the Scots Guards opened up for Wibb a whole new world of design and quality in flute making. At the beginning and end of the tour, the Band was based with the Marines in

Washington DC. Wibb got to know the flute players and their flutes, particularly a man called Michael Hamilton.

> *While we were there, we tried Powell flutes and Haynes flutes that were belonging to the people in the Marines Band where we stayed. They were so much better than what I had. Apart from anything else, they worked properly and, to me, it seemed they were perfectly in tune (it wouldn't nowadays!). But anyway, I thought Powell flutes were a gift from heaven and I bought a Powell headjoint—Michael Hamilton, one of the Marines, sold me a spare—and it was a Mariano model hole, which meant a deeper chimney: 5.4mm, which is deep even by today's standards.*
>
> *Then, a week later, the band went off the Rochester, New York, where Mariano himself was the teacher. We had two or three days there and I was listening to Mariano's teaching and playing. He had a huge input because he was, I think, the greatest American flute player. He had lots of different sounds and played perfectly in tune, he really did. He had a fast vibrato—the American type—but he could do so many things with the sound. I wanted to play like that.*

Wibb was so fired up by all this that he also adopted a particular aspect of Mariano's technique.

> *Mariano's pupils said: 'Notice that he plays with the headjoint well pulled out, about half an inch'. Of course, they didn't say how long the headjoint was, but I was so impressed with Mariano that I said: 'I'm going to do that—I'm going to pull out my head joint—and I'm going to do it for three months and see how it goes'. Well I did it for three months and forgot to push it in again! It was a good answer for me. It helped me open up the high notes quite a lot—I think I must have been covering too much of the mouth hole before, without realising it. I was just covering it to get the pitch down.*

There is more about the upper register and freeing the sound in the chapter on Playing, at the end of this book. Meanwhile, Wibb's Powell headjoint had cost him a complete month's Army wages and now he was determined to buy a complete Powell or Haynes flute. This time he had to borrow the money and he soon discovered that the instrument was far from perfect.

> *I bought a Haynes flute when I was in New York. It had allegedly been made by Powell when he was foreman at Haynes, and I think that was true, but I was aware that it was built on the old scale, like a Louis Lot, which is flat down the bottom and sharp around C and C Sharp. I bought it accepting that I would have to do something. If Geoffrey Gilbert could play his Louis Lot flute in tune, anything was possible, and a lot of American players played their instruments in tune.*

Before returning to England, the Band stayed again with the Marines in Washington and Wibb had a brilliant idea.

Wibb No.1 flute with Louis Lot headjoint No.2828

> *I got some long thin strips of paper and carbon copying paper which I inserted under Michael Hamilton's Powell flute, pressed on the keys and got a printed impression of where the holes were. I came back to London, drew all this out on my father's drawing board, and made a plan of what I thought the Powell scale was. I wasn't quite sure where the thumb hole should go, because it wasn't in the same line as all the others, so I had to bend the paper right round the flute and I was quite unsure about that.*

Wibb then began, rather like a flute making Professor Frankenstein, to plot the creation of a perfect tuned flute! First he went to Rudall Carte's shop in Berners Street, where incidentally he met the young Albert Cooper for the first time. Later he would collaborate extensively with Albert, but this time he was on a solo mission to create his own flute: Wibb No.1.

> *I bought a sharp pitch Rockstro Model flute from Rudall Carte. It was quite cheap (sharp pitch has no value). Very big keys and open hole keywork—good solid Rudall Carte stuff. That was my kit for the keywork. Then I went off and bought a tube of the right flute length and what turned out to be almost the right diameter from Johnson Matthey, the silver company. It was slightly under-bored and later I sand papered it out. I had to get more bits of tube to make the tone holes and I set about positioning the holes as near as I could from my measurements I'd taken from the Powell flute. I had to do everything. I took the keys, and transplanted the mechanism, and then started soldering them on the flute, according to my plan of what I thought a Powell was.*

How did Wibb manage for tools?

> *I had a little gas poker in the kitchenette of my room at home and a pair of scissors! I invented my own tools.*

It was a time-consuming job and it took Wibb about nine months to complete the whole flute. He fitted it with the Powell headjoint he had bought in America.

> *When I finally got it playing, with some pads that actually covered, the C was horrendously sharp. So I got something called plastic metal, a sort of aluminium-looking stuff out of a tube, that set hard in a few hours. I put a great wodge of this metal into the C hole to make it flatter. It got quite a lot better. Then I did a little bit with C Sharp, which was troublesome, and then I took it to a flute lesson.*

You can imagine the scene: the confident, twenty-year-old Wibb arriving at Geoffrey Gilbert's house brandishing his 'Wibb No.1'—just as he did while he was telling me this.

> *You need the opposite to dark glasses! It's a good shade of black!*

The tube and keywork were almost completely blackened from all the work on them, but in the eyes of its creator this flute was a great marvel.

> *Geoffrey feigned amazement: 'It works!' It didn't work very well, but the fact that it worked at all surprised him! He tried it for a few minutes and said: 'Yes... don't you think the E Flat is a bit low?' I tried it: 'Oh my God, it's awful!' I went straight back home that night and cut about a millimetre and a half off the footjoint with a hacksaw. There was no worry about doing it to my own creation, and it was better than before.*
>
> *So all this business about moving holes started with me making my own flute and then discovering I was unhappy with the one I'd made. I found that my position for the thumb was better than Powell's and then I started moving one or two other things. It's all by experimentation: 'That note's wrong, let's shift it!' Then Elmer Cole, a younger colleague of mine, got interested and started doing the same work. He's the one responsible for bringing back Boehm's Schema, with the aid of Alex Murray. He was impressed with my flute, but he was more scientific than me. He rebuilt himself a flute entirely on Boehm's Schema.*

And so with Wibb No.1 launched, Wibb began to play it often in the Army Band, where it was much appreciated.

> *It turned out to be very powerful. The Colonel was quite impressed and he told Sergeant 'Tiggy' Walker to make an arrangement for a Church Parade of a hymn tune for brass band, with flute. There I was: a not-brass instrument in the brass band! That flute always had this tremendous depth of sound, which I think may have had something to do with the very large tone holes. So this was quite a useful adventure, one way and another.*

Wibb's method of working, then and now, is a heady mixture of science, observation, invention and experimentation.

> *Rockstro's flute meant large keys. He liked maximum size holes. So I said to myself: 'Put foot joint size holes on the right hand'. Powell's are smaller,*

but I kept the larger holes of the Rockstro model, and that proved to be a good thing because I got the E and the F sharper than Powell. And then I thought, when I drew up the drawing: 'It doesn't look right. The proportions aren't right. The G looks a bit high'. So I left a little metal inside the G hole. It was alright!

To make smaller tone holes for the left hand notes, I had ordered a thin piece of tube. So I cut out the curve in the metal to fit the flute and then, with a hacksaw, cut through it, pierced it and left it too tall and then filed the top down. That was to make the tone hole. But there wasn't enough metal there to make a good join, so I got a pair of pincers, and just went round the lower edge tweaking the sides out so that there'd be a sort of flange around it—and that gave me the idea for the tuning patch.

When I wanted to shift the hole uphill, I could have a tone hole with a flange on the side, and with this very thin metal that I'd made it out of, I could make a flange that went all the way round by tweaking and then rubbing sandpaper on the tube. Later, I got thicker metal for the tone holes and I silver-soldered a piece on the outside, and that was my invention of the tuning patch, which enabled me to push the hole up a millimetre or two—and that's very much still in use. My flutes are covered in tuning patches!

This would all seem to require some quite sophisticated metal working, so what training did Wibb have for it?

I didn't have any training—I had to invent it! You've no idea how difficult it was to solder with only a gas burner and a sink. Soft soldering was a nightmare, hard soldering was much harder, but I picked up various things. I was never very good at it, but...

But Wibb would persevere throughout his career. The die was cast and an important principle was firmly established: the instrument is only a means to an end. Its surface beauty may need to be sacrificed to whatever it takes to correct the tuning and unlock its inner resonance. Incidentally, later on Wibb's colleagues in the ECO would say that they always preferred his blackened flutes to shiny ones because they sounded so much better. Occasionally, therefore, Wibb would artificially blacken up a new flute he was trying out, just to put them off the scent and keep them happy!

Meanwhile, soon after the creation of Wibb No.1, he had a chance to compare it with a distinguished Powell original flute.

An American gentleman came to London and he had some Powell flutes, including one that had belonged to Georges Laurent. This man had been one of his pupils. Laurent had had the foot joint cut at both ends—apparently he didn't like the Powell foot joint, it was too flat. My flute was better in tune than Laurent's Powell, but I must say that his flute was so beautiful. That was my ideal of what a flute should be like. That quality of sound,

> most particularly in the high notes, was just a constant inspiration to me. The American never sold me that flute, when he did decide to sell it, because he knew I'd take it apart and tune it and ruin it... but I wanted to have that headjoint. I think it was number 285, so it was a very early Powell.

If you listen to recordings of Wibb in the 1970s, the flute he is quite likely to be playing on is a Louis Lot, serial number 2828.

> My best flute still!

It has a chequered history. Wibb first saw it in the Rudall Carte shop on a visit to London when he was in the BBC Northern Orchestra, but it was already promised to Geoffrey Gilbert. So he had to wait until Geoffrey had tried it and decided he didn't want it. Then Wibb was able to take it on approval back to Manchester.

> It had the sound I was after. I thought: 'This is the sort of flute that Dufrène must have played on'. The sound went to the back of Manchester Town Hall (where we gave our Friday concerts) and it came back at me, and I knew that that was what I was looking for.

But when Wibb played it to Geoffrey Gilbert, and to his pianist Susan Bradshaw, neither of them liked it—maybe because the mechanism and padding didn't work very well—and they persuaded him not to keep it. So James Galway bought it instead, but couldn't get on with its uneven tuning and soon sold it on Elmer Cole. He in turn realised that the holes in the tube needed to be moved around, but he didn't complete the work.

> Elmer took the whole thing apart and never managed to stick it together so that it would work again. And so I bought that flute for £30—a tube and a tin of bits! It took me about a year to get it going and make it work again with new hole positions. And that's been my flute ever since.

Meanwhile, the headjoint of Louis Lot 2828 had its own story to tell. It wasn't with the tin of bits that Wibb bought, so he played the rebuilt flute with various other headjoints—notably a Bonneville, rescued from a not very good flute he bought for a few pounds.

> I realised that the nickel Bonneville had the right sound in it. It became the best one, the one I used for many years. Then an accident happened with it...

But by a stroke of luck, headjoint 2828 reappeared. Having passed through various hands—losing its gold lip plate on the way—it had been acquired by Trevor Wye, and Wibb was able to buy it from him.

> It was the original headjoint for that flute. So I put another lip plate on it and it worked. 2828 is the best flute—and it's actually back with its own headjoint. There's something I rather like about having a complete instrument!'

Mind you, the quest for perfect headjoints is never over. Along the way there was another Louis Lot, serial number 3616, that Wibb bought from a friend.

> I liked the head and I put a new lip plate on it—a Powell lip plate—and

I bushed the inside and made it small and started again and I made one that was bloody good! That was the best headjoint in the world, until one day the lip plate came unsoldered, because my soldering wasn't that good! And that's somewhere still being repaired. I'm always looking for headjoints like 3616, and the Bonneville, and they were both nickel.

As a postscript to all this talk of flutes, I wondered what Wibb had made of the revival of the baroque flute—the one-keyed traverso. How did he feel in the 1970s and 80s when he was recording the Bach Sonatas and much other Early Music?

Sketch of a baroque flute player by Wibb

I didn't like what I heard from the baroque flutes. I thought it sounded appalling! I haven't changed.

Strong words! But how to define *appalling*, what is it that Wibb doesn't like!

The sound is so unequal through the instrument, and the players do funny little swells and things which don't help the line. Mind you, they're fighting to play somewhere near the right note, and some of them can play well. I don't like it though. I'm so much in love with the way the good French players played sixty to a hundred years ago and I can't see any need to go back further. But I don't think the baroque players do go back to the baroque way, I think they've invented a new style.

Of course they are critical of players who use vibrato, because so many flute players now use vibrato totally indiscriminately, and it's good to have somebody to make them think. But I don't think what the baroque crowd has come up with has produced anything very exciting yet. Not to excite me anyway. I like the Romanian nai and the Arab end blown flutes—some of those have a marvellous voice. I've certainly tried to do things with the baroque flute, but oh my God it's hard!

Allied to this for Wibb, is a fundamental deficiency of design: the baroque flute cannot be for him an end in itself, it's merely a staging post in the evolutionary process.

The deficiency of the baroque flute is that it's a diatonic instrument with seven notes in the octave, which is basically six holes, which means that everything closes and then everything opens. Seven notes gives you a scale—any scale depending on where you drill the holes—but it's one scale. The way players got around that, to play in other keys, was by cross fingering, but the cross fingerings make a different, less pleasant noise.

> *G or A on the baroque flute are perfectly decent notes, but it's the ones in between—the G Sharps and the B Flats—which sound completely wrong, because they are cross fingered, and that's a makeshift way of getting the chromatic notes. They don't have enough vent and the harmonics are much less in tune, and therefore the sound doesn't ring right. It wasn't until Theobald Boehm came along and said: 'Look, there are twelve notes in an octave, let's have twelve holes in the flute', that it got better—or enough better—because he'd done more complete thinking. The first way had been to put closed keys on the flute, which were pretty unsatisfactory and cumbersome, difficult to use. Boehm said: 'Let all the keys stand open', hence the Boehm system. That was sheer brilliance—just plain thinking—but nobody else had done it.*

That said, Wibb is quick to point out that not all his flutes are modern or retuned instruments.

> *I've been known to play something like a baroque flute in the past... I have two wooden Louis Lots and Moyse's wooden Couesnon—not to mention five wooden, conical, early Boehm flutes.*

He has used some of those flutes on recordings, notably for the Handel Sonatas and Trio Sonatas in the early 1980s. Check them out!

Sketch of a Mediterranean harbour by Wibb

7—Music

When I asked Wibb which pieces he particularly remembered studying in the early years of learning the flute, the first things he came up with were the Mozart Concertos, the Bach Sonatas and *The Flight of the Bumble Bee*! Mozart and Bach have remained with him, *The Flight of the Bumble Bee* was a passing phase.

> *That was for thirteen-year-olds! I was trying to play the Bumble Bee within six months of having a flute. I always wanted to go as fast as possible, to play as many notes as possible per second!*

Wibb was also interested in 20th century music from quite early on, thanks to his enlightened music teacher at school, James Bayley, so he was learning works like the Hindemith Sonata and Lennox Berkeley Sonatina. He was also encouraged to write his own music.

> *I was already interested in not-classical changes of harmony. I liked the music doing different things harmonically.*

The results included a Concerto for Flute and Clarinet, and even some fragments of a Symphony, all written while Wibb was at school and quietly consigned to obscurity among piles of other flute music collected over the years.

Wibb's natural curiosity has always kept him in search of new flute music—and new music which could be for the flute—he has often commandeered pieces written (mistakenly, he would maintain!) for other instruments. His approach to something new is simple and effective.

> *I look at a piece and hum the tunes through to see if it seems any good. That's usually very quick. It'll grab you if it's worth anything, just by reading it in your head.*

Then he takes the music straight to the piano.

> *Why? Well, you hear the harmony as well, don't you? You get a much better picture than just playing the flute line by itself. The harmonic world is important—and the rhythmic.*

Even then, maybe picking up your flute isn't always the best way to understand how the music should go.

> *It isn't for me, no. Instead, see how it feels if you sing it. You don't even have to sing the right notes! I'm finding in master classes I'm always saying: 'Stop, sing it, find out what you do', because people are much*

One of a series of card designs by Wibb

better at singing than playing. They do things without knowing what they're doing, but they do it. They have much more feeling than is often apparent.

One of Wibb's recent discoveries is the long-neglected Flute Sonata by Mel Bonis, and then there was the Sonata that Schubert didn't realise he had written for the flute.

Quite often you get to know a piece because you hear somebody else play it first, but in the case of Mel Bonis's piece there wasn't a previous performance and there's plenty of pieces one meets like that. There's a Schubert Sonata which I'm very enthused about (in fact, there's more than one!) it's Opus 162. A friend of mine played me a record of David Oistrakh playing it, which was absolutely marvellous. I had to rush out and get it. I ended up recording it with Clifford when we decided to make a CD of Schubert, with the Introduction and Variations and Boehm's arrangements of the songs.

Wibb's enthusiasm for the music, and understanding of it, usually translates itself into narrative—a story is never far away and ideas can spring up anywhere. The idyllic surroundings of Pender Island in Canada, where Wibb was giving masterclasses and concerts, were a vivid inspiration for Schubert's Op.162 Sonata.

> *Our hotel was just on the edge of a bay: there's a tiny harbour and you overlook this wonderful stretch of water and the next island is about four, five miles away, just looming up with mountains all over it. There's this vast expanse of very calm Pacific water and this incredible light.*
>
> *So I told the audience: 'You know... surely Schubert must have come to Pender Island and seen this scene, or something very like it! This incredible still lake of water in the sunset. The music begins in the bass and then the flute comes in, very still. Then a little later along comes a police*

> *boat chasing some smugglers and the flute goes: 'Please stop! Now! Stop!' Finding silly little things like that to tell the audience, makes the piece much more vivid for me to play. I find I'm more and more conscious of what the music is doing.*

It's a quest to articulate meaning, to search out eloquence, and it's a given in everything that Wibb does.

> *Making the music talk is often a question of saying: 'This phrase goes up and this one comes down. This is the ninth floor and this is the basement, or whatever. That's the first thing, but then you should lead on to a more advanced level of communication, like: 'Oh, now we're feeling very miserable, this is a funeral parlour. Or this is a dance hall... or whatever it is'. The audience is more involved than if you just play those notes without thinking, which is what happens a lot of the time, I'm afraid.*

This story telling approach has been particularly illuminating in Wibb's understanding of the Mel Bonis Sonata. Her first name was actually Mélanie, but being a woman composer in a man's world in late-19th Century France was a handicap, so she shortened it to make her gender ambiguous. Her parents had initially discouraged her musical ambitions, then relented when her talent was spotted by the composer César Franck who arranged for her to enrol at the Paris Conservatoire in 1876. But they withdrew her after she had a love affair with a fellow student, Amedée Hettich, and persuaded her into an arranged marriage with a businessman nearly thirty years her senior.

For many years Mel Bonis concentrated on raising a family, then in 1893 she met Hettich again (he was now a music critic) and he helped launch her career as a composer. He also had an affair with her which resulted in an illegitimate child, a daughter, born in 1899. A full-blown scandal was only averted when the child was given to a maid to be brought up. In the middle of all this she composed her Flute Sonata, dedicated to one of Paul Taffanel's pupils, Louis Fleury—she was a close friend of his and his wife Gabrielle.

> *The story's good—it always goes down well when you get a bit of sex in it! Yes! For all illegitimate children, being one myself!*

But the process of discovering and unlocking a piece is more than just uncovering a good story. For Wibb, there's a particular exhilarating moment.

> *Yes, you suddenly find that the air comes rushing into you and you want to make the music say something. I got very enthused about this sonata by Mel Bonis (which I've just edited for a CD). It's absolutely superbly written for the flute. It has good melodies and a good balance between the flute and the piano. The piano part isn't just a tonk tonk accompaniment, it's a proper piano part and it integrates very well with what the flute does. They're both contributive and work very well—it's a proper duo sonata.*

As for the emotional range of this music, there's certainly passion and ecstasy, also playfulness, tenderness, wistful melancholy, and more than a touch of the exotic. But is there also a narrative? Can any of Mel Bonis's own turbulent history be heard in it?

> *Well, that's what is so interesting, when you know the story of Mel Bonis's life. The music seems to connect up an awful lot to what she's been through. Starting off with: 'I'm feeling so lonesome... I'm feeling so blue' in the first movement and then off to visit the boyfriend, waiting at the bus stop, in the second movement. And then this terrific gloom in the slow movement, with the very sad, big melody which she uses brilliantly. She gets this big Bach-like tune at the beginning and then makes smaller and smaller fragments. After a while, a little snippet of tune gets paired down into a three note figure, which is just like Moyse saying: 'Je t'aime... je t'aime', and then that becomes shorter—'Chéri... Chéri'—and finally, just 'Ooh....!' The last movement is so César Frank (he could have been one of her fanciers). It says Allegro Moderato but there's nothing moderate about it at all, it's totally immoderate and passionate—a wonderful tune! She was a really serious composer—I accept her completely.*

To complete the story: Mel Bonis was deeply affected by all this trauma in her life, although she had saved her career and reputation. When her husband died in 1918 she was happily reunited with her daughter, but during the First World War she had progressively withdrawn from musical life and was suffering increasing ill health. She lived on until 1937 and died all but forgotten.

Back now to a much earlier period in Wibb's life and to much earlier music. While he was a student at Guildhall he played in an amateur orchestra and was recommended to a group of friends who were enthusiastically playing baroque music.

> The violinist was called David Jack, and he said he'd been in the Busch Chamber Orchestra and had studied with Adolf Busch—I was very keen on my records of Adolf Busch. David had a pianist friend called Richard Hunt, plus another pianist, Richard McLaughlin. So there was Ricky and Dicky and Davey! They all lived in a flat in Paddington, just down the road from Geoffrey Gilbert. I used to go off and play chamber music a lot with them.
>
> They talked about learning about violin style, Bach bowing and things. I learnt about top note trills and things like that and they told me that in Baroque music you mustn't put in slurs, everything has to have a separate bow. Of course, they were right! I learnt to firmly disbelieve anything that was written in the printed parts, which was a very useful piece of education. All the editions of old music were full of editors' dots and slurs. So now I tend to disbelieve everything in all music! I mean, people are so literal about it: 'It's printed, so you must play it'. Death! It's not how it goes. Somebody who didn't know how it goes put the slurs in!

Wibb found that all this experience was a useful grounding in style and technique for playing early music and by the time he met George Malcolm he had been playing the Bach Flute Sonatas regularly—and some of the Violin Sonatas! Eventually he and George recorded the Flute Sonatas together on the Enigma label, which was run by John Boyden, a former Managing Director of the LSO. By then Wibb and George had played them together so often that there was little discussion about any of the finer points.

> George would just occasionally say: 'Make a little corner here... you shouldn't be too relentless'. He wanted odd moments of romanticism to creep in and he was, of course, right!

As for Wibb's own approach to playing Bach.

It was intuitive and influenced by my friends with whom I'd played so much of that sort of music. Bach is always fantastic. I don't know why, but his music is so perfect. Bach and Mozart are above anybody else, aren't they? They seem to have some inspiration from somewhere else entirely.

Wibb has never made a commercial recording of the Bach A minor Partita, but it's a work that has fascinated him for years.

A constant source of exploration. I even wrote a complete bass line—there obviously was a bass line that didn't get written in. You discover so much about the piece just by trying to find out what the bass line is. Working at that Partita and trying to get the sense out of it—it's thrilling! I get stuck on the piano for hours trying to find out: 'What is the harmony?'

The other day I was at it again and I suddenly got a new idea about the Bourrée anglaise. I remembered going to Borough Market and there were Morris dancers in the street. They had sticks that went 'click, click' every so often as they hit each other's sticks. The Bourrée Anglaise is a Morris Dance! I had great fun: I did it with Jonathan Leathwood at the Wigmore Hall, played the solo Partita for flute and guitar, with two taps on the sounding board at the end of that phrase in the Bourrée Anglaise!

For his edition of the complete Bach Sonatas, Wibb published his own completion of the opening movement of the A major. It had been in the back of his mind for years.

I was trying to do it whilst I was still at school. I was wrestling with the idea. I suppose that's because I was composing things myself. I thought it must be possible to do something to complete it. Of course, I didn't know then how long it should have been. Later, before the Berlin Wall came down, I went to Leipzig with the Academy of St Martin's and I bought all these lovely facsimiles of Bach. In the middle of the first movement, you can see that somebody removed the bottom of the page, so that bit is missing, but we know how many inches it was and you can calculate just about how many bars it might have been.

From baroque to contemporary repertoire was a musical leap that Wibb made with ease as a young player, particularly after he met the pianist Susan Bradshaw. But he distanced himself from new music after he began to study with Moyse.

> *For a long while, I wouldn't do any. I was fed up with being asked to flutter tongue all the time—it gets completely inexpressive and horrible—and I detested that idea of making double stops come out of the flute. When somebody does a double stop on the flute, it's impossible for either of the notes they're playing to have a good tone. My question would be: 'Which note do you want most?' My speciality is playing a good tone. You can have one note or the other with a good tone, but not both with a bad tone!*

Even back in 1962, when Wibb recorded the Boulez Sonatina and Berio *Sequenza*, he was looking for ways to find some more traditional lyricism in contemporary music.

> *I decided I wasn't going to make that awful flutter tongue noise. Three lines through the tail of the note means tremolo, so I did very fast double tonguing for a lot of it. Particularly when it was very soft, because to make the tongue flutter you're blowing about three times harder than normal and it makes a totally dead noise. I thought that some of the effects in the Berio Sequenza should be tremolando like a violin, with proper tone. So I did it that way, probably wrongly, but people didn't seem to mind very much!*

And of course there was that characteristic Wibb quest for narrative in the music.

> *The thing you have to realise is that in the Berio Sequenza, the silence is written and if you just do exactly what the little time clicks mean, you don't hear it, you just hear a whole lot of fairly fast, consecutive noises. You actually have to work on the theatrical aspect of it: here's a phrase, there's a contrasting phrase. This one says: 'Whaa!', the next one says 'Whoo!' and it's all romantic. You actually have to look for or create romanticism on some phrases, because what they're really doing is making huge contrasts and getting effects. With Berio those are particularly theatrical effects. In my music I've written: 'Top G, flutter tongue, try and make it romantic!'*

It certainly worked with audiences and after one ECO performance of a particularly challenging contemporary score, Wibb's agent at the time, Lilian Wick, commented: 'It's amazing: when you play it, you sound as if you like it!'

> *Just because I was pretending to be romantic in it. Trying to get some charm—like putting lipstick on a dead potato!*

More than just charm, however, for Wibb it's a search for shape, for direction, for meaning, so that the music does actually express something.

> *Well, you do hear quite a lot of music which is just notes and doesn't say anything! You struggle with a piece and you can't find the sense, you can't*

find where it goes. I pride myself on being able to look at the score and get a feeling of what it's saying—although I've got quite a lot of scores which I can't say I have any idea of...

Is the Boulez Sonatina one of those inexplicable scores for Wibb? Susan Bradshaw, who was studying with Boulez, was very keen that Wibb should play it.

She was coaching me heavily in how to do it, the idea of having different bar lengths—3/4, 2/8, 1/16, 11/32—which was quite a lot for me to take on board. I can remember the first rehearsal we did. I think it was an hour-and-a-half before I said: 'I've had enough—got to stop!' and we'd only done the first two-and-a-half pages, just sort of scratched the surface as it were. I had no idea whether it was a good piece, I was just trying to get into it.

But there was a breakthrough moment.

One day somebody played it on the radio. I remember listening to it and saying: 'It doesn't go like that!' I knew how it went—it was my piece—and I realised: 'Oh yes, I must like it a bit!' Now, if I think Boulez, I have all sorts of sounds in my head that I can remember from it. It's not just nothing. There are definite clear ideas in it. I can see note patterns in my mind's eye. I'll not say I'm really attached to it, but I have taught it once or twice.

Wibb was also receptive to *Winter Music*, the new piece that Susan Bradshaw asked Richard Rodney Bennett to write for them in 1960, after they came back from Paris.

I liked Winter Music, *yes. It's still got all those changing time signatures and funny rhythms and techniques, but it's quite accessible.*

As a fitting postscript to those contemporary music years, Wibb played *Winter Music*, with Richard Rodney Bennett, at the Memorial Concert for Susan Bradshaw at the Royal Academy of Music, after her death in 2005.

The repertoire that opened up for Wibb when he went to Moyse in 1965 (as noted in the chapter on Heroes) was the rich heritage of flute works that had been written in response to the playing of Paul Taffanel and the development of a new French Flute School in the latter years of the 19th century.

Moyse also had a fondness for the virtuoso pieces written earlier in the 19th century—Taffanel had used them as teaching pieces for developing technique—and for anything that focused on the expressive, vocal qualities of the flute. Moyse's *Tone Development through Interpretation* is a compendium of great moments from Romantic operas and over the years Wibb has developed a tradition of arranging short, light pieces in this style as encores for his recitals.

> *Virtuoso and sentimental stuff—all sorts of sloppy flute music! It's Moyse's fault! But it didn't half make me interested in doing that stuff properly. Moyse just showed one all sorts of things in the music.*

Clifford Benson's *Song for Wibb* sums up this musical world. Composed for Wibb's 50th birthday, it's a four-and-a-half minute romantic miniature, by turns lyrical and animated—often floating effortlessly in and out of the top register—and always eloquent.

> *It was quite a surprise. He didn't let on that he was preparing anything and then suddenly it was there: elegant little tunes that he was very good at. He heard countless masterclasses in which I was picking up on Rampal's idea of going to the top of the phrase, and the changes of colour which I got from Julian Bream, and from that record of* En Bateau *by Debussy, with the Paris Conservatoire Orchestra, that I quoted to Geoffrey Gilbert when I was sixteen. And I remember Clifford saying: 'Oh, I want that other, hollow sound there... Ooh...'. He knew it could happen!*

Clifford also composed a set of *Tango Variations*, intended for oboe, and while he was still writing them, suggested one to Wibb as an encore.

> *Tango Variations is my very favourite of the Clifford pieces. I tried quite a lot of it before it was ever performed on the oboe. It was written as a birthday present for someone else, but it ended up getting published finally as a flute piece—which it should have been anyway!*

What about Wibb's most favourite flute pieces of all? One evening we had a go at playing the *Desert Island Discs* game. If you could only take a handful of pieces, which would they be?

Well, the desert island would have to have a piano!

OK, that would be the luxury item—and it means you don't only have to take unaccompanied pieces.

Well I can play the Bach unaccompanied Partita from memory, so that's alright!

The rules of the game are there's no memorising: you don't get extra pieces!

Help! I don't know... these questions are so impossible to answer!

Of course they are... and we didn't get very far, but we did manage to identify some of the flute music that means most to Wibb:

Mozart: Andante in C

That's a superb piece. Fantastic, wonderful, a proper flute aria. It's so elegant. And when I first got a record of that as a fourteen-year-old—my lying godfather, God rest his soul, gave me the record of Jean Nada and the Zurich Tonhalle Orchestra—I was fascinated by the cadenza at the end with the fast notes, by Boehm.

Bach: Sonatas

The B Minor, first of all. I like it all and I think the jig at the end is so fantastic. It goes on and on and develops more and more—like horses galloping and they can't be stopped. The E Flat Sonata is more difficult in a way. That last movement is quite hard and not so gratifying to play. The C major is fantastic—and I get so angry when people tell me it's by another composer.

Gaubert: *Nocturne et Allegro scherzando*

That's my party piece from studying in Paris. It was what I took to the Geneva Competition in 1958 and the first piece I played for Moyse. I have a Gaubert Box of music and got it out recently. It's very good—and the first two Sonatas are wonderful. Gaubert has written some really good stuff. He's got a great, wonderful, romantic feel. Gaubert is very interesting: the Studies which he wrote for the Taffanel and Gaubert flute method really push the player to do something with the colours. He's a proper composer who is producing, understanding and feeling harmonies and harmonic progressions in a way that practically none of the others did.

I have the record of Gaubert playing his Madrigal, which I bought in Paris—my great treasure from there. Fantastic inspiration. How to do little bits of time alterations, changing colours, taking breaths in the middle of slurs and things like that. Gaubert was wonderful!

```
                    PROGRAMME
Zampa Overture                                    Hérold
  flute, harp, piano
Partita in C minor                                Bach
  flute, harpsichord
    Preludio
    Fuga
    Sarabande
    Gigue
Trio Op 26                                        Matiegka
  flute, viola, guitar
    Adagio: Allegro moderato
    Scherzo
    Rondo
                    INTERVAL
Bachianas Brasileiras No 6                        Villa-Lobos
  flute, bassoon
    Aria (chôro)
    Fantasia
A Song for Wibb                                   Clifford Benson
  flute, piano
    (dedicated to William Bennett on his fiftieth birthday)
Dolly Suite                                       Fauré
  piano duet
    Dolly Berceuse
    Mi-a-ou
    Le Jardin de Dolly
    Kitty Valse
    Tendresse
    Le Pas Espagnol
Sonate                                            Debussy
  flute, viola, harp
    Prelude
    Interlude
    Final
```

Programme of Wibb's fiftieth birthday concert

Martinu: Sonata

Yes! It's a fantastic piece. I've often said: 'That's the best piece of this century!' (when it was this century). Clifford and I used to love playing it.

The Martinu Sonata actually gave me one of my most tense, but most rewarding experiences in the recording studio with Wibb and Clifford. In just one three-hour session we had set ourselves to record for a BBC broadcast in 1993 the Milhaud Sonatina, Dohnanyi's Passacaglia, three Gershwin Piano Preludes, Copland's Duo and the Martinu Sonata. A tall order! The Martinu was last. We had completed two movements and were fast running out of time. I kept looking at the clock and realised we just had time to play through the Finale, but not to record any retakes. So, with supreme concentration, Wibb and Clifford did just that.

We finished it in the last four minutes and it went in.

You did the last movement in one take because you had to.

Had to, yes. That's the best way!

So Martinu would be on your desert island?

Oh, I think so, yes!

Sketch in Rio de Janeiro by Wibb

8—Recordings

I all started off with me using this very dangerous plaything—the gramophone!

By the age of three Wibb was already listening to recorded music and the gramophone would inform much of his musical education.

> *I think a lot of us hear music through recordings more than actual concerts, don't we? That's how it's come to me. It started with the gramophone more than hearing the thing live. I grew up with the gramophone.*

Pleasurable listening, and frequent accidents as a child with brittle old 78rpm records, soon yielded to much keener scrutiny of exactly what things sounded like—in particular, the flute.

> *I think I was fascinated by the sound and the expression of the flute for a lot longer than I know that I was. I had my recordings of Marcel Moyse at quite an early age and I was, without knowing it, hearing French flute playing.*
>
> *When I was just going to go into the army, when I was 18, I got a Christmas present, a record of the Boston Symphony Orchestra with Georges Laurent. Wonderful playing! And that's the Taffanel School. Gosh, that was the sound—and I couldn't make a sound like that. That wonderful, round top register and the life in the tone... and that was the school that Moyse came from.*

But Wibb wasn't content just to listen.

> *I was playing along with a lot of my recordings. The Mozart Concertos, doubling up with Marcel Moyse. A little while later I got the Flute and Harp Concerto, and I have a sort of part, not written down, but it's in my head, the second flute part of the Flute and Harp Concerto! I invented the whole thing so I could play along with Moyse, and I played it sometimes an octave higher, sometimes a third below, or a sixth below. So, the sound of Moyse was coming at me a lot.*

Wibb's own first recording was made in 1952, when he was still at school. He still has it: a slightly mildewed, but still playable, double-sided 78rpm shellac disc. It's a one-off, because the recording was cut directly onto the disc. At EMI studios in Oxford Street you could hire a studio by the hour, which is exactly what his music master James Bayley did.

> *I'm playing my own composition, a Prelude and Fugue, with flute, violin and piano, and also extemporising with the music master and the wife of the games master, who also taught German. We went along and did it*

> and we timed it. The Prelude took up one side of the disc and the Fugue was only about a minute and a half and I had two minutes or something to spare at the end. So we said: 'Oh let's improvise!' We did a waltz in E flat major and C major, alternating two bars of each. Then, when it was getting near the ending time, they said they'd turn the flashing light on, and so at a certain point the light started flashing and James, the music master, suddenly went into a sort of coda and we finished!

In true school outing fashion, there was also a slap-up meal.

> We all had a nice lunch in a lovely restaurant. It was a place just near Marble Arch and it was somewhere you could eat as much as you like for four and sixpence. So I was in good shape for the recording...

A recording made on a completely full stomach! Was Wibb nervous at all doing it?

> Not really, no. We used to improvise quite a lot. We used to improvise in school concerts when we didn't know what else to play!

A couple of years later, when Wibb was at Guildhall, he went back to EMI Studios with some student friends. This time the music was the C minor Trio Sonata from Bach's *The Musical Offering*.

> We recorded the whole of the Trio and something else. I booked the studio for an hour and thought I could do the whole thing. They thought I was going to do one side in an hour. 'Oh no, one after the other. I'll do six sides'. And I did!

Before I heard those recordings, I think I expected that they wouldn't necessarily sound like Wibb, because so much was still to happen to him afterwards to affect and develop his playing. I was wrong. It is recognisably Wibb playing, with already some of those distinctive elements that I've always associated with him: the extraordinary aliveness in the sound, the sense of shape and direction in the phrasing, the musical eloquence. Wibb's teachers and colleagues on the recordings sound a little dated and old-fashioned. He sounds modern. I began to develop a theory that he was born with a predisposition to play in this very vocal way, communicating the music.

> Help, I don't know! You see, I liked singing songs at school and I'd made my guitar and that was used mostly for playing all the lovely songs we'd learnt from music masters and anywhere—things that were pop songs at the time.

So when Wibb first picked up a flute, did he make a conscious connection with that?

> No. Not a conscious connection to singing.

But it does seem to be innate. Was he a very natural player?

> Well, I think so, yes. It all worked fairly easily for me. I mean, as you can hear, when I'd only been having lessons with Geoffrey for maybe six months, I can play! The connection between the flute and the voice became

much more developed when I went to Moyse much later. But you must realise, I already had records of Moyse when I did those recordings. I was already inspired by the wonderful sound that the flute could make and, even by that first recording, I was having lessons with Geoffrey Gilbert who was doing Moyse exercises, listening to Moyse records, and I'd been taught how to control the vibrato up to a point. We haven't got any recordings of me before I learnt anything proper—perhaps happily!

By the time Wibb joined the Army for his military service, he was already beginning to make his way in the freelance London music scene and getting involved in commercial recordings.

I used to know a viola player called Jimmy Verity who conducted the Ben Uri Orchestra in a synagogue just opposite Lords. He was tremendous fun. He was the fixer for Eric Robinson's TV orchestra and I used to sometimes go in and then I'd also get little gigs, going to Birmingham to play with some jazz group or other.

Army bands started when I was eighteen, and that was for three years, but all sorts of other things were happening—chamber music and all that—and during those three years I was already recording things at Lansdowne Studios in Holland Park with my colleagues. I was in a trio with the cellist Margaret Moncrieff and pianist Margaret Norman. It was called the Lyric Trio and I have a record of Leclair and Damase. I also did recordings of various sorts with the military band of the Scots Guards, including the odd film session, and then about that time, before I was twenty-one, I got through the BBC audition, with the Lyric Trio, and we did a nine o'clock early morning recital.

Wibb also invested in a tape recorder—in those days a bulky piece of equipment with reel-to-reel tapes—to record things for himself and learn more about the technique.

I think my cousin Nogin had something to do with getting me a tape recorder for my twenty-first birthday. So I started using tape recorders quite a lot. You can hear all the things that are bad and good!

Were there any particular surprises or revelations?

Sometimes, but I don't remember being totally surprised. Sometimes I'd have to modify something a little bit. I think my concern was if there were too many whiskers on the sound—and getting the right distance from the microphone so it didn't sound either too up front or too distant and sort of muffled.

At that time, tape was very expensive. Wibb had to use it sparingly and generally not for just recording ordinary practice sessions. But there were special projects. One was with the flute player Albert Honey, who recommended that Wibb should go to Paris for lessons with Caratgé. He and Wibb played the Telemann Double Concerto and the Trio from Berlioz's *L'Enfance du Christ* in a student concert at All Souls Church, next door to the BBC.

Albert was a lovely man who played the flute in the BBC Revue Orchestra and inspired me by his lovely tone and everything. He was kind enough to agree to come along and play second flute with me, which I thought was incredibly generous, a man who was fifteen or so years older than me. Anyway, we did it, and I had my tape recorder and I've got that on a tape somewhere.

Wibb also came up with an imaginative, rather eccentric idea for a solo recording.

I thought: 'I'm going to do the Bach Partita' and I did it two bars at a time and then joined it up every two bars. I had pieces of sellotape and stuck it together! 'Now I'll hear what it should sound like: no breaths at all'. But it was absolutely agonising to hear how bad it sounded without breaths in it. I suppose that's the struggle you have, to make those continuous pieces work. They've still got to have a flexibility, even if they are in perpetual motion. You always imagine it would be nice not to have to breathe and stop, but in fact it's quite good.

That was confirmed soon after, during a session deputising for Richard Adeney in the Melos Ensemble. Wibb took the opportunity to show the score of the Bach Partita to the principal violinist, Emanuel Hurwitz.

I asked him: 'What do you do with this?' He looked at me and said: 'With a piece like that, my boy, you've got to find the places to let the audience breathe!' Then he looked at the music and said: 'About here' and he pointed at that bit when it comes in C Major—about the third or fourth line. 'That looks like a prime place to let them breathe'. He just went straight to it. It's of course quite possible he'd heard the piece a few times, but he couldn't have been more concise—a wonderful teacher and person.

Meanwhile, Wibb was involved in an increasing number of BBC broadcasts—useful opportunities for observing and learning more about his playing.

All the time. If I was on a recording session, I would always go and listen to the take to find out how my quality was projecting, or blending, or whatever it was that was necessary. Sometimes I had a bit of a shock: 'My God that was out of tune!' and that's very salutary, of course. You need to be reminded that it was wrong. My first broadcast with the flute, cello and piano combination, I heard the playback, recorded off the radio, and there was one

CD cover designed by Wibb

> bit where I was quite sharp and I was terribly ashamed of that. I wish more people were ashamed! In fact, it was only for a bar or two. I don't remember whether I noticed at the time, but I was horrified when I heard the recording. I played it to Geoffrey Gilbert, but he didn't seem to mind at all!

Undeterred, Wibb continued to enjoy every chance to broadcast.

> It was an excitement, it was what I was living for, to do everything that I did. Quite often it was a live broadcast so there wasn't any chance of going back on things. You just had to get up and do it and I seemed to like to be in the centre of the action. It was fun!

> Later, when I made my first LP, the recording man said I was apparently completely at ease in front of the microphone. I had never thought of it as something I needed to address. I just got there and somebody came and put the microphone in front of me and I stayed there!

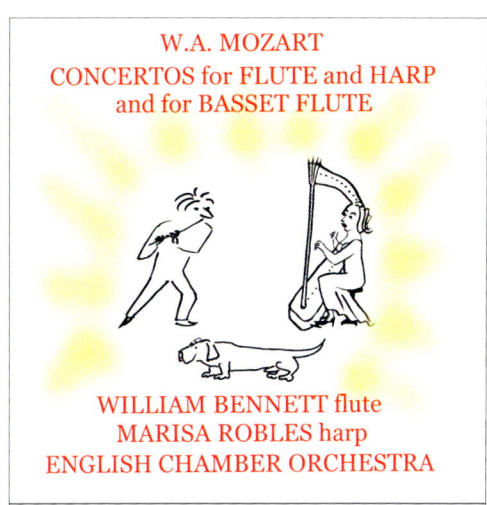

W.A. MOZART
CONCERTOS for FLUTE and HARP and for BASSET FLUTE

WILLIAM BENNETT flute
MARISA ROBLES harp
ENGLISH CHAMBER ORCHESTRA

CD cover designed by Wibb

I wondered, therefore, what were the highlights for Wibb from his early recordings.

> Help, I don't know! I remember I did a recording with the Pro Arte Orchestra, doing British Light Music, conducted by George Weldon, and I was sitting next to Peter Graeme (the oboist in the ECO and Melos Ensemble) and I was very proud because I played well in tune with him. There was a lovely melody in octaves and I was always pleased if I could get it to sound right, a bit like Oliver Bannister whom I worshipped by then—he always got his octaves in tune—and I thought: 'That is the epitome of good English playing: that the octaves are in tune!'

Then there was a curious recording of Ravel's *Daphnis et Chloé*.

> It should be a flute highlight... it was conducted by Jacques Cousteau, the underwater film maker. He hired the LSO. I don't know if it's ever been used by anybody in any way but it's the only time I've recorded it!

I've been searching out early recordings of Wibb playing some of the key solos in various orchestras. Not an easy task as individual musicians are not always identified, but there are some gems, including Berlioz's *L'Enfance du Christ* with the LSO and Sir Colin Davis in 1976. Beware if you look for this: Wibb's name was accidentally omitted from the list in the booklet notes, but he is playing first flute in the lovely Trio, with Richard Taylor as second flute and the harpist Renata Scheffel-Stein.

Then there was Bach's B Minor Mass with the Academy of St Martin in the Fields and Sir Neville Marriner in 1977. Wibb didn't altogether approve of how Marriner wanted him to phrase the solo in the 'Domine Deus', but it's still beautifully played and recorded, as is the radiant 'Benedictus'.

Wibb also recorded Haydn's *Creation* with the ASMF and Marriner, in 1980.

> *Those little bits of solo were played on a Lebret tin flute! I was terribly pleased with that. It sounded live and French.*

One of Wibb's earliest recordings with the ASMF was of selections from Mozart's *London Sketchbook*—a collection of short pieces he wrote on tour as a child prodigy in the 1760s. The 1971 analogue recording came up again all bright and new for a digital reissue in the final CD box set of 'Rarities and Surprises' in Philips's Complete Mozart Edition for the bicentenary in 1991.

> *I still enjoy those if I hear them. Perky!*

It's a good description of his playing of them, incisive and full of vibrant life in the tone.

An early recording of Wibb in the London Symphony Orchestra has also reappeared on CD. It's of Respighi's *The Birds*, conducted by István Kertész. Wibb was credited on the original LP cover in 1969 for the extended solo in the fourth movement, 'The Nightingale'. The recording quality is a bit muddy, but the flute shines through, hovering and glowing in the orchestral texture.

Turning to solo recordings, there are three significant early ones, but unfortunately none of them has ever been reissued on CD. In 1962 the Mabillon Trio (Wibb, Susan Bradshaw and Philip Jones) made an LP on the Delta label called *Avant-Garde* with a very sixties, swirling abstract pattern in mauve, orange and white on the cover. It included the Boulez Sonatina, *Interpolations* by Haubenstock-Ramati, Berio's *Sequenza*, Messiaen's *Merle Noir*, and *Winter Music* by Richard Rodney Bennett. It's a truly fascinating glimpse into that period when Wibb was devoting a lot of time to new music and playing it with great conviction. (See the chapter on Music for Wibb's observations about some of these pieces.)

The critic of *Gramophone* magazine deplored the 'singularly hideous sleeve-design', but praised 'this very accomplished group' and immediately picked up on the importance of the recording 'that anyone with a real interest in contemporary music (especially British) should take the trouble to acquire. None of the music on it is otherwise available in the English catalogues'. He noted that pieces like the Berio *Sequenza* 'must pose an almost undeclinable challenge to players such as Mr Bennett, who have the technique and intelligence for them'.

A second recording on the Delta label, this time a two-LP set of nine Handel Sonatas, followed soon after, with harpsichordist Harold Lester and viola da gamba player Denis Nesbitt. Delta was owned by the husband of the concert pianist Joyce Hatto, William Barrington-Coupe.

> *He was known as Barrington-Crook... I had recorded the Boulez and a whole contemporary music record for just £25! But that led on to me doing the Handel Sonatas with Harry Lester, with whom I performed a lot over the years. There was already a recording by Julius Baker of the Bach Flute Sonatas and somebody said that the Handel Sonatas hadn't been done. We recorded in Greenwich Town Hall, with a proper Goffsichord. I was very keen on performing that sort of period music—I was a Baroque maniac! That recording was played quite a lot on the BBC.*

Wibb in a recording session

Better known (and reissued on CD) is Wibb's 1981 recording of Handel Flute Sonatas with Nicholas Kraemer and Denis Vigay, followed in 1983 by the Opus 2 and 5 Handel Trio Sonatas with members of the Academy of St Martin in the Fields. The playing is delightfully stylish and the flute sounds particularly mellow and mellifluous.

> *The second Handel Sonatas recording was on my conical bore, wooden Rudall and Rose flute, made in the 1840s. I also used that for the Handel Trio Sonatas. It seemed to fit with the harpsichord better than the rather more powerful silver flute.*

A third significant early recording bridged the gap between baroque and modern music and reflected Wibb's growing interest in the romantic flute repertoire. *A Victorian Musical Evening* was an idea that Wibb and Trevor Wye came up with together.

> *We went to Moyse in 1965 and then in '67 we thought: 'Let's try and make a record of some of this music'. Trevor found this place we could record in, the Colt Piano Museum, and when we'd made the record, we gave a copy to Moyse and he went over the moon about it. He thought it was marvellous, which was not what I expected at all. But he could probably hear us doing the things he was talking about.*

Wibb with Trevor Wye

Wibb and Trevor took the finished recording to the new Pearl Records label, run by Charles Haynes and John Waite, and it was issued as only the second release in their LP catalogue. Interviewed by *Gramophone* for the tenth anniversary of Pearl Records, Haynes and Waite commented: 'We were bowled over by the splendid flute playing. We possibly foresaw the increase in interest relating to Victorian music and happily the disc still continues to sell consistently well'.

A Victorian Music Evening featured flute music by Köhler, Doppler and Godard and piano pieces by Schubert and Chopin. Clifford Benson was the pianist and the three of them collaborated again on a follow-up LP for Pearl in the mid-1970s called *The Romantic Silver Flute*. This time the music was by Reinecke, Paggi and Sullivan, plus more Köhler and Doppler.

Three other important recordings from this first golden period in the 1960s (happily reissued on CD) have already been described in the chapter on Heroes: notably the Bach Triple Concerto with Yehudi Menuhin in 1965; French music by Ravel, Chausson and Delage with Janet Baker in 1966; and Holst's Fugal Concerto in 1967, Wibb's homage to Janet Baker's *creamy, mezzo-soprano sound*.

More than forty more years of recordings have followed and maybe not surprisingly when I asked Wibb (as I did frequently) which ones he looked back on with most satisfaction, I rarely got a straight answer! Just occasionally he would come up with a typically trenchant observation.

> *One of the recordings that I do remember I liked was with Jean François Paillard. There was no bullshit, he just got on with it. He had something—and it was a nice sound. Nothing airy-fairy, and no artistic pretentions. He was healthy!*

That was a CD of Mozart's Symphonies 39, 40 and 41 with Paillard conducting the ECO in 1977. It's not brilliant recording quality, but the playing has such spirit. As I write this I'm listening to the exuberant Finale of the 'Jupiter' and Wibb's flute is glittering through this incomparable score.

Some years earlier than that is a recording of Mendelssohn's *Spring Song* (Op.62 No.6) originally issued on a Reader's Digest 45rpm EP.

> *It was done at one of those sessions fixed by Sidney Sax. I had an arrangement of the Spring Song in E flat major—the original was in A—and it was just right for the flute. It was all done in about an hour and then I went off to the country—just jumped in the car and roared off to Wiltshire! Alan Civil came along and did the next number, so he was waiting, having his cup of tea while I was finishing off Spring Song.*

This recording really gets the Wibb seal of approval.

> *It was alive, it was in tune, it had that proper French live noise in it, and the recording engineers captured what I did.*

You can hear an extract from it on Wibb's website:

> www.williambennettflute.com.

Wibb was accompanied by the pianist Robert Docker, well known as a composer and arranger of light music. The recording appeared eventually on a Reader's Digest CD compilation of *Mendelssohn Favourites from the Classics*. It's now deleted, but like many of the other recordings I've mentioned, you might find a copy if you search online, or in secondhand stores and flea markets as Wibb himself did when he was a student.

A complete Wibb Discography is yet to be compiled, and is beyond the scope of this book. However, there's a good, representative selection of recordings on Wibb's website:

> www.williambennettflute.com/disco_b_c.html.

There's a separate section on the website for Wibb's own CD label, Beep Records. His wife, Michie, is the Executive Director of this label that launched in 1996 with the complete flute works by Taffanel. Wibb sketched the cover design for the CD booklet and for various others in the series—an added bonus:

> www.williambennettflute.com/beepcatalogue.html

I was intrigued by the title: Beep Records?

> *We'd just moved into this house and I was driving my son Timothy to his school in Westminster. There's a tower on the north side of the Thames, it's the BP building. We were looking for a name for the record company and I said: 'BP—Bennett Productions—Beep—that's the name!' It fits*

perfectly with 'Après le bip sonore' (that phone thing in France about leaving a message 'after the beep tone'!) It just hit me as we were going over Vauxhall Bridge. Just what we needed—so it became Beep.

It's hard to choose among so many Wibb recordings, but for a hopefully representative survey of his career, I've compiled my own personal Top Twenty solo and chamber recordings. It's just a starter—and of course you can disagree with me and choose your own. So, here goes, in chronological order:

1965   J.S. Bach: Concerto for Flute, Violin and Harpsichord, BWV1044
           Bath Festival Orchestra/George Malcolm/Yehudi Menuhin (EMI)

1966   Ravel—Chausson—Delage
           Works for voice and ensemble
           Melos Ensemble/Janet Baker (Decca)

1967   Holst: Fugal Concerto, Op.40 No.2
           ECO/Peter Graeme/Imogen Holst (Lyrita)

1969   Mozart: Flute Quartets
           Grumiaux Trio (Philips)

1971   The London Sketchbook: Works by Mozart from K15 and K33
           ASMF/Neville Marriner (Philips)

1971   J.S. Bach: Suite No.2, BWV1067
           ASMF/Neville Marriner (Decca)

1978   Mozart: Flute Concertos, K313 and 314
           ECO/George Malcolm (Decca)

1978   J. S. Bach: Flute Sonatas, BWV1030-1035
           George Malcolm/Michael Evans (ASV)

1981   Handel: Flute Sonatas, HWV374-5, HWV378, HWV379
           Nicholas Kraemer/Denis Vigay (Philips)

1983   Handel: Trio Sonatas, Op.2
           ASMF Chamber Ensemble (Kenneth Sillito/Trevor Wye/
           George Malcolm/Denis Vigay) (Philips)

1985   J.S. Bach: Brandenburg Concerto No.5, BWV1050
           ASMF/Iona Brown/George Malcolm/Neville Marriner (EMI)

Letter from Geoffrey Gilbert

1985/   Taffanel: Complete works for flute and piano
1996   Clifford Benson (ASV/Beep Records)

1987   Beethoven: Flute Concerto in D (arranged from the Violin Concerto)
            Schwindl: Flute Concerto
            ECO/Steuart Bedford (Camerata)

1988   Celebration for Flute and Orchestra
            Works by Saint-Saëns, Hüe, Gaubert, Doppler, Fauré, Godard
            ECO/Steuart Bedford (ASV)

1990   Melodies and Encores (Works by Pierné, Robinson, Elgar, Drdla, Hüe, Fauré, Chopin, Purcell, Gounod, Brahms, Caplet, Mendelssohn, Donizetti, Clifford Benson and others) (Bravura/Beep Records)

1990   Ries: Quintet in B minor
            Romberg: Quintets, Op.21 No's 4 and 5
            Novsak Trio/Mile Kosi (Jecklin Edition)

1992   Great Works for Flute and Piano
            Works by Hahn, Schubert, Franck, Prokofiev
            Clifford Benson (Beep Records)

1995   William Bennett
        Works by Haydn, Hanson, Honegger, Griffes, Kennan, Foote
        ECO/Nicholas Cleobury/Shuntaro Sato (Beep Records)

2001   Four Concertos for a New Era
        Flute Concertos by Burrell, Mathias, Musgrave, Pineda
        ECO/Raimundo Lineda/Richard Bernas (Beep Records)

2006   J. S. Bach: Art of Fugue
        London Octave
        (Clare Hoffman/Dietrich Bethge/Sara Bethge) (Octave Classics)

The Beethoven Concerto recording (1987) is worth noting. It's Wibb's own transcription of one of the mainstays of the violin repertoire—a daring undertaking, guaranteed to raise a few eyebrows! It's coupled with a charming original flute concerto by the mid-18th century composer, Friedrich Schwindl. When the CD appeared, Wibb sent a copy to Geoffrey Gilbert and received this response in a letter.

> *Let me say how much I have enjoyed listening to both pieces. Your playing is amazing and I am full of admiration for all the wonderful things you do with the pieces. Nobody who listens to the Beethoven with the right attitude could fail to be impressed.*

'All the wonderful things' is an apt description for so much in this list of twenty recordings and it reminded me of a moment in the early stages of preparing this book. I hadn't heard Wibb's Mozart Concertos recording (1978) for some time, so I put the G Major in the CD player. Suddenly, in the middle of the opening movement I was transfixed. Wibb's flute seemed to be hovering high up in some airy, wide-open space. It was a gloriously luminous moment.

The phrase, just four bars long, comes twice in the movement—bars 72-75 and 190-193—and it was the second appearance that had caught my ear. On the CD it's at 6'37" in Track 1. The music soars up to five, repeated top Gs. These are often played very incisively and staccato, but not here. Here they just float. I listened to the phrase again—and again—and then I listened attentively to the whole CD. It really is one of Wibb's very best. The recording captures the performances with clarity and immediacy; Wibb is on top form throughout both concertos (glorious cadenzas, most of them by Wibb himself); and the ECO is directed with great sensitivity by George Malcolm.

> *That was wise of me to have George Malcolm. I would rather have had him than anyone else—a feeling of great enthusiasm and caring. He was a musician of that sort and he knew what I wanted to be known.*

The *Gramophone* review in December 1979 was ecstatic. 'This is a beautiful record, with solo playing of the first order allied to an equally splendid quality of orchestral playing'. The review goes on to single out various 'unexpected felicities' in the orchestra—points of detail that often get lost in less well prepared performances.

> I discussed quite a lot of these points with George and I said all sorts of things I wanted. There were friends in the orchestra, so if I said: 'Let's do it this way', they would change quickly and do it.
>
> I remembered George saying to me when we did the Bach Sonatas: 'Couldn't you take little bit more time on this corner?'. He was just subtly suggesting that I was playing too much 'tic, toc, tic, toc', like a metronome. 'Wouldn't it be nice to do something there?' So I tried it and I went on doing it.
>
> That's what I also noticed always with Clifford: he had time, all the time... There were these unmarkable rubati which were perfect—and I miss that so dreadfully now. It's all about little corners and taking time. I just accepted it and I went with him.

CD cover from 1992

And those four bars: floating, unhurried, the repeated notes articulated but not detached?

> The beat stops—it's one in a bar. I was thinking about that passage quite a lot recently. I did a class at the Academy and they were all playing the Mozart G major. If you actually hum that tune, it's not short and detached. It was Thea King who originally said something about that bit to me. She pointed out that flute players always play those notes short, but they should be long. And I keep on telling the pupils at master classes: 'Come on: dots on the notes can mean short, or long, or something... and sometimes legato!' La, la, la keep wai-ting... and then it moves along and becomes rhythmic again—the horns come in and the march begins again.

If you look at bars 190-193 and translate Wibb's *la, la, la keep wai-ting* into the five repeated top Gs falling to C, and then the five repeated Es falling to A, you get an idea of the subtlety of rubato, and of articulation within the sound to convey the eloquence of the music, that he cares so passionately about.

That's what I'm trying to teach people there. François Devienne writes in his Treatise, I discovered later, that a dot means 'coup de langue'—a tongue stroke—not necessarily short. I get almost angry, like Moyse used to get angry in classes, when I hear somebody going 'tic, toc, tic, toc' without any feeling for what's going on. It doesn't go like that!

You have to imagine at this point (and indeed all the way through this book) Wibb singing and gesturing while he is explaining this—living the music and communicating it. It's the heart of his artistry as a player and teacher and it leads us on to the final two chapters.

Sketch from a holiday balcony by Wibb

9—Teaching

Teaching has become a vital part of Wibb's life. He is currently a Professor at the Royal Academy of Music in London and travels the world to give masterclasses. When did he first decide he wanted to teach?

I'm not sure that I wanted to, as such, I just thought it was an obligation. You have some knowledge, you shouldn't hide it. The interesting thing is that in trying to teach, you find out an awful lot more about it for yourself. It's not like giving the stuff away and never getting it back. It actually builds you and it makes you analyse things in a different way. You're constantly improving—at least you hope you're improving—your understanding of how everything works and what you're trying to say.

Wibb's very first experience of teaching was when he was at school and it was rather thrust upon him.

The music master, Rudi Sabor, said: 'Will you teach Ollie Pritchett the recorder?' because he didn't have time. I was about fourteen and Ollie was about twelve. I did what I could. I didn't think I was any use to him at all. I wasn't very good at that time, I think it was mainly: 'Come on, do it like this!' but he got on alright, so it can't have been that bad!

Maybe it helped prepare Wibb, however, for a more significant teaching opportunity a few years later.

When I was seventeen or eighteen there was a young boy in the village of Speen, where my best friend Benedict Rubbra lived. Ben's Mum, Antoinette, said: 'Would you give Laurie Kennedy some lessons, he's begun to play the flute?' After a while I sent him to Geoffrey Gilbert because I realised he was far too good and needed somebody better than me! Very quickly he became first flute in the RPO and the Hallé.

Wibb later advised Laurie Kennedy to attend Moyse's summer school at Boswil, so he could benefit from the best of both teaching traditions that Wibb himself valued. Tragically, in 1970 Laurie died in a car crash (as noted in the chapter on Orchestras). He was only in his early twenties and his full potential was never realised.

The previous year Geoffrey Gilbert had left England for America, where he was to spend the rest of his career. His teaching posts at Trinity College of Music, Guildhall School of Music and Drama and the Royal Manchester College of Music (now the Royal Northern College of Music) devolved to some of his former students, notably Trevor Wye and Wibb. Not surprisingly, Wibb's teaching style owed a lot to Geoffrey.

> *I think I tried to get a lot of Geoffrey Gilbert's ideas through and put over some of my own as well. I'm still constantly remembering: 'Oh, he said that...' What an inspiration!*

And of course Wibb also owes a debt to Moyse for his approach to teaching.

> *It was so refreshing with Moyse, who actually said what he thought ought to happen, whereas Geoffrey would stand back and get most things in the right general proportions. He didn't want to say: 'Come on you must do it like this'. But Moyse often said: 'It does this'. It was so direct and refreshing and it was always right.*

Bit by bit, Wibb began to develop a style that would mature into a synthesis of his two great teachers. Some principles arrived early and have preoccupied Wibb ever since.

> *I remember being in Daytona Beach teaching for the first time in 1966 or '67, and Kathryn Lucas being there. She was saying: 'You know, you always ask: 'Where's the phrase going'. I was concerned that she, at least, went somewhere—and it's still the same question to all of them!*

I've already said that I suspect Wibb was born with an instinctive love of narrative, both in music and in art. It infuses his teaching.

> *Yes—and what I'm trying to encourage in people who come for lessons is to use that instinct, because I recognise I'm very much dependent on instinct for finding out how things work. I find I'm always having to sing something in order to find out where the phrase is. Everybody seems to be able to get things right, up to a point, when they sing, but they don't know that they're in touch with something. I just believe I'm in touch with something, and I know about it!*

The late 1960s and into the '70s were very busy playing years for Wibb. He wasn't able to devote significant amounts of time to teaching, but he was on the staff at Guildhall and at Dartington, there were summer schools with Trevor Wye at Canterbury and then Ramsgate, there were international masterclasses, and he had a few private pupils.

A turning point came around 1980 when he met Michie Komiya, a Japanese flute player who was studying with André Jaunet in Switzerland and had also been to Moyse's masterclasses in Boswil.

> *Michie turned up asking for lessons. She'd heard my record of the Bach G minor Concerto, with the famous slow movement, and she said: 'I want lessons with him'. She says she was terribly nervous! She was very keen on making notes about everything and she took things on board in a way that many students don't. She was very enthused about all the things that were happening with flute making and she got me spare parts from the flute factory in Japan. Then it developed from there...*

A young Wibb teaching

Wibb separated from his first wife and eventually he and Michie were married. After their son, Timothy, was born Michie's playing career was rather curtailed, but there was occasional freelancing.

> *Michie did a few dates playing with me in the ECO, and she made one recording with me of the mad scene from* Lucia. *She played second flute. It's rather fun. And then Michie started running our own Summer School and doing teaching and proving to be very good at it.*

Michie also encouraged Wibb to accept an invitation in 1983 to succeed Aurèle Nicolet as Professor of Flute at the Hochschule für Musik at Freiburg. That was a significant commitment: some twenty hours per week teaching individual students.

> *Quite often they came and listened to each other's lessons. I can remember the room having three or four people a lot of the time. I had a nice group of students with me. It must be said that I didn't have very many German ones—I didn't get on with them very much... but there were one or two good ones.*

Wibb remained on the staff at Freiburg for just over three years, commuting backwards and forwards from London and rubbing up against German bureaucracy!

I had an account at a bank in the town. I'd go there and they'd say: 'We haven't had your pay cheque'. 'Why not?' Then I'd go to the official Administrator's office and say: 'My pay cheque hasn't come in' and they'd say: 'Oh yes, it's because you haven't done such and such... haven't told the police your new address'. The number of times I had my pay stopped for some reason or other. Absolutely like the bloody Army the whole time. Terrifying!

Meanwhile, there was also a musical tussle with the Hochschule authorities in the teaching studio. Wibb was introducing his students to the technical regime he had inherited from Geoffrey Gilbert, along with Moyse Studies and his ever widening repertoire.

Learn your scales, do your studies and do your pieces—here's how you do them—and try to play in tune! That was part of the battle. They issued me with an old piano the first week. It was terribly sharp—A445 or something. I said: 'Right, next week I'm coming in with a tuning hammer'. I let it be known that they were all going to learn how to tune the piano and it was going to be at the right pitch.

Next time I came there was a grand piano in the room. They'd heard about it in the Office and issued me a better one. It was only A443, which they considered to be flat! So I got on with that and I didn't have to tune it—added to which it was a very good piano.

Wibb left Freiburg in the year that he turned fifty and was offered a professorship at the Royal Academy of Music in London.

I said: 'Well, why don't you give my wife some teaching as well, so she can do some assistant work?' and that went really well. Then Sebastian Bell and I shared the position and I got on very well with Sebastian, so that was fine—couldn't have had anybody better, frankly.

It was a defining moment for the Academy. Wibb and Sebastian (Bas) Bell were succeeding Gareth Morris, a last staunch defender of the English style of flute playing. Bas had been Gareth's student, Wibb was coming from the other camp and there had always been antipathy between Gareth and Geoffrey Gilbert. Wibb and Bas therefore represented a sort of reconciliation of flute playing styles. Sadly, Bas died of cancer in 2007 at the age of only sixty-five. Wibb has remained at the Academy ever since.

I give five masterclasses a year. I have some contact with all the people in the flute department and I have my pupils who get weekly or two-weekly lessons.

So what sort of experience does Wibb try to give his students? Do they get up close to his own playing in lessons?

Yes, sometimes it's a way of showing: 'Come on, you can do this' and sometimes people hearing that, get a way of doing whatever it is without you having to go through explaining every tiny inflection in words. But I do a lot with singing and making them sing, and teaching them how to observe what they're singing.

I don't think people do that enough. You don't have to sing well, but you do have to say: 'That's what I feel' and then you have to make the flute do that. An awful lot of people can sing, really quite musically, and you have to get them to hear what they're doing, and then say: 'Look, you did it this way, now do that on the flute'. But then you have to show them how they can do what they sang.

It's making the music talk—or making the flute talk—instead of just saying: 'I can do a million notes!' If you're obsessed with trying to play as fast as possible, then at a certain point it becomes boring.

It may not even be an obsession with speed and virtuosity. For some students there may be a more basic issue of the actual flute getting in the way of music making.

Well, I suppose the mechanics of playing any instrument are an obstacle, aren't they? You think: 'I've got to get the right notes. I've got to get the right fingering'. The problems are so many and various with fingers and lips and lungs and posture. We forget to make those basic musical shapes.

So how does Wibb unlock those problems? What if I'm a relatively shy person, trying hard on my flute, but the music is not really saying very much, and he declares: *No, sing it, put the flute down and sing it*—and then I can't do anything other than make a funny little noise with my voice?

In fact, it doesn't happen that way, there is always more shape when people sing it! They're not so bothered. If you can get them not to worry about a wrong note, or being out of tune, you take away some of the obstacles. Of course some of them are terribly embarrassed, but usually I say: 'It doesn't matter if you sing badly, just sing it, and if you can observe what you're singing, you're hearing your own inner voice'.

I maintain that we all instinctively know how things go, but most of us don't reach into what we know. It's like dowsing. You have knowledge of some water underground, somewhere, and when you get there the dowsing sticks cross. With music it's the same thing. There's a sort of knowledge if somebody's really good. You don't know what it is, but you know that they know. You unlock it.

Wibb constantly encourages his students to make this connection between their voices and their playing, their flutes and their bodies.

It's been a gradual discovery of mine, but it's been going on for some thirty or forty years!

It's all about mentally absorbing the instrument into your body, rather than only experiencing it outside, sitting on your chin.

From 1965 onwards I heard Moyse saying: 'When the singer do something they say the singer is stupid. But my God it's so beautiful! I try to do like that!' He got me listening in a new way. One day I was in the Queen Elizabeth Hall playing the Haydn Creation with the soprano

April Cantelo and she did one phrase and: 'Wow, I wish I could do that!' Like an answer from heaven, I had similar phrase a couple of bars later and I suddenly felt: 'It's in here. The flute is no longer outside me. The sound starts inside'. So you stop thinking about the flute as something exterior—it becomes the whole of you. That's why I say: 'the flute is your voice'.

There's more about Wibb's experience in that concert with April Cantelo in the chapter on Playing. It leads on to Wibb's fascination with colour in flute sound, and talking about colour when teaching. Did he do that before he went to Moyse?

I was already very concerned with different colours. Richard Adeney was the player in England who played with colours and I very much approved of that. Then I bought the record of Philippe Gaubert whilst I was in Paris—this was well before I met Moyse—and Gaubert had plenty of colours, like an even better version of Dufrène. The flute could also do what the guitar could do—the equivalent of playing near the fingerboard or in the middle of the string. Then there was changing the vibrato, which is what Geoffrey had been teaching us.

Wibb teaching

The significant change with Moyse, however, was discovering an equally colourful language in which to express all this.

Before Moyse, I was saying: 'You can play it tight there, make it hard or soft there...'

After Moyse, the music began to be related to sunshine, to the moon, to love, etc—a whole new emotional vocabulary.

I don't know how quickly it came in, but I know I'm not ashamed to do it!

But even if you can inspire a student's imagination, they may still not fundamentally be at ease playing the flute. There may be physical problems to be resolved, bad habits to be challenged.

It's very difficult, because you can't change those habits so quickly. You ought really to send someone to an Alexander teacher or Feldenkrais teacher to get completely unknotted. But problems can also come about from the flute not being good, and leaking, and that's an awful pest. With the old flutes, with only one key, there are no pad problems. Wonderful! All you have to do is put your fingers on the holes and blow and you don't have to press too hard.

If only Boehm flutes didn't have pads, you could play with the tips of your fingers, like a recorder. Wouldn't life be easy? People develop terrible habits from pressing too hard on flutes that have to be pressed hard to make them go well. If you have a flute that doesn't work, you press the keys until the pads cover, but you may be giving yourself all sorts of tension problems, RSI and everything.

And from a technical point of view, what are the most common things that people get wrong?

Mostly nowadays it's about tonguing. It's worldwide. They're taught to go 't' and that can be very explosive, and, worst still, they go 'tut', finishing the note with the tongue. Geoffrey Gilbert, right from the word go, taught me to stick the tongue out and withdraw it and blow, without a noise. I'm not that good at tonguing… but if there's somebody who's been playing for several years doing the hard explosive 't', and also stopping the note with the tongue, it's very hard to get rid of it.

From his own experience and experimentation, Wibb advocates the use of a range of alternative tonguing syllables to counter the problem.

I find I say to people: 'Tongue more softly, don't say 't', say 'nd''. I think 'd' means the air is already moving before you release the note and there's a sort of 'n' at the beginning of it. I got quite desperate when I was teaching in Germany—the Germans are even worse than the English!—and I ended up teaching some of them to tongue using 'n', just to try to get a different approach—'n' and 'd' being very similar. And for double tonguing: 'g' instead of 'k'. People write 't' and 'k' in the parts and they actually should be writing 'd' and 'g'. That's my solution—it's what I developed for myself.

Relentless and inflexible vibrato can be another recurring problem.

Geoffrey was teaching controlled use of vibrato, making sure we could do vibrato at many different speeds, so we weren't stuck at one speed. And that's why I say that we had the upper hand when we went to Moyse: Geoffrey's pupils could do what Moyse was asking, and the others couldn't.

During Wibb's lifetime, the French model of teaching in masterclasses has increasingly been adopted in England, although mainly as a way to supplement individual lessons. For Wibb, they require somewhat different teaching approaches.

At the Academy, with individual pupils, I have to uncover the dirt from the basics, which haven't been installed very well, and do a lot of what Geoffrey and Moyse would have done. At a masterclass or summer school, you don't have time to uncover things completely, but some people get a good message very quickly—and some people at the Academy just don't get it at all, so it's not guaranteed!

You try to throw ideas out at a summer school, whatever your priorities are, like we'd heard Moyse doing. I might start with intonation, and basic ideas about tone production, and what sort of beginnings you want on the note, and quite a lot about how to do it—as much as you can understand. Moyse's thing was about developing the line. When you hear Moyse playing, you hear this line that goes on and pulls you to the next place. It's absolutely marvellous—that life in the sound—and that's what Geoffrey wanted: the life of somebody using vibrato in a good and natural way.

I was intrigued by the concept of throwing out ideas.

Well, you throw out ideas about how to make the music go somewhere. The music has got to do something—you have perceived it. I've always said: 'Where is the point of the phrase, the summit of the phrase?' Phrases can be terribly short and a sentence has lots of little phrases in it, but then the sentence goes towards the most passionate bit. The learning of it is finding out which harmonies, which other sorts of stresses, lead to where.

Imagine a range of hills: there are a few little hills, and then some greater hills, and suddenly there's a mountain. But the first thing is that there's always the point of a phrase. Rampal was obviously on to the same thing. He was wanting the phrase to go to the top all the time—for him it was always the top. Sometimes I found that, with certain pieces, the top of the phrase was the lowest note, but that's quite unusual!

Faced with a technical or musical issue, Wibb's method has always been to devise exercises, for himself and for his students.

Thousands of things, yes! I was, for instance, very impressed with hearing Tubby Hayes playing his jazz stuff and doing great breaks, singing and playing two octaves apart. I cannot do this! I can't actually blow the flute and sing at the same time—singing and playing different notes. I find it makes my lips tingle so much. I must do some more study at it...

But I used to practise at the Festival Hall, when I was in the LSO, getting my diaphragm to go up as if I was singing. I used to sing a passage from Ravel's Septet—a simple, short bit of melody that has a small range—and then feel what was happening with my diaphragm. Then I'd hold the flute up and finger the same notes and make the flute resonate with my singing.

For instance, you finger middle F Sharp and you cover the right amount with your lips and you sing middle F Sharp. For me that's a high note in a male voice—it's low F sharp on the flute—you can do it

Teaching

Wibb teaching

> *at the unison or at the octave. You sing it and, at a certain point, you get the notes so that they're the same pitch. When you've got a good position of the lips over the hole and you've got it mechanically right, the whole flute resonates quite well. Then you move your fingers to the next note, and your voice, and you also get the resonance from the next note. But if you finger different notes to what you are singing, the flute doesn't resonate any more. If you suddenly move the fingers and don't change the voice, the resonance just completely dries up.*

If you are in a lesson or class with Wibb, it's never long before the taxis and elephants arrive!

> *Strong and weak. It's the stress thing. Somebody related the story of Isolde Menges, the violinist, saying: 'No dear! You've got to say, fetch me a taxi, fetch me a taxi!' Tax-i: strong-weak. Then I needed something with three syllables, it keeps on coming in Mozart, and elephant was the obvious word that came after taxi!*
>
> *There's an alligator as well (four syllables). It's limitless—but it's very difficult in Italian, the most musical language. They say ele<u>phan</u>to. The Germans say ele<u>phant</u>. You can't use it. So it's a question of finding a different word: in Italian finally I found Na<u>po</u>li. But very few words do that in Italian and that has been quite hard when I've given a class in Italy. I don't know enough Italian, I suppose!*

Sometimes the elephants take taxis...

143

Suggested Repertoire List

Technical:	Taffanel & Gaubert: Methode Pt. II
Moyse:	Sonorité; Tone development 24 Little Melodic Studies
Andersen:	Sudies Op. 15

Bach:	Sonatas, Suite, & Partita Sinfonia (Cantata 209)
Mozart:	Concertos D, G, & Flute and Harp Andante K215, and K616
Schubert:	Arpeggione Sonata Trockne Blumen 6 Songs arr. Boehm
Godard:	Suite
Gaubert:	Nocturne & Allegro Scherzando Fantaisie, & Madrigal, Sonatas
Griffes:	Poem
Hüe:	Fantaisie
Hanson:	Serenade
Hahn:	Variations on a Theme of Mozart
Beethoven:	Romance in F, Sonata in B flat, Spring Sonata, Serenade
Piazzolla:	L'Histoire du Tango

Solo pieces by Ibert, Debussy, Berio, Honegger, Dohnanyi, C. P. E. Bach, etc.

Sonatas by Poulenc, Prokofiev, Hindemith, Martinu, Reinecke, Dutilleux, Sancan, Franck, Mendelssohn.

Concertos by Arnold, Dodgson, Reinecke, C. P. E. Bach, J. S. Bach (G minor), Quantz in D (pour Potsdam), Haydn, Schwindel, Jolivet and Ibert.

Villa Lobos:	The Jet Whistle, Bachianas Brasileiras No. 6
Taffanel:	Opera Fantasies

William Bennett International Flute Summer School 2000

Clifford Benson piano
and
Michie Bennett, Katharina Zahn
teaching assistants
at
Bookham, Surrey, England

Course 1   24th July–1st August 2000
Course 2   3rd August–11th August 2000

Clifford and I used to refer to Bach's Chorale Prelude on 'Wachet auf' as the Elephant and Taxi Song. *The phrases have got to come away. Elephant-taxi-taxi-taxi / Elephant-taxi-taxi! I've got an arrangement of that for flute and piano.*

Wibb heard the Isolde Menges story back in the 1960s and it resonated immediately with what he had been learning from Geoffrey Gilbert, although Geoffrey didn't talk about taxis and elephants.

No, but he taught the idea very much. It was about the loud and the soft being in the correct order. I had the training from Geoffrey Gilbert: <u>one</u> two, <u>one</u> two... My job teaching is to make sure that pupils do the weak beats weak—and taxi and elephant just became the words I used.

Yet again, it's a logical extension of this idea we have noted so often: Wibb seeking narrative. An illustrative word personalises the music and illuminates the interpretation.

> It's just an easier way to understand. I use words an awful lot in order to describe inflection. What was I doing today? Oh, a Telemann Fantasia... and I was saying: 'Dad-dy, Oh Dad-dy', is a bad-dy, is a terrible daddle da dum!' Those are just the words that come when you try and sing it—you find your tongue doing things.
>
> George Malcolm picked up on this, he was interested in the words I chose when I was describing a phrase. I was obviously doing that a lot. Moyse would sing: 'Pi-um pi-ar pi-ar', because it described what you had to do with a phrase. He was vocalising what the music did for him.

So it's often quite spontaneous: a response of the moment to the music.

> The words are usually found when you're struggling to describe something to somebody else, like a pupil. If you're just singing to yourself, you find what's convenient to your own language. Like duba-duba-dub, the Swingle Singers' technique—it's very good.

Surprising things can emerge with words, for example in Bach's E major Sonata.

> I was doing it for the opening of the Second Movement, with 'The Grand Old Duke of York'. That becomes the 'The Grand Old Da-be da-ba da-ba da-ba..'. etc. It demonstrates that you can't breathe before 'Duke'. You sing quite naturally: 'Da-be da-ba da-ba da-ba...' I don't know why, but it's getting through to instinct. People do use words. If they sing things, they use something that comes naturally. 'Da-be da-ba da-ba da-ba...' might be totally wrong if you're Japanese or Czech!
>
> Incidentally, that movement is Bach's Rumba! When George played it he had the strongest stress on the second beat, and a slightly longer note, and a more jazzy chord, and it had to be right. He really made it into a rumba!
>
> And in the last movement, the penultimate bar of each half where there are two even quavers, George said: 'Would you mind if I dotted the first one?' When I heard it, I said: 'No—it's got to be that way!' And it's that way in my edition. George was a real jazzer! Then somewhere when we were doing the B minor Suite, he said: 'What do you think about this?' and he had figured out a whole series of descending jazz chords for the Polonaise. They were absolutely marvellous. But Bach was a swinger! There are all sorts of jazz rhythms there.

Incidentally, for anyone who has ever struggled with getting the opening of the Second Movement of that sonata incisive enough with the repeated E, E, E in the middle register, Wibb has a word of advice.

> *Middle E is one of those difficult notes. It's produced with the longest piece of flute tube, with an unassisted first harmonic, and possibly leaky pads not quite covering all the holes. I practise it without the tongue, only from the diaphragm, so that the air makes the note. 'Ho, ho, ho... Ha, ha, ha... He, he, he.' If you can do that, it's quite easy.*

Returning to putting words to the music, and for Wibb they don't necessarily have to mean anything, it's all about stress and forward movement. The music is always going somewhere and it has to make sense on the way—in whatever language.

> *In Bach it's <u>el</u>ephant, <u>el</u>ephant, never el<u>eph</u>ant, el<u>eph</u>ant, and that's what makes it difficult teaching people from some other countries—Japan, for instance, and the Far East—they have completely different sorts of stress on things. Quite often with oriental languages, all the syllables are the same strength and that makes it hard to get through to what that jazz thing is, which I subscribe to.*
>
> *But that's the point: to get the stresses and directions of the sentence. You have a principal syllable somewhere, and you need to find that, and then there's the next principal. It's usually the first note of the bar, or the top note of a phrase. George Malcolm wanted the phrase to go to the very highest note, even if it wasn't on the downbeat. He talked about going up to the actual top note of a phrase on the harpsichord, because he used to pedal crescendos in to make them interesting.*

There's obviously a lot to learn and I wondered if Wibb advocated a particular practice routine for his students.

> *I think it would always be an individual thing of what I thought you needed. It wouldn't necessarily be what everybody should do.*

There would, however, be some fundamental things to be got right, starting with the tone quality of each separate note.

> *For a note to have good tone the harmonics have to be in tune. People don't understand that, but it's the basis of what I teach. Note bending, followed by harmonics, is the first thing I make anybody do. You find out where you are in relation to the instrument, how much you've got to cover it for the basic note.*
>
> *Then when you've got a decent note—say a C—you do Geoffrey Gilbert's tone spreading exercise. You play a C and you go down chromatically to G sharp and back up again chromatically to C—with vibrato, of course, nice singing tone—and the aim is that you don't move the lips. You come back to the same tone on the last note that you had on the first note. It's a different form of doing Moyse's first* Sonority *exercise, leading by semitones. But in all this you're getting the notes with a good quality without moving the lips. The flute ought to be able to give you the low register with the notes in the right place—but they weren't, which is why I had to move the holes!*

There's more about note bending to help get the harmonics in tune—one of Wibb's early discoveries as a young player—in the chapter on Playing. Meanwhile, any course of study with Wibb would be likely to include Moyse's *24 Petites Etudes Mélodiques*—already noted in the chapter on Teachers. These studies have been a mainstay of Wibb's playing and teaching: an ideal place to start to identify, understand and apply the basic principles, as he sees them, of making music through the flute.

What it would be great to have, of course, would be Wibb's own flute method or flute tutor. From time to time—and none of his notes are dated—he has sat down and started to put some of his ideas on paper—but only started. Here is a page of advice about posture.

> · *Flute is an instrument which sings. Important that the holding of the flute does not impair the natural singing stance. Check that the body is ready to project a note, and, remaining in same position, lift the flute to the lips, keeping the flute well forward of the body and turning the head to the left. N.B. the flute should <u>not</u> be parallel with the shoulder line, but should be nearer 45 degrees to the shoulder line.*
> · *To make the flute parallel with the shoulders can produce a raising of the shoulders and a crick in the neck. Uncomfortable and cramping to the breathing. Right shoulder tense and throat not open.*
> · *The feet are important too, place them about 12 inches apart, and slightly turned out, and you should be capable of putting your weight on your toes and balancing on the ball of the foot.*
> · *About turning the toes out. Try making yourself pigeon toed and see if you can project your voice!*

At that point those notes break off, but here is page about note bending, a key element of Wibb's teaching.

> · *Note bending: to establish that it is possible to change the pitch of any note.*
> · *To make a note flatter, cover the mouth hole more with the lower lip.*
> · *To make a note sharper, uncover the mouth hole...*
> · *This can be done by moving the lips and jaw (particularly the lower lip) and sometimes by rolling the flute.*
> · *Some notes move very little, and other notes move a long way.*
> · *In order to move the least flexible notes a little, I believe that we should begin by moving the most flexible notes as much as possible.*
> · *The most flexible note is C'' and the notes become less flexible as they descend to low C, which will only move half the amount of the open C.*
> · *The notes in the middle register will only move about half the amount of those in the low.*

Wibb's notes on Note Bending

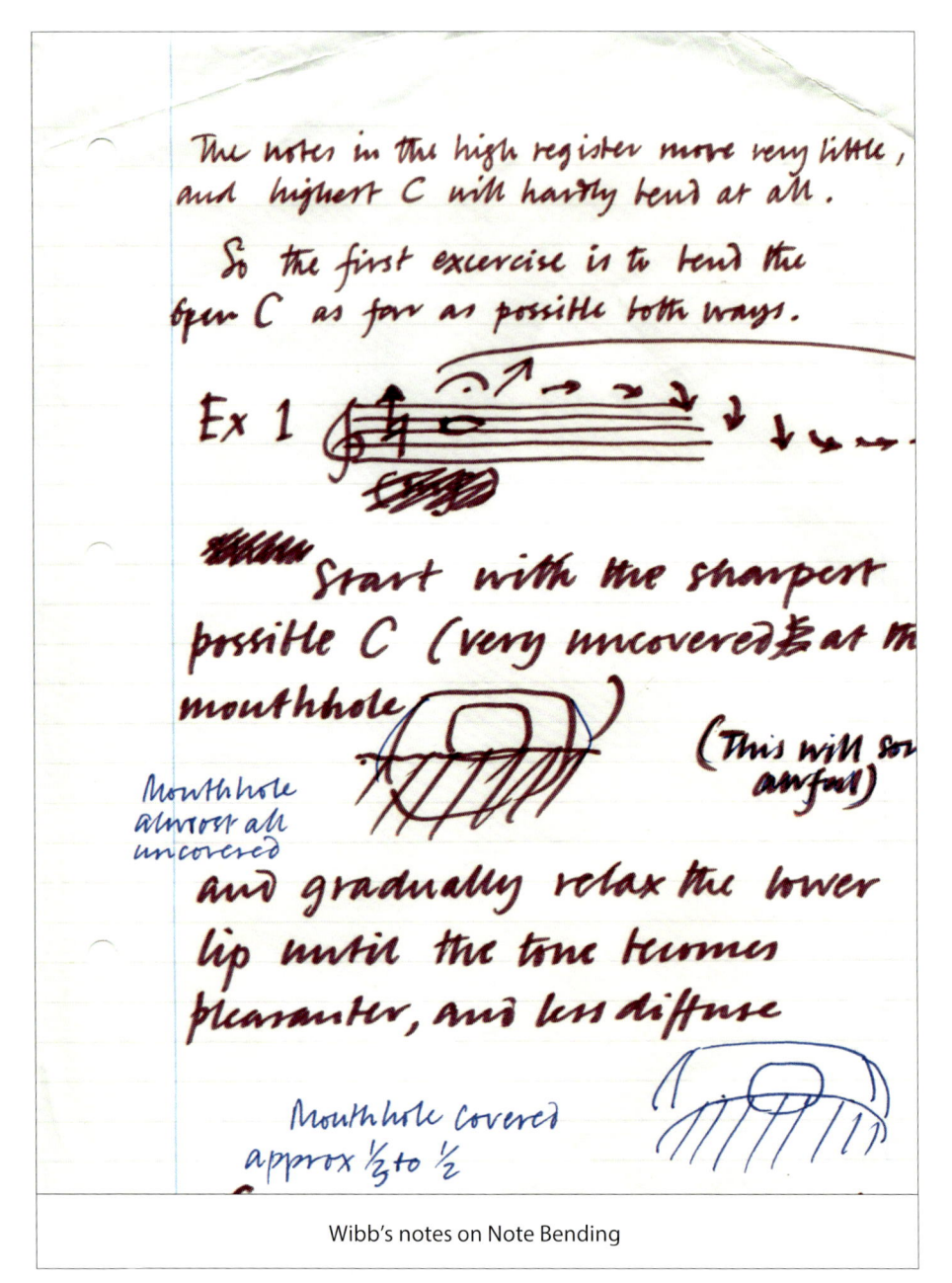

· The notes in the high register move very little, and highest C will hardly bend at all.
· So the first exercise is to bend the open C as far as possible both ways.
· Start with the sharpest possible C, very uncovered at the mouth hole (this will sound awful) and gradually relax the lower lip until the tone becomes pleasanter, and less diffuse and more resonant.

This next fragment is a thoughtful definition of the distinction to be made between exercises and studies.

> · Exercise or Study?
> · Exercise is the repetition of the difficult passage.
> · Perhaps a <u>study</u> is a short piece including the difficult pattern in many places, contrasted or compared with similar patterns which are easy, in order that the supposedly difficult pattern can little by little be played as easily as the easy patterns.

Elsewhere among Wibb's notes there are some initial ideas about approaches to exercises for the flute—a first draft only and one in which he seems to be engaged as much in a dialogue with himself, as with us. Wibb is analysing the problems and challenges and working out how he will approach them.

> · Essential Exercises for the Flute

Wibb's notes on Essential Exercises

> · The idea for this stems from the 'Essential Finger Exercises' for the piano by Erno Dohnanyi, in the introduction of which he says that the practice of finger exercises should be kept to a minimum to allow for the vast amount of time that the pianist must devote to learning the vast repertoire that is needed. This means that the finger exercises must be very concentrated. For instance, in the Dohnanyi the first page is devoted entirely to the independence of the 3rd, 4th and 5th fingers.
> · I have tried to find a way to adapt this same thing to the flute, but would advise all flute players to devote ten minutes per day to the first page-and-a-half of the Dohnanyi <u>piano</u> exercises <u>on the piano</u> if possible, as these are very beneficial to the working of the fingers.
> · With the flute it is necessary to also work at the lips and jaw movement, blowing and breathing, vibrato and expression, and articulation (tonguing).

Wibb's Dohnanyi Type Exercises for the Flute

· *I am trying to separate the work on the lips from the fingers, so that mind of the student can devote itself better to the concentration on one detail. This is of course only possible in a very limited way, as there may be work on the lips which does not employ finger movement, but there is much less effective work that may be done on the fingers that does not require participation of the lips, jaw, lungs etc.*

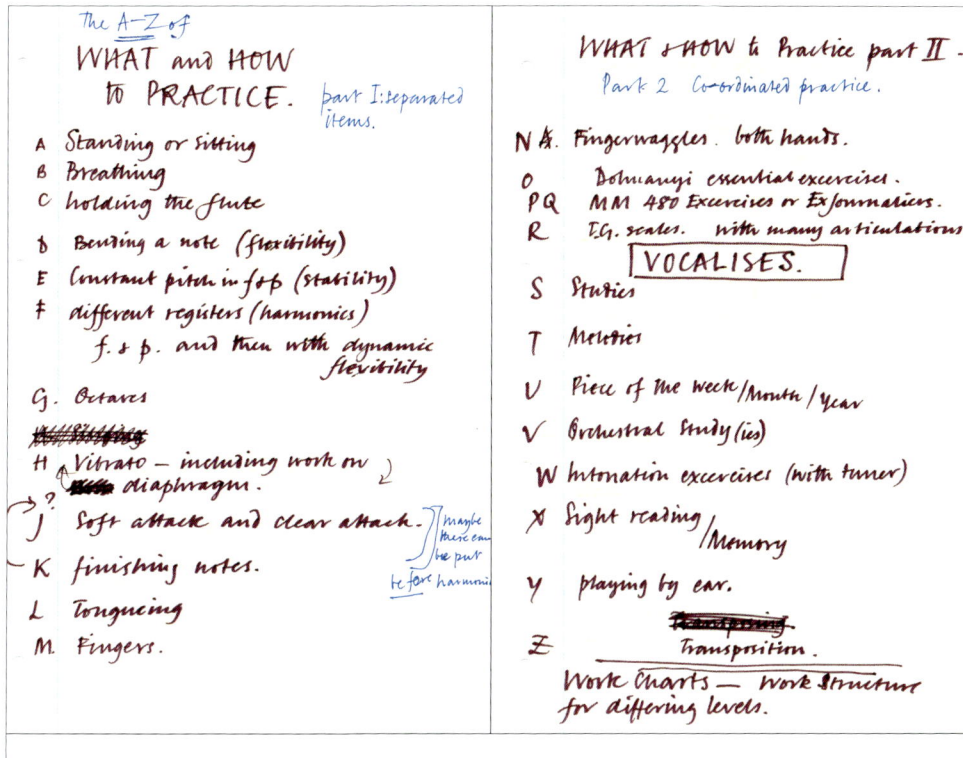

> **The A–Z of WHAT and HOW to PRACTICE.** part I: separated items.
>
> A Standing or sitting
> B Breathing
> C holding the flute
> D Bending a note (flexibility)
> E Constant pitch in f & p (stability)
> F different registers (harmonics)
>   f. & p. and then with dynamic flexibility
> G. Octaves
> ~~H Bending~~
> H Vibrato – including work on diaphragm.
> J Soft attack and clear attack. — maybe there can be put before harmonics
> K finishing notes.
> L Tongueing
> M. Fingers.
>
> **WHAT & HOW to Practice part II –** Part 2 Co-ordinated practice.
>
> N. Fingerwaggles. both hands.
> O   Dohnanyi essential excercises.
> P Q MM 480 Excercises or Exformaties.
> R   E.G. scales. with many articulations
>   ⟦ **VOCALISES.** ⟧
> S Studies
> T Melodies
> U Piece of the week / Month / Year
> V Orchestral Study (ies)
> W Intonation excercises (with tuner)
> X Sight reading / Memory
> Y playing by ear.
> Z ~~Transposing~~ Transposition.
>   Work Charts — Work Structure for differing levels.

Wibb's notes on the A–Z of What and How to Practice

· Also what starts out as being a lip exercise in isolation, is of course only a lip exercise with small finger participation, but the lips work in balance with the whole blowing apparatus, and cannot be isolated from the lungs (and this includes posture) and the jaw. But what I am attempting is at the outset to isolate the attention onto lips, tongue, fingers.

· What is referred to as work on lips, is in fact lips, jaw, breath pressure; and when it becomes articulation, this is not merely the use of the tongue, it is tongue, expression, and the whole blowing apparatus.

· Perhaps it would be better if I said: 'I am attempting to separate Blowing from Fingering'. But apart from a little practice on the piano, it is almost impossible to do any effective work for the fingers on the flute without calling the whole blowing apparatus into action.

· I therefore start with exercises for the blowing apparatus, in which the participation of the fingers is limited at the outset to holding one note.

First: <u>Note bending</u> to establish pitch control

· 2nd: Harmonics—to establish control of the speed of the air jet

· 3. Diminishing and augmenting a note without pitch change

· 4. Articulation: repetition of notes in different ways

Once again, at this point the notes break off. Growing out of them, however, sometime later, is this useful alphabet list of things to practise. (N.B. there is no entry for 'I' as Wibb decided that I and J are interchangeable letters.)

A–Z of What and How to Practice.

Part I—Separated Items

A · Standing or Sitting
B · Breathing
C · Holding the Flute
D · Bending a note (flexibility)
E · Constant pitch in f and p (stability)
F · Different Registers (harmonics) f and p, then with dynamic flexibility
G · Octaves
H · Diaphragm—including work of vibrato
J · Soft Attack and Clear Attack
K · Finishing Notes
L · Tonguing
M · Fingers

Part II—Co-ordinated Practice

N · Fingerwaggles—both hands
O · Dohnanyi Essential Exercises
P · Marcel Moyse 480 Exercises
Q · Marcel Moyse Exercices Journaliers
R · Taffanel and Gaubert Scales—with many articulations
V · Vocalises
S · Studies
T · Melodies
U · Piece of the Week/Month/Year
V · Orchestral Studies
W · Intonation Exercises (with tuner)
X · Sight Reading/Memory
Y · Playing by Ear
Z · Transposition

· Work charts—work structure for different levels.
· Guidance for Wibb—I need to introduce a yoga type exercise quite often, specially when structuring the work. Frequent vocal exercises and

references back to posture.
A. Standing or sitting
B. Breathing
C. Holding the flute
· These are very much linked together when playing the flute. Breathing is often made difficult by unwise, bad body usage.

Looking at the A-Z again after some years (he doesn't remember exactly when he wrote it) Wibb was fascinated by his thought processes then.

It's about the things one ought to be addressing in teaching—but it doesn't mean to say I necessarily do that!—and then it goes on with how to practise.

For Wibb, this is crucial: distinguishing between the *what* and the *how* of teaching.

You see, <u>what</u> and <u>how</u> are separate. That's something I picked up in a book about Kreisler. He said that you must separate the what from the how. I was terribly impressed with that. I find that lots of people give lessons and they say: 'You must do this...' and they tell you <u>how</u>, as if it's the important thing. They don't tell you <u>what</u>. They start telling you how: 'You've got to do this with your hands, or your lips etc'. But if you state the what clearly enough, quite often you just jump over the how.

For instance, <u>what</u> you are doing is blowing a jet of air, which needs to go up and down a bit, and at the same time you need to control the amount of covering of the hole, to make different amounts of opening to control the pitch, and different sized jets of air to get different velocities. Different tone colours are sometimes to do with focusing or opening the jet. But instead people tell you <u>how</u>: 'You do this etc' and it's not what you need to be visualising at all.

Wibb teaching

[Pages from Wibb's notes on getting back in shape after a holiday]

> But the moment you know that what you are trying to do is make a smaller jet and focus it down there, or lift it a bit, that's it! The how is very confusing if you don't know what you are trying to do. If you teach exercises, for example, they wouldn't necessarily relate to the flute. That would be getting the how before the what.

The section marked 'Guidance for Wibb' underlines this point.

> It means I'm trying to think about *what* to teach and *how* to teach. More what again! That's about what's going on in my imagination. It may have been when I was trying to sort out what to do because somebody wanted me to write a flute method. I never got anywhere near it—far too difficult!

The final phrase in the A-Z about *unwise, bad body language* reminded Wibb of a disconcerting experience that took him right back to the beginnings of playing.

> I tried a Finnish flute made to be played on the left side of your body. It was the most terrifying thing, because you pick it up and you cannot hold the thing the wrong way round. You try and hold it, play a C or a C Sharp. Holding the flute for C Sharp is almost impossible. Well, that's what a beginner feels like when they play. Try it that side and the muscles

Teaching

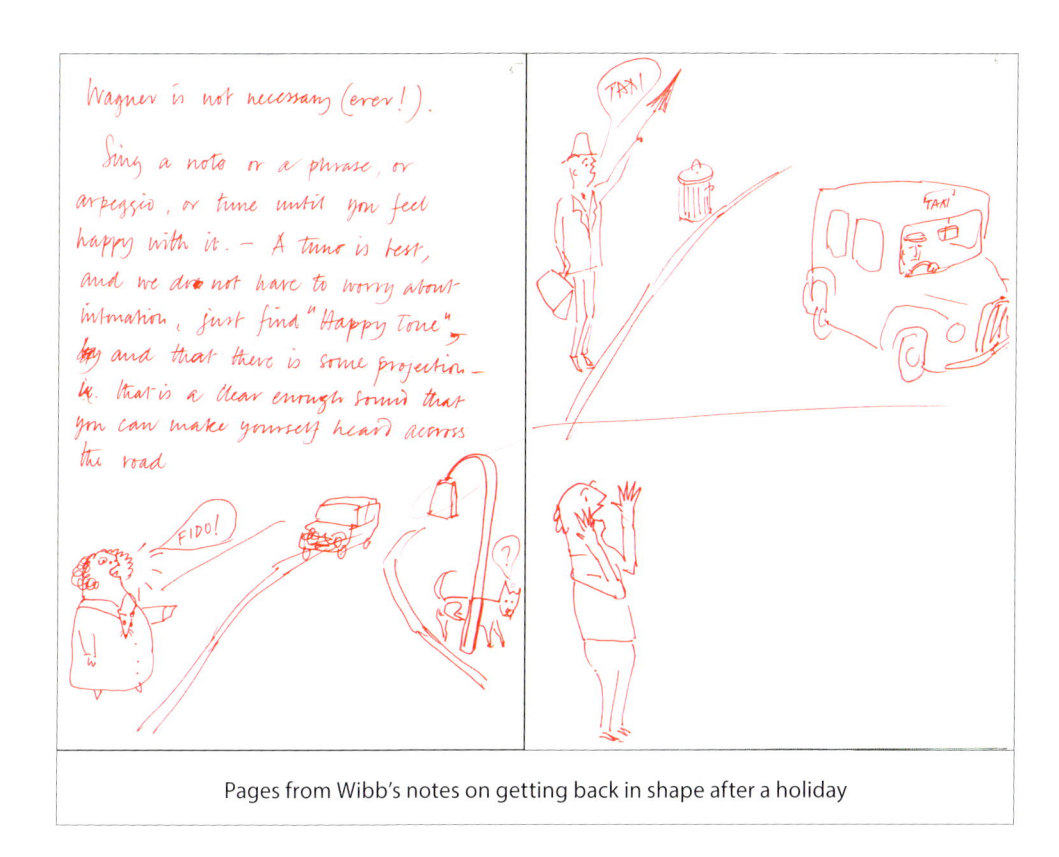

Pages from Wibb's notes on getting back in shape after a holiday

of the body don't do it. Very salutary for any teacher—just try playing a left-handed flute. It's hard. Your face feels wrong, your arms and hands feel wrong, the air doesn't come in the body and it's quite shocking how much practice you have to do before you get at the music.

Finally, here is some practical advice from Wibb about how to get back in shape after a break from playing. We found this collection of pages, along with the A-Z, sifting through a pile of notes and jottings. The illustrations are Wibb's own and so is the experience of coming back rusty from holiday.

I think I went away on some trip to the Lake District, with a friend on a bicycle, and I didn't have a flute with me. When I came back, I couldn't play. I asked Geoffrey about it and he spoke about things not working very well for a few days when you come back off holiday. And so I haven't let it happen very often. I've usually made a point, after that, of having a flute and staying in shape.

What we have here is in effect a continuation and expansion of the notes on posture quoted above (*Flute is an instrument which sings...*)

Well, these are many of the things that I have been taught by different people. I wonder if that was also when I was trying to write a flute method? I only did some bits and pieces...

[Pages from Wibb's notes on getting back in shape after a holiday]

It's significant that the focus is on reconnecting your whole body: how you stand, breathe, sing, hold the instrument, and so on.

> You come back from holiday happy and ready to enjoy playing, but it usually sounds awful. You feel clumsy in the fingers and thick and parched in the lips and the flute pulls you down on one side, or has grown incredibly long and heavy. And when you blow, your air disappears in an instant, and you feel faint or giddy after a few puffs.
>
> The point of this book is to help you to re-start quickly and perhaps avoid some of the bad habits which you had before.
>
> The first thing to recapture is the basic idea that the flute IS your voice, and that for the flute to sound well it is important that your body is held in the same way as when you sing, or project your voice. So the first thing you have to do is <u>sing</u>.
>
> Wagner is not necessary (ever!). Sing a note, or a phrase, or arpeggio, or tune until you feel happy with it. A tune is best, and we do not have to worry about intonation, just find 'Happy Tone', and that there is some projection—that is a clear enough sound that you can make yourself heard across the road.
>
> Notice also that you often come up on your toes when you project—with a feeling of life travelling up your legs. Sometimes of course this projection

Wibb's notes for a projected flute method

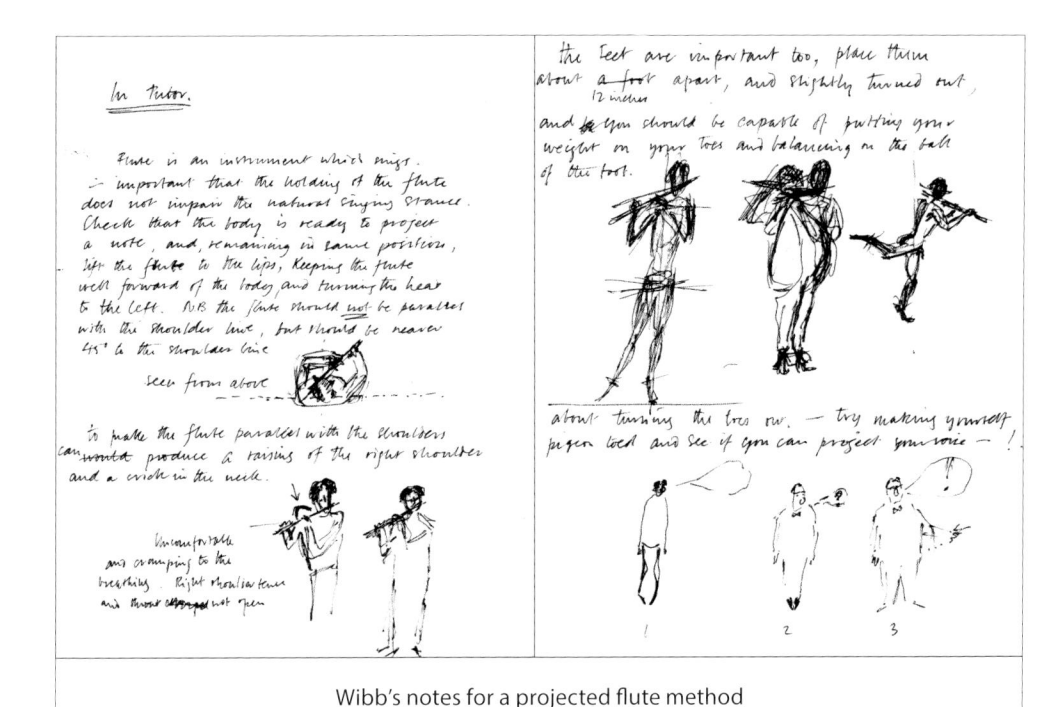

is not suitable. But sometimes it is necessary to <u>project</u> this intimate and soothing voice softly across a room.

Try all these different sorts of projections, and notice in all of them that your body lifts you up as you project, like a marionette with strings attached to the head and the front of the chest. Your head sits on top of your spine like a pudding on a broomstick, but notice when you project your voice that your head <u>lifts</u> your spine like a gas-filled balloon might lift a pencil.

Sing some notes, enjoying this lifting sensation, and notice how the head can turn in any direction without destroying this sensation. In fact you can project your voice to the right or left by turning the head and not moving the whole body...

Sing a note, and then the same note an octave higher, and then return to the lower note. Notice that there is a resonance, or focal point in the middle of the chest for the low note, and that this 'focal point' is higher in the body for the higher note.

Observe a singer or an actor doing their stuff, and notice that their feet are slightly apart. This gives them strength on the ground. Your feet should be about one foot apart. If you play with your feet together the wind can blow you over. With your feet apart you are strong like a wineglass with a good sized base.

So, standing with your feet apart, sing a note until you find a little resonance. (This will ensure that your spine is lifting upwards and that your chest is free and open.) Still singing, turn your head so that it is pointing to the left of your shoulder by about 45 degrees. Then pick up the flute (still singing) and hold it in front of yourself more as if it were a trumpet than a flute.

Turn your head to the left, singing a note (this is to ensure that your spine is lifting upwards and that your chest is free and open). Lift up the flute. Then bring the flute to your lips <u>without</u> moving your neck forward.

LH fingers: Hand position.

Take the flute like a violin, with the foot joint under your chin. The flute will sit just above the first knuckle joint. Notice that the thumb is straight, and that the middle of the thumb rests on the B natural key. Swivel the flute round to the normal playing position.

And then? The notes stop at this point. Will Wibb perhaps continue writing one day and give us more ideas?

Sketch of a villa by Wibb on tour in 1975

10—Playing

A phrase from the writer Robert Louis Stevenson kept coming to mind in my conversations with Wibb.

...to travel hopefully is a better thing than to arrive...

For me it sums up Wibb's attitude and activity: playing the flute is for him an ongoing quest.

There's an ancient legend concerning the search for the Philosopher's Stone, the alchemy that could turn base metals to gold. While we can't apply this literally to Wibb—gold flutes have never really worked for him!—there is a sort of alchemy that time and again transforms the various and often blackened metals of his flutes into the musical gold of his playing. Does Wibb sound like any other flute player? I don't think so. Some of the differences are identifiable, others are harder to define, but no less tangible.

This final chapter explores that alchemy, bringing together all the explanations and reflections on flute playing that were threaded through our conversations. Elements of some of the ideas have already been touched on earlier in this book, but this is where everything comes together.

Nature and Nurture

I've always felt that there are two sorts of flute players: those who seem as though they're made to play the instrument and others who have to find a way to master it, to mould themselves to it—it's not so natural.

> *Well, I was obviously made for it up to a point. What Geoffrey Gilbert did was to set up most of the principles of playing.*
>
> *Geoffrey was fantastic. I'd been playing for three or maybe four years by the time I went to him, and I could play quite a lot of pieces like Bach Sonatas and Mozart Concertos and so forth, so I wasn't a total beginner. But it was about how you hold the flute, how it is in your hands, where you balance it, and how you move your fingers. All of that had to be sorted out into scale practice and looked at every day.*

It certainly gave Wibb an extra security about his playing.

Well, I got it in plenty of time. Geoffrey said: 'It's very good that you came early' (because I was fifteen when I went). 'Many people come to me when they're eighteen, nineteen or twenty and it's already too late really to get their habits changed, to accept the right information'. That was his sort of intellectual clear thinking, trying to get rid of already acquired bad habits.

Was anything difficult about the flute for Wibb?

Well... what is difficult about the flute, as Marcel Moyse expressed it: 'Flute is like a fish. It get away!' It loses the tone. Geoffrey taught you how to make it equal and strong—equally strong all over. That is the principle he laid down right from day one. He also laid down a rule: 'If something isn't right, do it slower'. You've got to have even rhythm and even tone, and somehow I'd picked up something about intonation, even before I came to Geoffrey. It was already necessary for me to try and get in tune.

Since then, have there been particular physical or psychological problems for Wibb to overcome on the flute?

Help! There are things that constantly worry you... It's about getting the instrument to respond in the right way, or pitching things. Not being able to get the right pitch of a note is why I put plasticine in the hole—or 'chicken shit', as Bas Bell called my mixture of superglue and sawdust!—or I carved something out. That may be where I'm somewhat different to quite a lot of flute players who won't touch their precious jewel, the flute. I've made the flute less of an obstacle, for me.

I'm sure Wibb's general character has played a large part in this: an extrovert personality, an attitude of treating obstacles as opportunities, the advantage of an enquiring and encouraging family background.

Yes, that's being dogged by good luck, isn't it?

Has he ever lain awake at night worrying about anything?

Oh yes, but not too often!

Wibb would be much more likely to get up and do something about it. Anything practical that can be fixed, gets fixed. So when, for example, there was a broken piece of keyboard action in his grand piano, what did he do?

I had the screws out from under the piano, keyboard out, the whole mechanism out, vacuum cleaned inside the piano and had the broken part fixed ready to go in. I think most people wouldn't have bothered, wouldn't have dared take the risk. When it went wrong I had to take the keyboard out to find out why things were stuck down there. Then this little piece of wood came out, so I knew that was it. I sorted it.

And sorting the flute has been a lifetime preoccupation. But for Wibb, that is inseparable from sorting out the player.

The flute is a voice, not a machine for playing a million notes per second.

The body and the flute resonate together.

Hold that thought. It's the key to all that follows.

An Open Sound

One obstacle for many players is retaining the quality and equality of sound across the whole range of the flute, particularly in the top register, which can easily become tighter, less expansive.

That gives us a lot of problems. We are always trying to find out how to make the top as good as the bottom. I'm still struggling! That is the quality of the great players like Dufrène: he had this wonderful something in the top register, which I was very jealous of. Moyse wasn't as good in the top as the bottom. In Gaubert's records, the top register is less wonderful. I think that was one of the things the English players found, that the Rudall Carte wooden flutes had a rounder and more generous top register, although I was more critical of what wasn't so good in the bottom register—it didn't seem to be so clear—but I'm not in any way anti-wooden flute.

I wish I knew the answer. Somebody brings a flute and I say: 'Well the top register is too thin'. You get up to top E and it's a terrible note. Sometimes it's the scale of the flute. When it gets to the third octave it's too sharp, and the player has to do something about it, and they close something up to try and push the pitch down, whether it's conscious or not.

So it could be a problem with the instrument, but we should beware of thinking that that is the only answer.

I didn't like my wooden flute because it made an awful sound and then when I got my first Louis Lot silver flute it was just as bad, showing me that it was me, not the material of the flute that mattered.

That's a clear challenge to any player, and I've often thought that a lot of flute players make very good mezzo-sopranos, but they don't really make very good sopranos. They sound comfortable in the bottom and middle registers, but much less comfortable at the top.

Oh, well, I thought we were all trying to be mezzo-sopranos rather than note canaries!

Maybe, but the soprano range of the flute is there nonetheless and surely you have to love being up there.

Yes, but it's very frustrating when it doesn't work. I'm fighting the thinness of it. One reason is that if you take the easy way of getting the low notes by covering a lot more, those notes will come out quickly—you get the easy beginning of the notes—but when it gets to the third octave, you're closing off too much of the wall of the mouth hole you're blowing into—the air is entering too steeply. But if you have a slightly bigger opening, it gives you a different angle of wall to blow against. You blow against a whole wedge and that wedge is at a different angle and it has a tiny bit more resistance.

I remember Wibb once saying to me: *I turn out as much as I dare!* And there is certainly an openness which sends his sound soaring luminously into the top register. For me, it's a defining part of the alchemy of his playing.

I can't say I always feel it! If you play a difficult solo like Daphnis and Chloé, you're straight up to the G Sharp—such a hard note—and you've got E and F Sharp and they're all thin. Very difficult. That's addressed in Moyse's Sonority Book where he talks about going up from the B through the D and trying to get the roundness of the upper notes of the middle register carried into the depth of the third octave. That, I think, is one of the hardest things to get a flute to do.

You see, the top register is easy about tonguing and things like that. You can slip the notes out: 'pop, pop, pop'. I wish you could in the low register! Unless the harmonics are perfect, the low register is much more difficult.

Nevertheless, for many players the low register feels safer and the top register more hazardous. Wibb's playing at the top always sounds as if he could still go very much higher. There's no feeling of precarious height, or straining. He enjoys being in the top register!

When I was at school, I had a fingering chart and very quickly I could go up to the highest F, the last note of the Boulez Sonatine. I could play all the notes. I used to play them quite often to the discomfort of my school friends! But I can remember going to Geoffrey Gilbert aged fifteen, and saying: 'The high register is the most difficult'. I thought it was difficult because of the cross fingerings. Geoffrey said: 'Oh no, the high register is the easy one: you just put the right combination of fingerings and blow— it's maybe easier than the low register. You have to learn to do the finger movements in the right way, but it's not difficult to play the high notes.'

> *He didn't want anybody to believe that anything was difficult. That was the most wonderful philosophy.*

It was also clever psychology and it obviously worked for Wibb.

> *It was most important: 'No, there's nothing difficult'. All you need is the right combinations of fingering, the right air speed, and the note will come out.*

If that sounds just a little too simple, Wibb would also add that a decent flute is also vital, particularly for the top register.

> *I think a lot of people castrate themselves by playing on instruments where the third octave is too sharp because the scale is wrong. A long scale flute makes it very difficult to play at pitch in the third octave. That's what I discovered when I suddenly heard myself playing a Boehm study terribly sharp and that's when I did my first big tuning job. I put plasticine in almost all the holes from, I think, G upwards. I made them progressively flatter, then I could play without having to bite down.*

And then he could begin to put into practice what Geoffrey, and later Rampal, were advising.

> *There's a particular passage in the Boehm Opus 26 First Capriccio, going up into the high register. When I was in Paris as a student I couldn't do that. I'd always get a compressed sound. Nastiness! Geoffrey said: 'Just leave the lips alone and relax and don't do anything', but what I learnt from Rampal was to go up with the air column. He didn't talk about that passage, but I found it and suddenly it got better. It got added into the recipe. You don't have to pinch the high notes!*

Rampal's insight connected to ideas from Caratgé and indirectly from Dufrène.

> *When you play an octave, the air goes much faster to get the higher note. On the flute the air has to double its speed as it passes over the front edge of the mouth hole to go up the octave, and then go faster still for higher harmonics, but doubling the speed is not merely making the hole smaller.*
>
> *There was something I picked up from a Canadian flautist who had a lesson with Dufrène. He was told to practise the register changing studies in Moyse's* Etudes et Exercices *in two ways. One using the diaphragm alone, and one using the lips alone, and then finally combining the two. Dufrène was thinking of two ways of getting the high register different*

from the low notes. One was purely what Caratgé might describe as the 'pince des lèvres'—pressure to make the hole smaller—and the other would be what Rampal would talk about as elevating the air column.

Changing the lips alone is changing the direction of the airstream. I took diaphragm alone to mean don't change the direction, but you have to change the pressure, you can't just simply blow harder for the high notes. You tend to think that lifting the air column up and down means being fairly relaxed—that's maybe my interpretation being put on that—but then the interesting thing was to combine the two and that helped me a lot in the high register. When I started doing that, it opened up the problems I was having, it overcame them.

The Triangle

Back in the 1960s, Wibb had a powerful moment of revelation that has since informed all that he believes about the relationship between the flute and the human body.

I was doing Haydn's Creation *with the conductor Michael Dobson at the Queen Elizabeth Hall and the soprano April Cantelo was singing. I had already heard Moyse saying: 'They say the singers are stupid—but my God they are beautiful!' and April sang something—one phrase—and it was marvellous. I just heard this phrase and I thought: 'Oh, I wish I could do that!' Then I had a phrase which more or less answered it, and I found I could do it, and I suddenly felt it: a triangle in my throat. Gosh! I'd always thought of the sound of the flute coming from where the air comes out from the lips, but I felt the flute wasn't outside me at that moment, it wasn't perched on my lip. The sound started under my Adam's apple and I was quite convinced the sound was a little triangle, where there's a hollow there, and I could feel it.*

That was one of the most exciting breakthroughs: I actually felt it was no longer something that had to be manipulated with the lips, over the hole, the actual sound production was inside me. In other words, the air came from inside my body, as when you sing. You have to have the air to generate the voice and you have to have the air to generate the flute. The whole apparatus is you—and I could actually feel it very strongly and definitely as a place in my throat.

I was so excited, I went home and practised. I got the flute out at eleven o'clock and practised a vocalise, which the school music master, Rudolf Sabor, used to make us do in choir, going through several keys, just to get the voices warmed up. So I did that and did it in many keys, trying to recapture what I'd felt in the concert. And then I was playing a lot with another very good singer, Eilidh McNab, and she gave me one or two exercises that she used, which I found terribly useful. Changing the colour and getting this tremendous vibrancy. I've used those quite a lot.

Then I got this feeling: 'I can get that triangle bigger'. It went out broader and deeper. I practised for a month or two and I could feel the triangle going down to the bottom of my ribcage. I was terribly excited by that. I was doing all sorts of vocal things, singing and playing and trying to relate the two things.

I found that's what I needed to do to make the flute resonate, because my body was in tune with what I was fingering—and that may still be a new breakthrough from those many years ago. The oboist Roger Lord said: 'Sounds as if you're singing that!' and I was probably—I don't know which I was doing, but I was very consciously trying to do that.

Not long after, during a tour in Germany with the Philomusica and George Malcolm, a meeting with Aurèle Nicolet provided further illumination.

Nicolet was always talking about the diaphragm. One evening at supper he said: 'You know the diaphragm does a jump when you go up an octave. It goes upwards'. And I just thought: 'Oh yes, it does!' just by imagining I had the flute. He said: 'Do you see? The diaphragm follows the contour of the melody?' That's absolutely true: you feel the note going up and down in your body—focal point low, focal point higher. There are definite different spots where you feel this and the diaphragm moves and it's very soft and easy. What that showed me is how to try to feel the body as if you are singing.

It led me to realise that when you sing, something moves here in the throat, but there is a small, very small complementary movement in the diaphragm. The pressure changes from down there and getting the feeling in your body helps you to get the expression that you hear and have no trouble singing. You sing something, you get the feel of it, and then you can get the same feeling on the flute. It's making the flute talk.

About the same time, Wibb travelled down to Wales, to play a concerto with the BBC Welsh Orchestra, and found himself on the same train as Janet Baker.

I knew her a little bit and she was lovely and we had lunch together on the train. I described the triangle and talked about the diaphragm and asked her: 'Do you feel this?' She said: 'Oh, well, not there, but I feel the sound comes from right down at the back, beneath my ribs, and she was pointing to her kidneys. When I sing a high note, I send it from right down there and I bounce the sound off my soft palate'. And I said: 'What's that?' She said: 'Well, it's the bit at the back of your throat where you feel cold when you breathe in'. That was to give a reflecting point for the sound to come out. I learnt a lot about breathing from that! Just cool the back of your throat. You don't think about how this works. The air comes in and it's enough.

These encounters with various other musicians crystalised for Wibb a whole set of connections, in his mind and in his body.

At a certain point it became internalised: 'It is in my body, yes'. And you also feel tone colours in your body. You feel the note inside and you can feel it coming from there. The sound doesn't start as the air comes out of the lips, it's actually in the body, and somehow the body is part of the resonance of the instrument.

Has that stayed with him?

Of course! I'm now so used to hearing a lot of resonance when I try to express something. Do I use it? Yes. The feeling of singing a phrase, I feel it in different places: a low note I pitch lower in the body, I feel something down there if I'm singing a low note. A high note I feel up here, I feel a change of focal point inside the body. It's important that you also think of the lips, but that's not the centre of it.

To enable the body to be the centre of this resonance, however, the basic challenges of holding the flute have to resolved. It's not the most natural position for ensuring good posture.

> *No—I used to be very worried about that when I first played the flute. You get awfully tired holding that piece of wood up! (It was a piece of wood then.) Geoffrey taught us how to use our bodies and gave us the exercises for the diaphragm. Hold the flute in the right place so that the lungs aren't blocked and ribs aren't squashed, the arms are free, and breathe from the diaphragm. Push the stomach out, take the breath in, and pull the stomach in to push the breath out. It's just a simple bicycle pump!*

And is there an external role for the body in performance?

> *Geoffrey was very concerned that we should not move around and distract the audience. He didn't like weaving around of any sort. Michie used to try and persuade me to move a bit more while I was playing. She thought it would communicate better. Moyse would do funny things when he played. He would look up towards the ceiling when he got to the top of a phrase. Rampal also did quite a lot of gestures going upwards—he was thinking upwards all the time. He was remarkably light and balloon-like for a rather heavy man!*

Lips and Airstream

The flute playing world that Wibb was born into was sharply divided on the subject of embouchure: the appropriate formation of the lips for flute playing.

> *At the time I was a student, the big divide was the English versus the French: the straight players on wooden flutes, versus the vibrato players, the free players, on metal flutes. But then, the wooden flute forced you to use more pressure with the lips because it lacked brilliance. To get some upper partials you had to use more force and that engendered a different type of tone production. You worked a hell of a lot harder, and the danger was it could make you get quite hard at the sides of the lips.*
>
> *For instance, Richard Adeney, who played most of his life on a wooden flute, had the old sardonic smile, a constant, pulled-up smile, but he found some completely other way of changing his colours. Whereas Geoffrey had the other way, the French way, and used to make his pupils turn their*

lips down. You know, the French themselves just weren't bothered. They were talking about what happened in the middle of the lips—and not very much about that either!

Many British players of Geoffrey Gilbert's generation had little sympathy with the French style of embouchure, but what are the essential qualities of the lips in flute playing?

The French style was described by some English players as being 'loose-lip playing', relaxing and becoming soft. I don't think that's the case at all. In the case of Marcel Moyse he was very relaxed, but there was a pressure at the same time. He was criticised by Caratgé for being too tense: 'Il a cassé les lèvres' (he strained his lips). Pushing too much. I don't think that was true either.

The lip is something that you can move and do things with: you can make it softer and harder. If you want a soft, floppy sound you can relax the lips. But more than anything else, that makes the hole in the centre round—you get a one-sized air column. But when you use more pressure and play like the English players used to, pulling the lips, or stretching them over the teeth, they become thinner and harder and the air passes over them in a different way—and of course the air goes in a different direction because the little piece of tube pushing the air towards the flute is a different shape.

Wibb feels that there are actually real advantages in combining something of both flute playing worlds.

You can make all these different colours that we have on the flute by changing between loose and tense lips, and by changing the shape of the column of air, and varying its width going into the hole.

But for Wibb, the musical intention and the results obtained have always overridden any doctrinaire edicts about what is right or wrong.

Players like Richard Adeney made the flute sound wonderful. He had this very hard pulled smile, but then he invented his own way. He got the sound in a way that nobody else has. It can't be wrong because it's so good! He made lots of colours, but he invented his own system. He used to get this terribly intense sound with lots of harmonics, and then this other completely hollow sound.

It's all to do with the quality and quantity of the airstream: along with changes in the shape of the column of air, go adjustments in the speed.

> *If the air is going the same speed for one sound or another, whether the hole is small and flat—it might be horizontal, it might be vertical—that will make a different sound. I suppose (you can never know) that when the air comes from your lips as a jet and it goes into the flute, some of it might go slowly for the low register, but part of that air column is going faster and that contributes to getting more harmonics in it. In Moyse's case, for example, he produced a sound rich in overtones.*

So does Wibb. Meanwhile, there's also the temperature of the air stream to consider.

> *You make a small jet to cool the soup! An exercise for blowing and getting control is to blow a cold spot onto your hand and move it up and down, then make a warm spot. You have to get your hand a bit closer to feel the warm spot and to make the warm spot you've got to have a bigger space. It's warmed by your body—the temperature that's coming out, having been in your lungs, is warmer. The fact of compressing the jet makes it come out cold.*

So what are the lips and airstream doing to make that distinctive Wibb sound?

> *I can only guess! I've noticed, by looking in the mirror, it's not a round hole between my lips, it's a slit. Then you have to make the hole larger and smaller, which is part of making the air go faster and slower and is necessary to produce the different harmonics. Obviously to go from the low register to the middle register you've got to double the air speed. You can either double it by pushing more air out from the stomach, or by making the hole a little smaller. And to get the higher notes I think you've got to aim the air higher.*

> *Supposing the hole between the lips is only half as much as it was for the low notes, the air's going to come out twice as fast, and when you make the hole smaller it can feel as if you're raising the air using your chin. I'm doing what Geoffrey might call 'pushing the jaw forward'. But now what I think is that I'm lifting the air column.*

> *I remember Geoffrey talking about how to finish notes. He would say:*

'Push the lips forward' and he gave us a sort of mechanical description of what the chin does. I think I've slightly modified that way of keeping the air moving at a certain speed, by making the hole smaller and by lifting it. Then you make the note softer not by letting the air speed get slower, but by letting less of the column of air that you're blowing hit the opposite edge of the mouth hole.

Note Bending, Harmonics and Intonation

When I asked Wibb what advice he would give anyone about how to start each day with their flute, he replied it would be tailored to each individual person, but does he have a particular way for himself?

What do I usually start with? I can remember having trouble with the flute and beginning again after I'd had flu or something, and the flute not working, and I'd got to find out: 'How much should you pull out, how much should you cover the mouth hole?' I must discover all the possibilities. That was when I'd been to America and got my out of tune American flutes. 'Where is the right place to play any note?' With out of tune flutes, you've got to move your lips to get each note at the right pitch. So I decided: 'Well I'm going to find out what's the maximum amount I can bend any note?'

I started playing some notes in the low register—the easiest notes are the shortest bits of tube—B or C. C sharp is already hopeless because the hole is wrong. So I started the note C in the middle of the treble stave, played it as sharp as I possibly could and gradually went flatter. How to you make the note flatter? By making the mouth hole smaller. And how do you do that? Do you do it by rolling? Some people say you shouldn't roll the flute, so I tried starting as sharp as possible—that means as open as possible—and then gradually bringing the pitch down, trying to hold the flute steady without rolling. I found I could go quite a long way, moving my jaw but not rolling the flute.

Then I said: 'I can go about a semi-tone or a tone down—that's quite easy', but then, if I looked in the mirror, I could see some mouth hole showing: 'I can cover more than that'. So I made my exercise start as sharp as possible, go as flat as possible without rolling, and then try rolling the flute, turning your head—nothing is forbidden!—and I could go down another tone, just, and then come back again.

Then I tried to make a variation on this. I went down as far as possible, rolled the flute in, and then came back the opposite way. In other words, kept the flute rolled in, pulled everything away, and I found I got a completely different sound. You see, one way is relaxing the lip and the other is rolling back and tightening it—a completely different harmonic spectrum.

Then I asked from that: 'Well, of all those possibilities, where does it sound best?' And it sounds best quite near the sharpest point. Best is strongest! When you play the very sharpest you can blow, the harmonics are completely out of tune and they make that awful puffy noise that a saxophone player makes when he can't play the flute! When you play a bit flatter—about an eighth, or a quarter of a tone flatter than the sharpest point you can blow the note—it sounds healthy and then you can go quite a lot flatter by gradually closing the mouth hole and rolling the flute in.

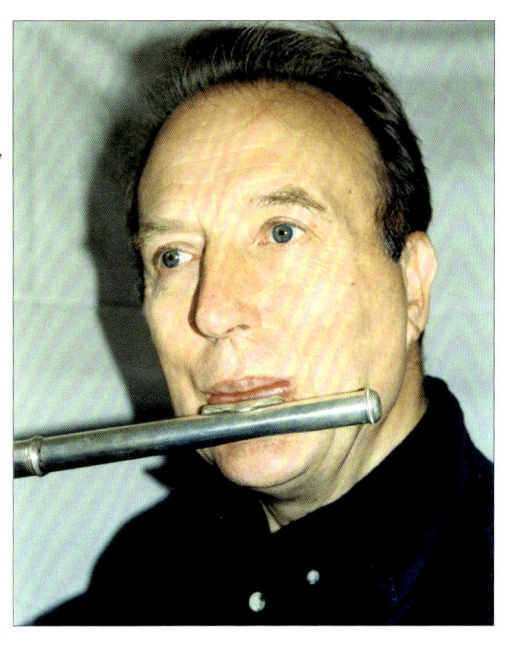

Those sounds, when it gets very covered, are almost unusable, partly because the sound comes out of both the mouth hole and the far end of the tube. With the top ends blocked up, the vibration can't get in and the vibration also goes out through the mouth hole as well as the far end. So, up to a point, a larger mouth hole gives you more sound, but, if it's open more than a certain amount, the harmonics go dreadfully out of tune—the octave in particular.

And that is the whole point of it: you need to be able to bend your tone on the flute because your flute is out of tune, inevitably. Even if it's built perfectly at equal temperament you'll want it better than equal temperament, and it's out of tune because it goes sharper when you blow stronger and flatter when it's weaker. So you've got to be able to move the pitch around anyway. We have to have flexibility.

Maximum flexibility was what Wibb wanted—and he found it.

I found that I could get a major third downward movement on fingered C and gradually a smaller interval as the flute tube got longer. I could get half as much on low C. I could get a B Flat, just, out of bottom C fingering. You wouldn't be able to use it, it wouldn't be strong enough, but the very sharpest sound is no good at all—nobody wants it. Then, as I said, you find that the place quite near the high point has this decent signal which is strong and you can modulate as you wish. The place where it's good is where the harmonics are in tune. If you go too sharp the harmonics are flatter than the fundamental. If you go flatter by more than a little bit, the tone goes out of focus once again and the octaves get wider and wider—like ninths instead of octaves. For a note to have good tone the harmonics have to be in tune.

Rampal knew that. He didn't always play the flute completely in tune, he did fairly well, but he mentioned once: 'Oh if you play in that position, the harmonics are out of tune, bad tone'. His tone production was always in tune with itself, impeccably. He might have been a bit sharp in forte sometimes on some notes, but basically it sounded lovely because he had an in tune tone. Same with Marcel Moyse, a fantastically in tune tone.

Wibb has inherited from Moyse the ideal of homogeneity of sound, achieving evenness of tonal spectrum across the range of the flute.

Yes, as in Moyse's Sonority *book, the ideal is that you can play up a scale chromatically and you can't detect a change of sound from one note to the next. If there's a change, it's very gradual and absolutely equal as it ascends or descends, whichever way it is, but on the flute it's often horribly unequal to this day.*

It's like establishing an artist's basic palette, the tonal spectrum without which the colour blend will be unbalanced. It's something to which Wibb instinctively relates, given his skill as a visual artist.

You can't make a properly shaped phrase if some of the notes drop out. No! It sounds like a different instrument playing. I'm always chiding my students: 'Don't play that C Sharp like an ocarina!' There's a basic colour... you are struggling to make the flute equal and not have unequal notes. If you're trying to build a phrase, you don't want to have to have the phrase dropping back on one note simply because it's bad on the flute. You're constantly trying to balance it so that you don't have these awful unequal notes.

We are still working on things like that, trying to improve the nasty note that comes out with a C sharp—that tiny C sharp hole! The trouble with a dodgy note like C sharp is that its octave is so appallingly out of tune, unless you do exactly the right thing with the lip. The C sharp hole is too small and it blows a flat octave and it's very hard to get the mechanics just right. I've got someone trying to make a new mechanism with a large and a small C sharp hole. It's not the first time it's been done, I've made a couple over the last forty years, but it's fraught with troubles. But we're constantly looking at things like that so that there isn't this sudden awful sound in the middle of the flute. It's the thing that trips most people up, makes it into a difficult instrument.

Only when you can make the notes sound near enough the same, can you then choose to make them sound different for effect.

Once you've got the instrument right and you're capable of playing a good sound in the low register, with equal participation of the octave harmonic, or the harmonic at the twelfth, then you can blow it in a different way and make the notes have less of those harmonics, and that gives you a very obvious, distinctly different sound. You can just open the mouth and make it loose, but still the harmonics have to be in tune.

Wibb demonstrating a flute embouchure

The science behind this has fascinated Wibb for as long as he can remember.

I can remember at school reading the Oxford Companion to Music *and seeing pictures of the different spectrums of the different instruments, the oboe, flute and clarinet, and the clarinet was distinguished by having only the odd numbers strong. It has the fundamentals strong and then the second harmonic is weaker. It doesn't want to play an octave, but the third harmonic is much stronger. At school I tried to practise the flute to see if I could get the third harmonic to sound a bit like a clarinet. Of course I didn't succeed very much!*

On the flute, the strong harmonics diminish as they go up. On the oboe the higher harmonics are more present than on the flute. On the flute it's principally the octave in the low register and then, as you get in the high register, less of the higher overtones show. Funny lower partials come into it and make the flute unequal in the top register—which is a pity. For instance, take top F: you're playing harmonics of low F and B flat at the same time and they happen to coincide—where those two harmonics resonate is on that note. Some of our very high notes have three fundamental notes. For top A, you've got a vent hole at the top, which is effectively a D hole, and you've got the A, which is an A hole, and you've got an F, and all those things will give you an A of sorts. It's not a terribly satisfactory note.

Understanding the science not only explains the imperfections of the flute, it can also give you insights into how you might go about achieving what you want to hear in the sound.

You have to accept that the flute is a certain amount out of tune and that there are things you have to do to modify it. You've got to be careful that the top register doesn't go sharp when it's forte, and then for quite a lot of the range of the flute you've got to make sure it doesn't go flat when it's piano—which is also a bother! So, my contention is that you have to have the holes in the right place, which is exactly what Boehm said. There's a right place for the pitch you're playing at, and you can have a small amount of leeway, but there's only a very small amount where you can still get the octaves in tune. So you find that where the note has a good tone, the octave is in tune.

Wibb at the piano

The third octave has far fewer overtones, because if you had a lot of overtones, you'd have an intensity of sound more like an oboe. We often try to play like an oboe in the low register, with a lot of harmonics pulsating in the sound, but the higher overtones are much less present in the high notes of the flute. And to get a generous sound in the flute high register, you want fewer overtones in the third octave. So I think the objective is to get quite a lot of harmonics in the low notes and then, gradually, as you go up through the middle register into the high, to get fewer and fewer overtones to make it as equal as the piano.

This emphasis on harmonics inevitably informs something else that Wibb talks about a lot: intonation.

That has two parts: one is learning to hear it and then the other is learning to bend the notes.

And the process of sensitising the ear to intonation isn't just confined to the flute, as Wibb's students know well.

> *When I go to teach at the Academy, the pianos are all frightfully out of tune, because people have been playing them for donkey's hours, so I take my piano tuning key and a piece of felt with me, and I say to my students: 'Hey, this note's bloody out of tune! You tune it!' And I get them to learn to listen to beats in the sound and then from that you get into learning to listen to difference tones, so you can judge intervals.*

Once again, this is something that has preoccupied Wibb from his earliest years.

> *On the guitar I made as a boy, the fret board was so out of tune I couldn't use the recognised way of tuning it. Mostly the guitar's tuned in fourths, with one major third stuck in the middle. The tutor books all instruct you to play your low note, E, and then stop the fifth fret, which should produce an A, and then make sure the A is the same note. Well, on mine, that didn't work, so I had to learn to tune the fourth, and very quickly I found that out just by thinking of the harmonic series. The low E has a fourth harmonic of middle E on the piano, and the lower A has a third harmonic of middle E on the piano. If those two harmonics coincide, then you've got a correctly tuned fourth, not an equal tempered one. So, in fact, I was already into perfect intonation rather than equal tempered.*
>
> *As I said before, I was very aware of harmonics from early on because I was teasing myself with banging out the low C on the school piano and listening to the harmonics and noticing how the major third (middle E again) was always too sharp. And I've always been interested in the variation between the effect of major and minor. The jazz singer, Josh White, had a flattened blues third, which isn't as flat as a true minor third, and it's not as sharp as a major third!*

As for the technical means of controlling intonation on the flute, for Wibb the end result is more important than precise rules for how to get there.

Wibb with a tenor ukulele

Somebody sent me a flute tutor and they talked about moving the jaw in and out like a drawer in a chest of drawers—and that's very painful! My jaw mostly goes up and down, like when I talk, and only a very little movement backwards and forwards. After I'd met this idea of the nasty little chest of drawers, I thought maybe we've got to change that concept!

The main thing is to know what you're doing with the air and just to say: 'Move the jaw backwards', doesn't tell the person what they're doing. When you're flattening the pitch like that, what you are doing is covering the mouth hole, first of all by relaxing the lip and pulling it forward over the hole, and when you can't go any further, if there's any more, you do it by turning it in. Some people say: 'You're turning the flute! You must never do that!' But Quantz said to roll the flute... and if I can't move my lips any further and I've still got a little bit more room that I can cover, I can do it by turning my fingers. It's a last resort. You know, people get doctrinaire... you have to watch it with yourself.

Wibb teaching

Difference Tones and Whistle Tones

These two tonal effects are not connected, but they are further examples of the far reaching demands Wibb makes on himself and his students about listening and technical flexibility.

I can remember having composition lessons at the Guildhall and the teacher introducing me to difference tones. When two notes are sounded together, you hear two more notes. One is a low note—the difference tone—which is the difference between the two frequencies. The other is the summary tone—which is the sum of the two frequencies, but less easily heard. For example, if you play A440 and E330 together, you will also hear the difference tone of A110 and the summary tone of G770. It's all to do with the mathematics of sound. Hindemith said you can find the centre of any chord through working out the difference tones—even the most complex discord has a centre. I got very fascinated by that and that was part of the intensity of different harmonies.

I was also interested that the BBC used to broadcast A440 as a signal on the radio. When I was young there were no things like tuning machines, so I could tune my A to the BBC and I could also tune a D. If you play D and A in the right proportion, you will hear the difference tone of middle D in the bass clef, and if I play E and A, I get a difference tone of A at the top of the bass clef. I was fiddling around with it for hours. You quickly become a total intonation freak!

Whistle tones were a great speciality of the American flute player, William Kincaid, who taught generations of flutists at the Curtis Institute in Philadelphia. Wibb encountered whistle tones for the first time on his tour to the USA with the Band of the Scots Guards.

I couldn't do them at all at first because I had tight lips at that time, but the chap in the Marines Band who showed me said: 'Play low C, or a note somewhere down there, with the softest possible, relaxed sound, and then try to go to the first harmonic—the octave harmonic—and sometimes you get a whistle tone instead'. Almost at once, because it's very soft and relaxed, just at the moment that I thought the note would go up an octave, suddenly I got E above the stave—the fifth harmonic—and that was my first whistle tone. After some practice at it, I found that I could get one or two others. I could get the C and the G and quite quickly I could get up to the B Flat of the harmonic series.

It's exactly the same harmonic series, but it's only the edge tone, coupled to the frequencies of the air in the tube. It's something on the front edge of the mouth hole connecting to the resonance of the tube that makes the sound, but the whistle tone is just the edge tone itself, with the length of that defining the pitch of the whistle.

When Wibb returned from America he proudly demonstrated his new discovery to Geoffrey Gilbert.

Geoffrey said: 'Oh, very interesting... but do you think there's any practical application for it?' That stumped me for a while! But it has a useful purpose: it shows you how to get the air going at the right speed for that harmonic without any actual effort. It teaches you control of the lips. To get the very high whistle tones, you make a much smaller hole and the amount of air is almost nothing, but the further up the harmonic series the whistle tone is, the faster the air is going. That is the difficult part of playing the flute: aiming the air and modifying its size.

All I can say is I find it helps me to practise whistle tones. It helps me direct the air without becoming tense. You get a feeling of where the front edge of the mouth hole is, which is where the sound is in part made— except I say it actually comes before that. The sound is produced out there and reflects back into the mouth and chest. You're blowing your flute, you're blowing the air out there, and the resonance of the tube, according to how long or short it is, gives you the different basic pitches. Then if you blow twice as fast, it will get the next octave. But it's quite obvious that your body and head do affect the sound—there's a resonance chamber back in here—and although you think the air jet is coming out fast, it may only be at four or five miles an hour and the speed of sound is about six or seven hundred miles an hour. So you can create a sound wave and it can reflect back up through the jet of air that is coming out!

This is fascinating, but complicated, and introduces a whole new concept of resonance. It's maybe helpful to have a picture to explain it.

It's like if you have two escalators and you come with your dog and you go down the escalator together, and you throw a ball and the dog chases it, and it goes so fast that it can get up the down escalator much quicker than the down escalator can come down!

Which begins to explain why the head is a resonating cavity and how it works.

Well, anyway, that's my silly explanation, or guess!

And Jumble would certainly have approved of running up the down escalator!

Sensitive Fingerings

In the pre-Boehm era, players would of necessity routinely employ a repertoire of alternative, or sensitive, fingerings depending on the key of the music, or the dynamics, or particular articulation required. The baroque flute and the hybrid instruments that came after, with varying numbers of added keys, absolutely required this for full control of the chromatic range. Even after Boehm—when everything was meant to have been sorted out scientifically, with acoustically correctly placed holes and an integrated system of keywork—Richard Rockstro in his famous *Treatise* of 1890 still supplied a range of alternative fingerings. Although the tide of opinion had generally turned against any departure from the 'normal' fingerings, Rockstro argued for them: 'It is, however, sometimes absolutely necessary to employ different methods of fingering in order to obtain smoothness in execution, and there are occasions on which it would be almost impossible to play, on any flute, certain rapid passages of music without the use of these extra fingerings.'

For Rockstro they were 'indispensable' and for Wibb, reading Rockstro as a young player, they opened another door into the world of effect and colour—and control.

Rockstro's book on the flute is fascinating—he has all these extraordinary fingerings. I use quite a lot of tricks for playing loud, to open the sound,

Wibb's notes on Sensitive Fingerings

> *so that you can play naturally in the top without having to suddenly do something with the head or the air stream to pull the pitch down. I find a fingering that will get me that note at the right pitch without having to do a frightful bend of my lips. I think people aren't aware enough of what they can do with fingerings.*

Many of these alternative fingerings relate to the harmonic series, as Wibb discovered, and have the added value of pointing the way to better tone production with the traditional fingerings.

> *When I was doing my note bending, and realising that the harmonics were important, I found that I could get a better sound sometimes, more vocal, with a larger resonance, on a note like C above the stave, by fingering F rather than just the one finger for C. I found that I could get more amplitude in the sound using the longer length of tube. Something was relaxed there. So I tried then to make it that I could get the one finger fingering of the same note with the same depth, and there was something in that about opening the space behind the lips. I found that I did increase the vocal quality when I did those harmonics. I would play the more generous sound of the harmonic and get the expression in the sound and then somehow find the way of getting the short fingering natural with the same depth and resonance.*

French players generally made little use of alternative fingerings, so Wibb was rather taken by surprise when Moyse advised him one day in a masterclass to modify the fingering for the upper C sharp (see the chapter on Teachers). The point was that for Moyse, unlike Rockstro, the reason for using a change of fingering was more musical than technical.

> *It's a way of getting the note the way your ear's telling you it should be, without strain in the lips.*

Wibb also found approval from Geoffrey Gilbert, who shared his practical and pragmatic attitude to fingering.

> *Oh yes, he used all sorts of funny fingerings, particularly in the high register. Quite often he didn't use the regular fingerings. He came up with some very strange ones! Who knows whether he invented them, or discovered them from other people. I remember Geoffrey telling me about B natural, taken like low D without the thumb. It gives you a very sharp middle B, and he said you use that for the end of the* Fingal's Cave Overture. *I've always done that since he told me. You have to lip it down madly to get it right, but you can disappear to nothing with life in the tone, which you can't if you're breaking your jaw off to get it up to pitch the other way! I used to think that that fingering wasn't really acceptable. It's a piccolo fingering and I expect Geoffrey got it from some piccolo player, and thought: 'Well I can use that on the flute!'*

For Wibb, alternative fingerings are an ever-evolving resource in his technical toolkit—there's no end to the quest for them.

> *If there's a new fingering somebody gives you, maybe you use it sometimes and then you find yourself using it more often, you find it's more comfortable. You don't have to do so much to get the right pitch. It's a mixture of technical and musical. I needed a B for the Reinecke Concerto and I've now got ten different fingerings for a sensitive B! They're not all acceptable, but I'm extending the way in which sensitive fingerings can be used. I'm constantly working at them and inventing new ones.*

Articulation

Not surprisingly, the subject of tonguing has come up several times already in this book (see the chapters on Teachers and on Teaching). Eradicating the hard, explosive attack of the tongue has become a crusading mission for Wibb and if you listen to his recordings you immediately hear how his much more subtle approach to articulation has paid off. As we have seen, he has Geoffrey Gilbert to thank for that.

> *Almost the first thing Geoffrey did with me was taking the tongue away and then blowing and getting rid of the 't'. He was trying to cure me of that for years! He taught me about placing the tongue between the lips, withdrawing it gently, and then allowing the air to enter the flute, without tongue noise. That's frightfully difficult for most people to understand, but I find I'm having to do it more nowadays because everybody goes 't'—a nasty little spitting noise, what I call 'Zungenstoss'!*

As so often for Wibb, the solution is to observe what singers do.

> *Really, if you think about it—and this is the way I would now express it—when you sing 'aahh', you don't have to go 't' to make 'aahh' come out. It's not necessary to go 'aahh' with a glottal stop. Normally there's a moment when the air goes through the throat before the note comes out, and it doesn't begin as suddenly as most people think it should.*
>
> *I had some singing lessons recently with Jenny Miller, and I asked her: 'How do you begin a note when you're singing classical music?' She said: 'Generally we try not to do it too sharply' and that was a great revelation to me. People on wind instruments think they have to get this super-clear attack with a hard beginning to the note, but that can kill a lot of things. Only about fifty per cent of the notes, in my opinion, need hard attack or clear attack.*

Pianists have a similar challenge: how to liberate the instrument from always being percussive with hard hammers.

> *Pianists are also trying to get 'aahhs' into the notes and they spend a great deal of time working out how to use the weight of the arms to get an acceleration of the hammers. Clifford Benson was always talking about the way the hammer accelerates to get the sound. God knows how that works, but it does, and I was telling someone recently: 'You've got to do this as if you've got great big fat arms! Go slowly into the piano, but play big, like Brahms' and it worked. Pianists do talk about that sort of thing—using the weight correctly—and it makes an enormous difference to the sound of the piano. I saw a pictorial representation in the* Oxford Companion to Music, *or some such book, of how a note on the piano looks. It doesn't start at full volume, it takes a micro-second to get up to full volume. It blooms and then has a long tail away.*

It follows, therefore, that it would help to have a mental image of what the notes on the flute should look like.

> *There's almost never a sudden beginning, so almost all notes are faintly lozenge shaped, they're never quite square!*
>
> *I think a lot of us flute players are over-concerned about the beginning of a note—hard and sudden—it sounds most brutal. If you're playing in an orchestra and you have the conductor doing a slow gesture, if you come in with a quick attack, you're wrong, you're invariably first. That sort of curved, generous gesture requires an appropriate 'whaa' attack and there are so many variants of the different consonants—'dah', 'nah'—which take time to come out as the 'ah' bit. The 'ah' is the main part of the note, but the 'n' at the beginning takes a little time, the 'n' and the 'g' and the 'd'. There's a funny release with the 'd'. I use 'd' an awful lot and even 'l'. In the Altès Tutor (Caratgé edited it) he writes 'de', 're', obviously something he thought of.*

Unusually in my conversations with Wibb, articulation was the one subject about flute playing on which he laid down the law.

> *There's a time and a place for almost everything. I quote Geoffrey Gilbert on this and he said: 'Even that nanny goat vibrato, you know where you can use it? In the* Danse de la Chèvre, *when you want life on the top note of that upward leaping phrase—that's the only way you get the vibrato quickly in the time!' It's useful.*
>
> *Stopping the note with the tongue is the thing I try to forbid pupils doing, and I notice that the oboist Heinz Holliger and other people did the same thing. They couldn't bear the note being cut off with the tongue, it had to be finished properly. It's just like putting the cork in a champagne bottle before you finish pouring! That's why I don't like the organ: it can't imitate a flute, even though it has flute stops. It doesn't have any human inflection, does it? It doesn't have any vocal part. It has a different set of qualities...*

Vibrato

This is a minefield! British flute players before Geoffrey Gilbert supposedly didn't use vibrato, whereas French players did. But what French players understood by the word 'vibrato' was generally something wobbly and intrusive in the sound—not at all what they approved of—and they didn't really have a viable alternative term to describe the life and animation in the tone that was so obviously an intrinsic part of their playing. So the term vibrato will have to do...

> *Geoffrey Gilbert taught calculating vibrato—controlling how many beats per second—so you could control it at any speed you desired. That was the idea. I asked Geoffrey if this vibrato control come from René Le Roy or somewhere else. Was it part of the violin school which he'd learnt with*

Carl Flesch? Geoffrey said the control came from Le Roy, but I'm not quite sure if I believe that, because it's not like Le Roy. He wasn't very controlled in many ways, but Geoffrey was very impressed with Le Roy's brain power. He said he didn't play very well in tune, which is an understatement! I'm not Le Roy's greatest fan—although he sounds quite nice, quite often—but I suspect vibrato control for Geoffrey came more from Carl Flesch.

Marcel Moyse would have none of this idea of calculating vibrato.

He talked once about some 'Americain' who said he could control the speed of vibrato. Moyse said: 'This is stupid. What it mean? Nothing'.

Another French player, Maxence Larrieu, would have agreed.

Larrieu, when questioned about vibrato, said: 'Oh you don't practise vibrato, you play a straight tone and the vibrato comes', and that seemed to be very much the French way.

Fernand Dufrène, however, was closer to Geoffrey Gilbert in outlook and therefore, maybe, closer to René Le Roy and the previous generations of Philippe Gaubert and Paul Taffanel.

Dufrène said to somebody who went for a lesson: 'Don't always vibrate in fours. Sometimes in three, or perhaps five, or perhaps even seven, but keep changing it'. Dufrène was famous for changing expression in his playing and it seems as if it wasn't just him. Dufrène was a pupil of Gaubert—we've got pictures of Gaubert teaching him—and Dufrène was talking about counting out pulses, which shows that he was thinking that way, and I don't think he invented it.

Wherever it came from, and however it was explained, there was a common aim: to make the music more expressive. Geoffrey Gilbert's technique of counting out vibrato in beats per second was not an end in itself.

No. Geoffrey's teaching was not about applying numbers. He was talking about vibrating at different speeds and different depths to make the music more or less expressive. On one occasion he said: 'If I can count your vibrato, it's probably wrong'. He didn't say it was definitely wrong—that wouldn't be like him. He had these terribly high ethical standards about what you should and shouldn't say, for which I'm very grateful and full of admiration!

Moyse's response was similar, but expressed a little differently.

He used to talk about life in the tone, but he didn't want to say what.

If you listen to Wibb's recordings over the decades, you will hear an enormous range of vibrato—a technique used variously, and often sparingly, for musical effect.

Flute tone doesn't need automatically to have vibrato in it to sound nice. You do hear occasional vibrato-less playing that sounds absolutely marvellous, but as a general thing, I don't like most vibrato-less playing. I say most, but I can remember going to one of the concerts of the French National Orchestra—Pierre Monteux was conducting—and they were playing Petrushka. *There was one bit when Dufrène played a complete solo and it was as clean as a whistle—straight—and it was spine-chillingly perfect and absolutely marvellous. But he's the only French person I know who could play properly without vibrato and it was quite astonishing to hear it. Dufrène had obviously been asked by Monteux, or he himself had decided for some reason that that was the thing to do.*

So how much of what Wibb himself does is a conscious calculation?

A lot of the time it comes as part of your 'joie de vivre'. It's vibrant. But I think about what Geoffrey said: 'I'm not going to tell you how many vibratos to use per beat, I'm merely going to say more expressive or less expressive'. That's been going on since I was sixteen and it's not something to be forgotten.

I heard somebody say about one of the recordings I made of the B Minor Suite: 'Oh, you're using a very fast vibrato on that one!' Maybe I was very excited and it was going fast. I hadn't actually noticed! Somebody else picked up that I was doing something different. I haven't heard many recordings where I don't use any vibrato—I think The Art of Fugue *may be one.*

Phrasing, Eloquence and Communication

I've already described listening with Wibb to a recording of him playing the Bach Trio Sonata from *The Musical Offering* when he was a student at Guildhall (see the chapter on Recordings). Even then he was playing so much more than just the notes. There was an eloquence to the musical line—wordless, obviously, but I felt I could have put words to it.

I think the point is that there is always a direction to the phrase. There's always what I used to call 'the point of the phrase'. I don't know exactly when I started thinking about direction that much, but I think I've always been trying to find out where the phrase goes. That ties in with following Geoffrey Gilbert's rules of which beats are strongest in the bar. You've got to get the first beat in the right proportion to the third beat, and the second and the fourth fitting in, and then you sub-divide each of those beats into two quavers, or four semi-quavers, and there's the same hierarchy of the beat. If you obey that, half the music is revealed to you, and sometimes it's going much further than just one bar at a time, but there's a hierarchy of what you do and where.

You could, of course, do all this analysis, learn the musical language with the correct words, even make a sentence, but not still actually communicate.

Probably because I was playing the piano a lot, I was finding my own way

> *of making expression. I used to get a piano piece and experiment with it—do something with the tempo here and there and make it my own. The next time it might be something totally different, but I was always trying to do something with it. I can remember going to the Rubbra's house, where I spent a lot of time. Edmund Rubbra wasn't there very often, but his wife, Antoinette, was and her sister the artist Elisabeth Chaplin. I was quite often playing the piano, at the age of twelve or thirteen, and Elisabeth said: 'Oh, very interesting... he plays the piano like a grown up'.*

And Wibb would soon be playing the flute in an equally adult way, imbuing this single line melody instrument with his understanding of harmony.

> *Yes, because of the amount of piano playing I did as a boy, improvising and trying to create my own music. I was composing quite a lot of things and trying to write them down. I was never very good at it, but I was very interested in certain, particular harmonic changes.*

In taking on harmonic character and meaning, individual notes would cease to be neutral, together they would unfold a persuasive musical narrative. Wibb's playing always says: 'Come and listen'.

> *I was interested in finding out—I never did!—about the Elizabethan idea of different 'humours' that you get from different chords. A different harmony has a different meaning or atmosphere. Moyse used to talk about it: 'When you practise you must try to find atmosphere'. In other words, it's not merely mechanical, about tongue or fingers or something. A phrase I always remember from Moyse: 'When I practise, I try to evoke something'.*

Tone, Colours and Pictures

Listen to any Wibb recording, and I think you will be struck by how tone and colours combine to make musical pictures. It's clearly a vocal approach to playing, noted so often throughout this book.

> *It's completely easy to change the colour of the voice. It's almost the same thing to make the flute change its sound. And yet there are many flute players completely locked into only doing one sound. That's a pity.*

But what does the basic sound of the flute mean for Wibb?

> *I'm not quite sure what I originally thought flute sound was, but it was a definite voice that wasn't a recorder. The trouble is I was sometimes inspired in some way by things that I don't like now. I had a record of Robert Murchie playing the Rondeau from the B Minor Suite and it was good enough to inspire me when I was eleven or twelve.*

What were the elements that caught his attention?

> *I'm trying to think when I first noticed the flute. I remember the music master playing us Beethoven's First Symphony and there's a bit in the*

> *slow introduction where the flute has crochets—F, D, D—and this wonderful sound came through. It was the New York Philharmonic, probably John Wummer playing, or somebody like that. Then I remember the* Fifth Brandenburg Concerto *being played quite a lot, before I had a flute. The Rubbra family and their friends the Ashcrofts both had wind-up gramophones and I heard the recording of Roger Cortet, Jacques Thibaud and Alfred Cortot playing the* Fifth Brandenburg. *Things like that were in my habit as it were. But the Beethoven Symphony... suddenly the flute coming through like that, having a noble voice, which I recognised wasn't something I could do on the recorder.*

And Wibb's reaction?

> *Well, obviously, I wanted to have a flute. I wanted to do it. It was quite direct. I've quite often heard playing that makes me think: 'That's it—I want to do that'. I can remember one record I had—some French orchestra—of a Haydn Sinfonia Concertante and it starts off with a flute playing an octave above the violins. The most gorgeous, extrovert French playing, and I said: 'That's the sound I want!' I don't know who it was, but I've heard lots of French players who have this quality. Then, as a student, I was thinking: 'These French players make a nice sound right through to the end of the note. Sometimes they play it a little too long, because they are enjoying it. I'd rather play it too long than have a nasty note!'*

What then does Wibb see in his imagination when he plays the flute?

> *Quite often I see the notes as a piano keyboard. I play the piano quite a lot. I think of E Flat and C, or whatever, on the piano.*
>
> *Somebody said: 'I think you come out of the body when you play'. I can't say I've ever felt it! I've not been up there, observing it going on down here, and I haven't caught myself seeing anything. I'm usually looking at the dots!*

Not at all the answer I was expecting from someone with such a strong visual sense and awareness! I was intrigued and returned to the question at various times in our conversations.

> *If I've got a difficult passage, I may see my fingers, but I usually see a piano keyboard rather than a flute. I'm also conscious of mechanical connections. I can sense the whole mechanism—and you can't explain that.*

Well, there's something rather more visual there, but still not really a connection to the world of the imagination.

> *I don't know... I talk about colours...*

That was my cue to show Wibb something I had found: a publicity paragraph he had drafted just before he began teaching in Freiburg in the 1980s.

> *William Bennett grew up among artists and was seriously thinking of becoming a painter before he became fascinated with music. He thinks in terms of colour, light and shade, which he translates into ideas of sound.*

Watercolour of sunlight on the sea in Ramsgate harbour by Wibb

Yes, I've been known to say lots of things along those lines. I talk about making a bright blue sound, or bright yellow, or dark brown. I often say something like: 'What about the blue sky and the green leaves, that bright wonderful thing?' trying to get a clear middle D.

Does Wibb then see that colour?

I'm not sure if I'm actually playing and seeing colours like that, but I'm often thinking about it. I can remember going to America for the first time when I was nineteen and having two months touring around in a Greyhound bus. It was the Fall and it was the most exciting thing. I'd never seen anything like the colours. I had a little window seat and this bus had these funny lozenge shaped windows and I'd have my window open with my head looking out at these fantastic colours everywhere. My colleagues, some of them, were complaining about the draught, but I had to have the window open because the colours weren't any good through the tinted glass!

I was certainly making a connection with the sounds I was wanting to make. I'd seen Disney's Fantasia *and heard the sound of William Kincaid playing the* Night on the Bare Mountain, *and other things, and it was vivid in my imagination. I saw* Fantasia *when I was about thirteen and it stayed with me. I went to see it again when I was a student in Paris and I was terribly disappointed—it wasn't as good as I remembered! The sound in my memory had developed, as I developed, and then when I heard the actual sound again, I was expecting what I had developed it to be... But anyway, I was on this bus, and I remember likening this to my memories of what I'd heard. These vivid, vivid yellows, oranges and purples and everything mixed up seemed to have to do with the sounds that the flute could make.*

Did Geoffrey Gilbert talk about flute playing in terms of colour?

He was very reserved about saying it, or anything over suggestive. He was confining himself, I think. He was always putting a boundary for himself. He let me be the way I was. He wasn't interfering and he wasn't inhibiting me with anything—which was wonderful of him. But I can remember him talking about colour when I came back from Paris with the Gaubert Nocturne et Allegro scherzando *as my chief piece.*

I did it with him at a lesson and he was talking about the sound: 'Can you get that open quality of sound, that you've got in the opening of the Gaubert, for the third octave?' And getting an open sound in the low register is something I found was conducive to getting the third octave. When you get a focused sound in the low register, you make a smaller jet of air, so that some of it is producing the octave harmonic, or maybe the octave and the twelfth, but when you play with a bigger hole, softer lips, you get more of the lower partial. When I did that, opened it and kept it generous—in fact, blew more air than I needed, but not under pressure—I found that I could get the top octave to have the same space in it as the lower. I do remember finding that that's what I should be doing to get the top register with depth in it.

I've got a picture somewhere I did of Ramsgate Harbour when we were all swimming there in the summer school. I've got waves and little sort of lozenge shaped bits that I've coloured in bright yellow as the reflection of the sun. Most of the water is blue and these little lozenges are slashes of yellow, flecks of light, sunlight coming off the water.

There are times when one wants the sound to be luminous—and luminous to me means like the lamps here, where we are talking, with a glow coming out—but I'm thinking of those other colours as a highlight.

Exactly! I immediately felt I could see Wibb's picture (reproduced here)—although at that point I hadn't—and translate it into what I could hear in his playing. It's tantalising, therefore, that pictures seem not to be in Wibb's own head when he's playing. Or maybe they are and he's just not consciously looking at them?

> *Come to think of it, there's one bit in the first movement of the Reinecke Sonata when I always think of light. The beginning is all grey and rainy and then the tune comes later in this completely strange key, and there are the most brilliant colours you could possibly imagine. On the second page of the flute part it goes into F sharp major. The tonality of it is fantastic, there are sharps everywhere! It's really sparkling little jewels—just like that piece of sea. There's the sea and there are sharp spots of sunlight being reflected off it. I did several pictures with that sort of sea. I was interested in lovely brilliant flashes of reflection in the waves—lots of them.*

There was definitely something visual about memory that was very potent for Moyse.

> *I was interested in Moyse's memory and he said to me: 'You cannot study memory like mine. Mine is memory by love!' I showed my amazement and he said: 'For instance when that young man, the tall one, played Bach, there was some wrong note. I not need to look at the music, I remember. I know where the note is on the page. I remember when Cortet played this piece in 1935, the same piece at the Conservatoire. I remember the faces of all the other people and the light in the room'.*

> *He said: 'Once Taffanel play something and next day when I practise I draw curtains to get the same light because previous day was about three thirty in the afternoon in December. I want the same half dark'. So the light was important for him! I'm not quite sure if I'm as vivid as that about it. But I do often say to people: 'Can't you play with such and such a colour—light green, or red or something?'*

At that point in the conversation, on a sunny afternoon in Wibb's sitting room, just as I was about to ask another question, he spontaneously demonstrated just how visually acute he is.

> *I want us to change places now, because I think you're missing something. I feel that you're not having the same pleasure that I've been having. You're framed by the window, rather fantastically, and the tree! And those other colours down there that we don't normally see in this room. This is sort of a special occasion and it's going to go in a minute because the clouds are coming. It's a moment that I won't forget in a hurry.*

We changed places. Wibb was now framed by the window and his face was different, back-lit, with sunlight haloed around him. Then the clouds began to move across the sun.

> *Now it's going, you see? So I wanted you to enjoy the light! It just shows, these things are sometimes important...*

Wibb's Octave Exercise

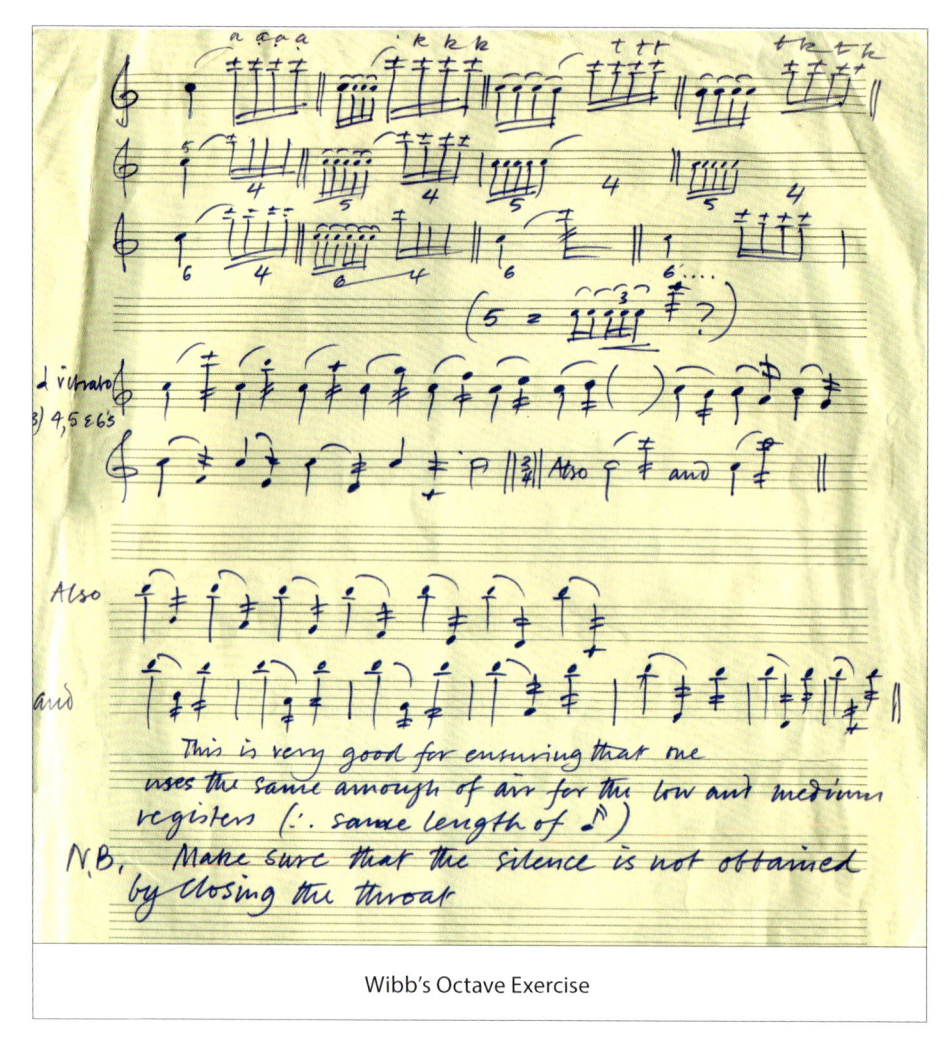

Memorising

Solo pianists almost invariably perform from memory, it's expected of them. What about flute players? Has it been important for Wibb?

> I haven't done a great deal of playing from memory. I could do it very easily when I was at school. I used to get a piano piece and learn it, and then it would be permanently under my fingers. Same with the flute. But I've never set out to play everything from memory, although I find that I do know a great deal of music just by having played it and listened to it. When you teach something in a masterclass, you may never have played the piece, but you know it by the end of the class.

Does he feel that memorising frees a player in any way, or gives any extra insight into the music?

> *Yes, I did find that, when I thought I'd better play the Mozart Concertos from memory. You have to sort out the actual process of making sure that you don't take a wrong turning—which you can do very easily when you're playing from memory. A phrase begins one way and the first time it ends like this, and the next time it ends like that. You have to sort that out and you find from the process of memorising that you understand it much better. It enforces understanding—and that understanding makes you project it to the audience. Quite a lot about the emotions that you're trying to show comes out of learning it in that way.*

The drawback of having the music on a stand in front of you, therefore, is that it may inhibit this process of communication.

> *It puts a barrier between you and the audience. But the moment you are playing without the dots you're thinking more about where the phrase is leading to and the actual shape. The first phrase leads up a bit, the next phrase takes you further, and then it turns a corner and does something else. Then the next time that particular series of phrases comes, it's different, it goes somewhere else. That's what you have to remember. That's where you are taking the audience for a ride to, saying: 'Come up with this phrase... this phrase goes higher... this phrase is the top... and it comes down like this... and then it changes mood'.*
>
> *While I'm saying that, I'm thinking of the slow movement of the Mozart D Major Concerto—which is Mozart's magic box of tricks! Tonic going to dominant... dominant going to tonic... subdominant... and coming down the scale again... and then it suddenly goes to E minor. That's fascinating, because when it comes round again, it goes somewhere completely different. It goes through a great range of stuff, from the most insanely simple beginnings. But the moment he suddenly takes you into E minor, the powers of darkness have arrived. Mozart is there!*

The ideal for Wibb is that the flute player should feel as if he or she is speaking directly to the audience, leading them through and explaining the music.

> *I was very much inspired by Moyse about this. When he was talking about it, I could see him look up and direct his attention up there, towards an imaginary audience. And I'm often telling people: 'Don't play to down there!' I'm playing for somebody over the other side of the road! I must think about projecting the sound.*
>
> *I remember being at the Rubbra's house, in a valley in Buckinghamshire, and I often used to go up and play the flute in the open air. The sound coming off the pine trees had a good echo, and I found that if I got a good staccato you could hear the note coming back off the trees. I used to practise in that sort of place and hear the long decay of sound from the trees. In the sunshine today, I went out into the back garden and played and I*

> thought: 'There's a wonderful echo here!' A short note has a great decay on it. I've got it out here as well. I hadn't realised. I've lived in this house for twenty years, but it's not often warm enough to go out there!

Practice

Nowadays, Wibb's starting point for practice is always the basic sound.
> Getting a reasonable note—which means getting the harmonics in tune—because without that it's unbearable!

But his practice has changed quite a lot over the years.
> As a very young player, I was concerned mostly with trying to play as many notes as possible per second! With Geoffrey Gilbert I was learning to control these things a bit and I've finally realised that I can't play as fast as quite a lot of other people and that the actual priorities when you play are rather different. They are finding where the phrase is going, what atmosphere it has, and how it fits in the general scheme of events of the piece that you're trying to revive. You're trying to get the dots off the page, to be something.

Studies are important—although they can be a mixed blessing—but for Wibb they must have musical value.
> Andersen's studies are marvellous! I spent hours playing them when I was in Paris. They're very musical—and so, of course, are the Gaubert studies in the Taffanel and Gaubert Method. Quite a lot of studies are bloody boring!

It's also been important for Wibb to analyse his technical needs and make up exercises for himself—a sort of bespoke tailoring on the flute!
> Oh yes, I've got lots of folders with little ideas of things to practise for certain passages.

Indeed—we went through pages and pages together of examples of Wibb over the years working out his thoughts on paper, not in words, but in musical notation. As needed, and when relevant, they get incorporated into practice routines.
> I have variations of things I do and then I will focus on a problem I meet. The other day I played some scales and I was finding trouble in the high notes and so I organised my fingers to work better. I find myself doing Geoffrey Gilbert exercises to concentrate on very specific finger movements. The most usual one is the co-ordination of G to B flat, so you don't get a blip in the middle of it. That's one of the hardest things we have on the flute. That's practice without atmosphere, purely mechanical stuff. I do quite a lot of it, but I don't do too much!

What would Wibb's advice be, therefore, for those of us wanting to organise our practice?

St John's Smith Square

LONDON SW1P 3HA   Director Paul Davies

Saturday, May 17th, 1997 at 7.30pm

OPERA FLUTASTIC!

An evening of great moments from Opera as they should have been - as seen by

William Bennett
Adrian Brett   *Flutes*   **Clifford Benson** *piano*
Trevor Wye   **Presented by Edward Blakeman**

Do what I have been made to do! Marcel Moyse Daily Exercises *and the* 480 Exercises. *Actually I wasn't made to do the* 480 Exercises, *but I discovered them and got into them and realised how very good they are. They've been a mainstay for me for the last ten or more years. I find if I can get through a set of ten of those each time, it's enough to get me*

going. Then there's the Moyse Sonority *book, Andersen studies, Moyse/ Kreutzer studies—they're wonderful because they put you in touch with real violin style, which is the backbone of our music making, I think. Then you should try melodies like Saint-Saëns's* The Swan *in different keys, from memory. That sharpens up all sorts of intellectual things about finding where the notes are and you get different problems in each key with the different intervals.*

Nerves

Confident... outgoing... it's tempting to imagine that Wibb hasn't had to grapple with the problem of nerves which confronts most other players.

I expect I was more confident than quite a lot of people, but there are times when you feel: 'Oh my God...!' But it's alright, everybody has something that makes them nervous. I remember being very worried about nerves. Sometimes before a concert I'd have a large black coffee—to make sure I was awake!—and then get up on the stage and my mouth would dry up. I learnt that black coffee is the worst thing for that. It stimulates the adrenalin and when you get too much adrenalin the mouth dries up. It's the worst thing you could take—makes you more nervous still.

That was about the same period as being in the Army and playing in the Trio with Margaret Moncrieff and Margaret Norman. I had a lot of concerts with them. I was about nineteen and I had a twitch in my eye, a jumping muscle. It was most disconcerting and I thought: 'Why can't I relax this? I should be able to tell my body to stop and it should work out alright'.

When that didn't work, Wibb's reaction, as so often, was to tackle the problem by doing something practical about it.

I went to the Central Music Library in Victoria and found the right section for a book on relaxation. I found a book on yoga as well, so I borrowed them both. The relaxation book talked a lot of twaddle and the yoga book seemed to make such very good sense.

Wibb began practising the exercises and they paid off.

I remember being away on a recruiting tour with the Army Band, in some barracks somewhere up in the North of England, feeling nervous with the whole business of the Colonel shouting and throwing music stands around. I started doing these breathing exercises—eight heartbeats in, eight heartbeats out—and things ceased to be so worrying.

The benefits of yoga were mental as well as physical.

There were yoga aphorisms at the back of the book I got. One important one was: 'Face up to fear and it will vanish'. It worked remarkably well. In the Band practice there were these terrible things happening and I was the only person really transposing all the time, so I had a lot more to worry about than the others. I was terrified and the fierce music stand throwing Colonel didn't make any allowances for me transposing most of the parts up a semitone. Most band music was written for flute in D flat and the normal flute is in D. It was wonderful for me—I had to be so much better at reading than everybody else just to hold my own. And I was thinking: 'What am I afraid of? What's the worst thing that can happen? They can put me in prison for playing a wrong note! But I think I might survive being put in prison for a few days...!' Suddenly I stopped worrying—and breathed instead.

Yoga consequently became an everyday part of Wibb's life.

I remember going to Boswil, to the Moyse course, and I would always go out at tea breaks and stand on my head! Sitting down listening to a class is a very tiring business. I revitalised myself with a few yoga asanas. Very useful.

Nerves never completely disappear—and Wibb would argue that they shouldn't. The secret is to channel them.

They are always there... and they are useful. You get heightened awareness when you have a concert. You've got to—you're on full adrenalin, ready to perform. But if you get too much adrenalin it suddenly seizes you up. It's that ability to switch something on in a moment of need, that's what gets you through a concert.

All of which reminded Wibb that he hadn't done his yoga exercises so much recently...

I must do more!

Nobility of the Flute

The aesthetics of the flute, and what you might call the philosophy of it, seem to me to have preoccupied Wibb throughout his life. Going through some of the reviews and clippings he had kept over the years, I came across an article on the flute in *The Economist* from July 1988. Towards the end it noted how diverse an instrument the flute could be in the hands of three leading players: Jean-Pierre Rampal, James Galway and William Bennett. 'Mr Rampal excels at the elegance of French baroque, Mr Galway conveys the extrovert pleasure of the flute bands of his native Belfast, and William Bennett has extended the nobility and subtlety of the Moyse legacy.'

Wibb had underlined that last phrase.

I was pleased that somebody had written that. Moyse would talk about nobility sometimes and noble is what I describe Dufrène as being. He had that quality which I'd not heard in anybody else.

But what exactly does the nobility of the flute mean to Wibb?

It's not always a fluttering little bird! I think Moyse may have been so kind as to use the term noble about me. He liked me in the first place because

I could sound like a French horn: 'Noble like French horn.' Players get nobility in their own way. Moyse had a lot of fantastic drama. Dufrène was always aristocratic, never out of place.

The sound, style and a seriousness of intent combined to produce the particular quality of nobility which attracted Wibb in Dufrène—but he also admired Rampal, for different reasons.

That Dufrène quality wasn't something you found in Rampal. Nobility is the right word for Dufrène and Rampal was much more happy bird! Very good, but it was different. I'm very interested at how much I'm actually influenced by Rampal, although I tend not to say I think he's the greatest. But certainly he's a very big influence—I loved his happiness.

Moyse was much more serious than Rampal, but when an American played the Chaminade Concertino in his class and the opening was very noble and deep, Moyse said: 'You must find happy tone for this'. I knew exactly the sound he meant: changing the vowel from 'or' to 'ee'. I realised that the American flutes had a lot of depth—I admired Mariano for his depth of sound—but I also wanted that happy French sound. That is why I liked nickel flutes—more like the light on the waves. I also heard that light in recordings of Gaston Crunelle, the Conservatoire professor before Rampal. He had something sparkling and clear.

Wibb at the piano

Soul of the Flute

It was one of those times when Wibb and I had been chatting generally about all sorts of things after the end of a session. Part of his mind, however, had gone on turning over the range of subjects we had just grappled with. He fell silent, looked thoughtful, and then took me by surprise.

You're trying to get to the soul of the flute, aren't you?

Yes. The soul of the flute sums it all up perfectly. Something beyond technique, musicality, aesthetics, even philosophy.

For me, there has to be a heartbeat in the sound...

Something I've visualised about this: I used to have some pet mice and if you hold a mouse and then release it, put it down, you can sort of see its

> *heart beating in the way it's breathing. You're very conscious of a nervous mouse and you think that's its pulse. That tremendous life! I often think of a heart beating in terms of a mouse and its very flexible body.*

How does that relate to the flute?

> *It's got something moving in it. It's not a tube with a straight line down it. There are no straight lines—no Mondrian here!*

So, no straight lines in a flute sound?

> *Not really, no. Not a good one.*

Postscript

This book has essentially been about Wibb in his own words. It's enlightening, however, to discover how others, particularly non flute playing critics, have identified and commented on the essentials of his playing, right from the beginning of his career. They picked up on so many of the things Wibb himself cares about. Here are a few extracts of some of those early newspaper and magazine reviews.

In January 1960, not long after after Wibb came back from Paris, he appeared in a Wigmore Hall concert with the Mabillon Trio. They gave the premiere of a Trio by Peter Racine Fricker and played a series of solo items. This response from the critic of *The Manchester Guardian* set the tone for many others to come.

> 'All three (Susan Bradshaw, piano, William Bennett, flute, and Philip Jones, oboe) are gifted players, and a combination of careful rehearsal and spontaneous responsiveness to the music and to each other gave their concerted playing its elasticity, vitality and polish. The flautist is perhaps the finest of the three. Both in Bach's C minor Partita and Poulenc's attractive Sonata his playing had such shapeliness and ease of line, and was so variously coloured and subtly modulated in tone, that each separate phrase could be admired as a beautiful musical entity. Any composer would be happy to write a work specially for him.'

Another review from the early 1960s noted a concert of the Vesuvius Ensemble at the York Arts Centre, including Berio's *Sequenza*.

> 'William Bennett made the difficult virtuoso music, written to explore the different possibilities of the flute, sound not only technically brilliant but also—music.'

A *Times* critic was present in November 1964 when Wibb and George Malcolm gave one of their many concerts, playing Bach and Couperin.

'The myth of the inexpressive flute was dealt a final blow last night at the Wigmore Hall. It happens to be the chosen instrument of Mr William Bennett, a musician of authority and insight, who handles it with a mastery as complete as it is unobtrusive... and with Mr George Malcolm as his percipient partner an evening of rare delight was created.'

When the two of them played a similar programme in Cambridge in May 1971, the local critic declared:

'Style is a very tricky thing to define, but whatever it is, both George Malcolm and William Bennett possess it.'

He went on to praise Wibb's 'formidably rich and pure tone', 'wide emotional range' and, in a CPE Bach Sonata, 'a fine sense of line and phrasing and an impeccable understanding of the harmonic implication of the sinuous melodic line'.

Meanwhile another critic from *The Times* was obviously not only delighted but also amused at a concert of the Geraint Jones Orchestra in May 1971.

'With his dress trousers hitched a regulation two inches above the ankles and his hips swaying elegantly to the music, William Bennett is an unmistakable figure among modern wind players. He is also, as he showed last night, a Bach flautist in a thousand. His account of the B minor Suite was quite outstanding not only for technical virtuosity (though few players would attempt to ornament the Badinerie repeats) but for sheer natural beauty of phrasing and tone...'

You can still savour that phrasing, tone and swirling ornamentation in Wibb's recording of the Bach Suite with the Academy of St Martin in the Fields and Neville Marriner made that same year, 1971. 'Every flute note a pearl', as the critic of *The Sunday Times* wrote of a later performance in August 1976.

In 1974 an initially reluctant critic from *Music and Musicians* began his review like this:

'A large audience of masochists came to the Elizabeth Hall to face the prospect of all Bach's flute sonatas at one go. Presumably the attraction was that William Bennett and George Malcolm were playing them.'

He soon changed his tune.

> 'That Bennett and Malcolm held everybody's attention throughout their marathon is one pointer to the fabulous artistry of their playing. I could write pages about the subtle articulation of running phrases, the colouring of sustained flute notes, Malcolm's unfailingly buoyant sense of rhythm, the sensitivity with which the two players were listening to one another's music, but I will just say that I have never learned as much in a single evening about the techniques and spirit of baroque duo playing. In fact I am almost going to say that the 'masochists' were nothing of the kind.'

In 1978 when the first disc of Wibb's recording of the Bach Sonatas appeared, Nicholas Kenyon, who was at that time a critic for the magazine *Classical Music*, responded with pleasure—and a dash of playfulness.

> 'The playing is delightful: fresh, relaxed, purring with good humour in Bennett's flute playing; perfectly matched in rhythm and inflection from Malcolm, whose right hand really duets with the flautist... a genuine sense of music-making which is both enjoyed and enjoyable comes from the disc. And more importantly, the music is well served, which is more than can be said for the self-advertisingly superficial performances of... oops...'

There are many other appreciative reviews from later in Wibb's career that I could quote—the critics have been remarkably consistent in their response to his playing. Here is just one from *The American Record Guide* in May 1996, reviewing a recording with Clifford Benson of the Reinecke Sonata, the Franck Sonata, Schubert's Variations and Taffanel's *Mignon Fantasy*. It says it all.

> 'Bennett plays his flute much in the style of a singer with excellent enunciation. He uses exciting colours and vibrato, maintains perfect intonation, and has a beautiful open sound in all dynamic ranges...
>
> 'Bennett and Benson play the opening of the Taffanel *Mignon Fantasy* with the range of colours that I normally associate with great string players or great singing. They offer each variation as a treat the way a gift box can bring out beauty in an everyday object.'

Sketch of Copacabana Beach by Wibb

Conclusion

The phrase from Robert Louis Stevenson that I quoted in the previous chapter is worth repeating it in its fuller context.

> Little do ye know your own blessedness; for to travel hopefully is a better thing than to arrive, and the true success is to labour.

That fits rather well with Wibb's own pronouncement.

All my life I've been dogged by good luck!

Talking with Wibb, you get a clear sense of a life that has been hugely rewarding and of a still continuing journey that is its own reward. Early on I asked him what had kept him playing the flute all these decades. At first he laughed and ducked the question.

You think I should have stopped much earlier?!

No—I absolutely don't think that!

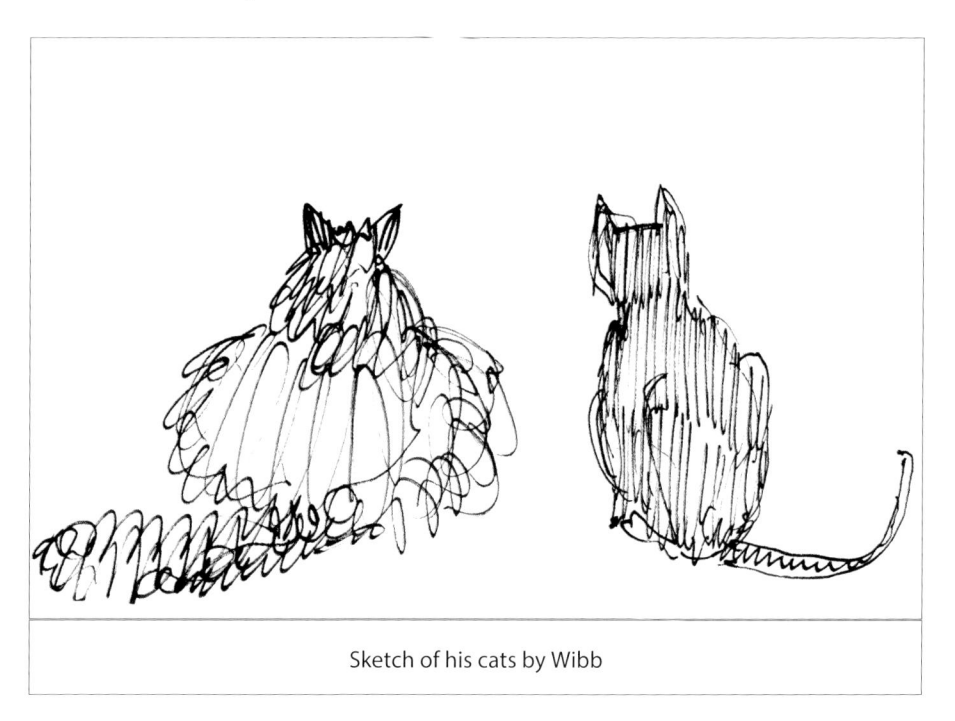

Sketch of his cats by Wibb

I think I just like playing it. I wouldn't have done any of it if I hadn't been really passionately wanting to do that above everything else. It's this fascination with the sound and all the problems of it. Getting the note at the right pitch and the right colour and the right attack—and the phrase shapes and making the flute a voice. It is a voice isn't it?

It most certainly is when you play it. Did you feel destined to play the flute?

I heard it and I wanted that voice. I wanted to play the flute, yes. I'm not sure whether it found me or I found it. It's been almost seventy years now, if you think I was getting interested in the idea of the flute when I was approaching ten years old. I was playing the recorder and I already liked the flute better without having one. It seems as if I had an association with it built in, some sort of an attraction.

It may have been that I was lucky to be quite good at it. I don't know. I was genuinely fascinated by it. I'm also fascinated by making things and what it is that makes something.

In all those years of being faithful to the flute, has it ever let you down?

There are moments when it doesn't work, and you think: 'Oh God, I've got to stop, this is ridiculous!' But then you clamber out of that—a bit of practice and you make it work again. There are all sorts of challenges. As a fourteen and fifteen year old you are concerned about playing as fast as possible—and that's quite normal and healthy—but then it becomes something else, which is to get the voice of the flute and to get it in tune. Things like that become more important than the velocity aspect. I think I was fascinated by the sound and the expression of the flute for a lot longer than I knew that I was.

Can you ever imagine not playing the flute?

No. It would be very hard because it's all I know anything about! It's very upsetting when it doesn't work, but I've given so much attention to it. A large section of my whole memory bank is to do with wrestling with the problems of the stupid tube! And it's still going on.

Would you have had it any other way?

No.

Did you never think that there was something else you might have done?

I can remember at some stage at school thinking: 'What shall I do?' I did think I might like to be a cartoonist. I might have been able to. I think I was just lucky... I got sucked into something in which I could use my imagination.

So you're never going to get to the end of the road, are you, with the flute?

No—it's a bloody pain! Some days, I can't even get to the beginning of the road!

But it sounds as though it's going to outlive you in its challenges and fascinations.

Conclusion

Wibb on tour in France

Yes. We don't understand enough, you know...

I think of Moyse as a very old man. Trevor Wye and I went to visit him in Saint Amour and he was his room playing something—he was over ninety at this point. Trevor asked him: 'What are you trying to do?' He said: 'I'm trying to get a note at all!' Awful come down, having been the best flute player in the world, to be struggling to get a note out of it at all, but it's an instrument which is like that. It sometimes cuts you off completely. You can always get a noise out of a keyboard by hitting the key. It might not be nice, but it's there. And the voice, if you push the air through the throat, unless you've got a bad cold, the vocal chords will produce something. The flute sometimes gets nothing! It's a bit terrifying.

Has that been the case at other times in your career?

That's what a momentous off day is, isn't it, when the flute does very little that you expect it would do? Off days have featured all the time. That's why there's this mechanical fascination of how to make the flute work—trying to make sure that the flute itself isn't the obstacle to you producing the note. You've got to have an instrument which is pretty perfect to be able to get the note. You can't have any leaks in it—and yet we do try to play on flutes which leak, to a greater or lesser degree. The tuning is never perfect, so you've always got to adjust a bit for some reason or other, whether it's getting away from equal temperament to slightly better intonation, or just pitching it right.

You did an enormous lot of work on flute tuning. Was there ever a point at which you just said: 'OK, that's it. It will never be perfect'?

No—I'm still at it! That's really the point of my life: to make the flute a little better for other people.

How do you sum it all up?

You ask yourself: 'What do I do with the sound? How do I want it to begin, and how do I want it to end?' I want some life in the sound. And then, finding where the phrase is going... I think I've always been thinking about those things.

As for what may lie beyond?

I can't help feeling there's something somewhere, some force that we can't possibly understand. Think about Mozart. Where did he get all that from? Couldn't have dreamt that up in his own lifetime...

At the end of one of my conversations with Wibb—it was when we had been exploring the idea of the nobility of the flute (see the previous chapter)—I was reaching for the recording machine and, not quite sure whether we had really finished or not, I turned to him and said: 'Now, if you promise not to say something really profound, I'll switch it off'. Wibb's reply was delivered with a characteristic loud guffaw.

I never say anything really profound!

Not true.

Wibb in relaxed mood